Beyond Quality in
Early Childhood
Education and Care

Beyond Quality in Early Childhood Education and Care:
Postmodern Perspectives

Gunilla Dahlberg, Peter Moss
and Alan Pence

FALMER PRESS

Taylor & Francis Group

UK   Falmer Press, 1 Gunpowder Square, London, EC4A 3DE
USA   Falmer Press, Taylor & Francis Inc., 325 Chestnut Street, 8th Floor,
        Philadelphia, PA 19106

First published in 1999

A catalogue record for this book is available from the British Library

ISBN 0 7507 0770 4 cased
ISBN 0 7507 0769 0 paper

**Library of Congress Cataloging-in-Publication Data are available on
request**

Jacket design by Caroline Archer

Typeset in 10/12 pt Times by
Graphicraft Limited, Hong Kong

*Printed in Great Britain by Biddles Ltd., Guildford and King's Lynn on
paper which has a specified pH value on final paper manufacture of not
less than 7.5 and is therefore 'acid free'.*

Contents

Acknowledgments

In preparing this book we have benefited from the comments of a number of colleagues, including Chris Pascal, Tony Bertram, Mary Jane Drummond, June Statham, Sally Lubeck, Katie Cooke and Bob Glossop. We appreciate their support, while emphasizing that the views expressed in the book, as well as any mistakes, are entirely our responsibility. We would also like to acknowledge the many people with whom we have worked in the First Nations and Stockholm Projects recounted later in the book, as well as from Reggio Emilia. Their commitment, enthusiasm and insights have been a great inspiration.

Chapter 1

What this Book is About

The Language of Early Childhood[1]

Over the last 30 years, increasing attention has been paid to 'early childhood education and care services' — by governments, by parents, by employers, by local communities and by researchers. The reasons have been varied. As women have joined men in the labour market, the demand for non-parental care has grown. The importance of early learning has been increasingly recognized, both in its own right and because many believe it may enhance subsequent academic performance. Early intervention has come to be seen as a means of preventing or ameliorating problems in families with young children and in later childhood, as well as protecting children deemed to be at risk. Early childhood education and care services are discussed as a condition for urban and rural development and as part of the social and economic infrastructure of healthy and wealthy local communities.

There are wide national variations in how early childhood services are delivered, organized, staffed and funded, as well as in the number of places available (cf. Lamb et al., 1992; Woodill et al., 1992; Cochran, 1993; EC Childcare Network, 1996a). But in many countries, increasing demand for non-parental care, education for young children, social intervention and local infrastructure has produced the same response — more early childhood institutions (we discuss later in the chapter why we use the term *institutions*) and more young children attending them. This can be seen as part of a process by which *reproduction*, in particular the care and education of children, has gone increasingly public, emerging from the 'private' domain of the household in response to new economic and social conditions (Benhabib, 1992).

As early childhood rises on the agenda of private and public issues, more and more voices are to be heard in more and more settings talking about early childhood education and care. Yet despite the growing volume and diversity of these voices, most seem to talk the same language of early childhood. Not only is it often literally the same language, as English becomes ever more dominant in the worlds of business, culture, science, technology and research[2], but it shares the same vocabulary: promoting development; ensuring readiness to learn and readiness for school; enhancing school performance; early intervention for children deemed to be in need, at risk or otherwise disadvantaged; developmentally appropriate practice and desirable outcomes; models and programmes; plans and cost effectiveness; regulation, standards; and most pervasive of all, the language of quality.

This dominant[3] language of early childhood generates its own questions. How do we measure quality? What are the most cost effective programmes? What standards do we need? How can we best achieve desirable outcomes? What works? The common feature of such questions is their technical and managerial nature. They seek techniques that will ensure standardization, predictability and control. They aspire to methods that can reduce the world to a set of objective statements of fact, independent of statements of value and the need to make judgements. They avoid the ethical dimension arising from what Rorty (1980) refers to as the 'burden of choice', the responsibility for making judgements, instead reducing choice to an issue of managerial rationality in which questions of value are systematically transformed into technical questions (Gergen, 1992). They are not questioning questions, which ask about value, acknowledge the probability of multiple perspectives and meanings, diversity and uncertainty, and which open up for democratic participation, dialogue and further questioning. In short, they express a desire for a clean and orderly world, devoid of messiness and complexity.

During its three years in the making, this book has become an exploration of ways of talking about early childhood and its institutions. Why does so much of the early childhood world choose to speak this sort of language? Why has it become so widespread, so dominating at this particular time? What other languages can we choose to speak? What are the consequences of the language we choose to speak, what does it mean for children, parents and others, what practices does it produce? As we have discussed such questions, the current dominating language has come to seem problematic. We have found ourselves talking about early childhood differently, having different conversations with other ideas, other questions, other words, other consequences.

We are not arguing, however, for the replacement of one dominating language with another. That would be to use the 'language of necessity' (Bauman, 1991) which manifests itself when we say that 'this is how things are' or 'this is how things should be' or 'this is what must be done'. The language of necessity also manifests itself by what is *not* said — when the possibility of alternative positions, understandings and approaches is not acknowledged, and when the choice of a particular position, understanding or approach is not presented and explained as a choice that has been made but rather is assumed and taken for granted as the only one available.

We try to avoid this in the book, although we may not always succeed. We are not uncommitted; we choose to understand early childhood in a particular way, which is reflected in the language we use. But we value a multiplicity of languages about early childhood, drawing on 'the potential infinity of vocabularies in which the world can be described' (Rorty, 1980: 367) — for we value the diversity of thinking and understanding, practices and purposes that a multiplicity of languages and vocabularies reflects and sustains. From this perspective, we do not claim that what we write is *the* truth, or that we have found the one and only language in which to speak about early childhood. We are not trying to show others the supposed error of their ways or to sell a new line, claiming to have arrived at some definitive and final conclusions.

Rather, our intention in the book is to be 'evocative rather than didactic' (Lather, 1991), to continue a conversation rather than attempt to discover truth

(Rorty, 1980). We want to encourage critical enquiry and dialogue about such subjects as the purposes of early childhood institutions in the world we live in today and how we might understand the child, knowledge and learning. In this way, we may contribute to enlarging spaces in which alternative possibilities are explored and different languages spoken. We want to invite the reader into some of these spaces, to engage with ideas we are struggling with, for we see our work as provisional, not definitive; a year earlier or a year later and this book would have been different. We are walking towards a horizon which always recedes before us, but as we walk we see new landscapes opening up ahead while the landscapes we have passed through appear different as we look back.

The Age of 'Quality' . . .

In past eras, quality was seen more as a luxury than a necessity, merely a handmaiden to quantity . . . [Today] quality matters and it matters a lot. On the heels of this realization, quality enhancement efforts are sweeping through US business and industry, bringing with them revitalized commitments to workers, to collaboration and to a new culture of quality. Those concerned with human services in general, and with young children in particular, are seeing similar developments. (Kagan, Cohen and Neuman, 1996: 2)

As authors we have come to the understandings and perspectives that we share in this book in various ways and over different periods of time. What brought us together originally was a shared unease with the concept of *quality*, and a shared interest in better understanding the 'problem with quality'. We first addressed 'the problem with quality' in a book edited by two of us, *Valuing Quality in Early Childhood Services* (Moss and Pence, 1994), in which the third author of this volume contributed a chapter, together with a Swedish colleague (Dahlberg and Åsén, 1994).

For most people, quality remains a challenge, something to be achieved, rather than a problem, something to be questioned. As the quantity of provision in early childhood institutions has increased, so too has the attention given to the subject of quality. Research in this field started in a big way in the early 1980s (Singer, 1993), since when hundreds of articles, papers and books have been produced. Interest has spread out from researchers until now 'almost every publication on early childhood institutions contains the word quality in its title . . . early years workers, managers, inspectors, funders and researchers are seeking to understand what quality means for them [and] parents as carers are also interested in the debate' (Williams, 1994: 1). Everywhere people are seeking answers to the same questions: What is quality? How do we measure quality? How do we assure quality?

Much of this work on quality has been undertaken in the United States. The upsurge of interest in quality in early childhood institutions can, in part, be understood as a consequence of the particular conditions of that country. A dominant ideology of private responsibility for children, reliance on free market solutions, high levels of demand and large economic inequalities between families — all of these conditions have interacted to produce disturbing, if (some would say) predictable, consequences. The report of the *Quality 2000* initiative concludes:

> Quality services for young children [in the United States] are rare, deteriorating and inequitably distributed. Indeed recent multisite studies indicate that the typical quality of programs, whether based in centers or homes, is substandard . . . [in one study] 86 per cent of the centers studied in four states were rated poor to mediocre in quality . . . with fully 40 per cent of infant and toddler rooms in this study found to be endangering children's health and safety . . . Another recent multisite quality study found 89 per cent of the family day care homes observed to be only inadequate to adequate and merely custodial in quality . . .
>
> Adding to this, there are serious concerns regarding quality deterioration and equity across family income. Data indicate that the quality of early care and education in the United States has seriously deteriorated over the past fifteen years . . . Children without access to either government or business subsidies and without a high family income are at particular risk of being in low-quality programs. (Kagan et al., 1996: 3–4)

Given this situation, it is perhaps not surprising that the subject of quality in early childhood institutions has high priority among those concerned with the welfare of young children in the United States, producing a large body of research. However, the issue has resonated elsewhere. The search for quality in early childhood institutions has fanned out to many other countries. Whatever view is taken of the concept of quality, there is no denying that it now plays a dominant role in our thinking, our language and our practices. The 'age of quality' is now well and truly upon us, and not just in relation to early childhood institutions, but every conceivable type of product and service. No day goes by without the word appearing in countless places attached to countless activities and institutions, goods and services. It is what everyone wants to offer, and everyone wants to have. It makes us feel good that we have chosen a 'quality' item, an item that marks us out as a discriminating and resourceful consumer, an item that shows we have done our best for ourselves and our loved ones, an item we know we can trust without needing to understand.

If there is an issue admitted to the current discussion of quality, it is about definition, for example what constitutes *good* quality in early childhood institutions. (Although, it should be added, this does not inhibit the frequent use of the term without definition, rendering quality meaningless, so that like its kindred concept, *excellence*, 'the general applicability of the notion is in direct relation to its emptiness' (Readings, 1996: 23)). But the *concept* itself has achieved such dominance that it is hardly questioned. For the most part it is taken for granted that there is some thing — objective, real, knowable — called quality.

It seems to us, however, that the very concept of quality does need questioning — because there is a problem with quality.

... and the Problem with Quality

> Quality in early childhood services is a constructed concept, subjective in nature and based on values, beliefs and interest, rather than an objective and universal reality. Quality child care is, to a large extent, in the eye of the beholder. (Pence and Moss, 1994: 172)

> I challenge the global distribution of any one single framework of quality. Such a framework might inevitably lead to a world of uniformity, a standardised recipe for the quality of childhood ... There are many potential criteria for quality which are closely linked to beliefs about goals and functions ... These beliefs are in turn shaped by perspectives on childhood, by cultural patterns and personal values. (Woodhead, 1996: 17, 37)

Much of the work on quality in early childhood institutions has been concerned with exploring the relationship between various features of these institutions — mainly resource and organizational features such as group size or staffing levels and features of what actually happens such as the activities of children, the behaviour of staff and child–adult interactions — and various outcomes, usually defined in terms of child development, but also sometimes in terms of later school, social and economic performance. This has been supplemented more recently by another outcome: the satisfaction of parents as the assumed consumers of services. The exercise has been relatively straightforward: to identify and measure indicators of quality defined in terms of their predictive significance for children's development (Phillips, 1996) or other desirable outcomes. It has been assumed that both indicators and outcomes are universal and objective, identifiable through the application of expert knowledge and reducible to accurate measurement given the right techniques. We examine in more detail the main features and assumptions of this work, the early childhood thread within the broad fabric of quality, in Chapter 5.

More recently, in the 1990s, the concept of quality in the early childhood field as some universal and knowable entity, waiting 'out there' to be discovered and measured by experts, has been questioned or problematized. In particular, there has been a growing awareness of context, complexity, plurality and subjectivity. An increasing number of writers on quality (see Balaguer, Mestres and Penn, 1992; Dahlberg, Lundgren and Åsén, 1991; European Commission Childcare Network, 1996b; Evans, 1994; Farquhar, 1993; Moss and Pence, 1994; Munton, Mooney and Rowland, 1995; Pascal, Bertram and Ramsden, 1994; Pence 1992; Williams, 1994; Woodhead, 1996) have:

- identified the importance of the *process* of defining quality — who is involved and how it is done — and questioned how that process has operated in the past, arguing that it has been dominated by a small group of experts, to the exclusion of a wide range of other stakeholders with an interest in early childhood institutions;
- understood quality to be a *subjective, value-based, relative* and *dynamic* concept, with the possibility of *multiple perspectives* or understandings of what quality is;

- argued that work with quality needs to be *contextualized*, spatially and temporally, and to recognize cultural and other significant forms of *diversity*.

This process of problematization in the early childhood field originated in Europe. But recently it has begun to make an appearance in American literature. Leading American researchers in the field now refer to quality as needing to be contextualized and as a 'construct' (Phillips, 1996), and recognize that 'conceptions of quality early care and education vary throughout the world . . . (and) according to the particular stakeholder, the socioeconomic status and culture' (Bush and Phillips, 1996: 65).

> The subcultures and plurality of values in societies often mean that no one definitive definition of quality exists. It is a relative concept that varies depending on one's perspective . . . Indeed, quality is both a dynamic and relative concept so that perceptions of quality change as a variety of factors evolve. (Bush and Phillips: 66–7)

What seems to underlie the 'problem with quality' is a sense and an unease that what has been approached as an essentially technical issue of expert knowledge and measurement may, in fact, be a philosophical issue of value and dispute. Rather than discovering the truth, and with it certainty, we encounter multiple perspectives and ambivalence. The critique by Readings of the concept of 'excellence' in relation to universities could equally well be applied to quality and early childhood institutions:

> Measures of excellence raise questions that are philosophical in that they are fundamentally incapable of producing cognitive certainty or definitive answers. Such questions will necessarily give rise to further debate for they are radically at odds with the logic of quantification. (1996: 24)

The question now is where to go. Seeking some provisional answers to that question remains at the heart of the book and is the main theme of Chapter 5. Without giving the game away, we can say that our search leads us to the view that the concept and language of quality cannot accommodate issues such as diversity and multiple perspectives, contextual specificity and subjectivity. To do that we must go beyond the concept of quality. A new concept is required, what we term the concept of *meaning making*.

Asking Critical Questions

The Italian historian Carlo Ginsburg (1989) argues that the Minority World[4] lives in a culture where we are constantly being offered solutions, *before we have asked the critical questions*. In the three years it has taken to write this book, we have had to formulate questions that have been helpful to us, first in understanding the problem with quality, then in getting beyond quality. Our questions have started with the child. How do we construct the young child and early childhood? What is our understanding of who the young child is, can be and should be? Such questions have led us to problematize, in Chapter 3, commonly held images or constructions of the young child, including the child as knowledge and culture reproducer, a *tabula rasa* or empty vessel needing to be filled with knowledge and to be 'made ready' to learn and for school; as nature, following biologically determined and universal stages of development; as an innocent, enjoying a golden age of life, uncorrupted by the world; or as a supply factor in determining the labour force. What these ideas or constructions have in common is that they produce a 'poor child', passive, individualized and incapable, and a pedagogical[5] practice to match. Instead we choose to see the young child as having 'surprising and extraordinary strengths and capabilities' (Malaguzzi, 1993b: 73), a co-constructor of knowledge and identity in relationship with other children and adults. This construction produces a *rich child*, active, competent and eager to engage with the world.

Next have come questions about early childhood institutions. What are their purposes? What do we think they are for? From asking these questions has come understandings that have been particularly important to us, and which we explore in detail in Chapter 4. Early childhood institutions are commonly referred to as *services*, implying the delivery of a product (for example, *child care* or *education*) from producer to consumer. But in one chapter in *Valuing Quality*, they were referred to as *forums* or *plazas* (Dahlberg and Åsén, 1994). One of the main projects of this book has been to explore what this conceptualization of early childhood institutions might mean. This process of exploration has opened up for us the possibility of understanding the early childhood institution as a forum in civil society where children and adults meet and participate together in projects of cultural, social, political and economic significance, and as such to be a community institution of social solidarity bearing cultural and symbolic significance.

Early childhood institutions are widely seen as contributing to developmental and economic projects. We problematize the developmental project because we have an understanding of the young child in which the concept and language of development is problematic (we discuss this issue further throughout the book). We accept that early childhood institutions can serve important economic purposes. But, as forums located in civil society, early childhood institutions can make important contributions to many other projects of social, cultural and political significance, some of which we consider in Chapter 4, and that though less widely recognized and discussed in research literature or public policy statements, these social, cultural and political projects are as important as economic projects. Furthermore, understood in this broad way, early childhood institutions can play an important part in constituting civil society, and become the primary means for fostering the visibility, inclusion and active participation of the young child in civil society.

We have travelled a long way in our understanding of the problem with quality. It seems to us now, as the result of our journey, that this problem needs to be located within a far larger context and in relation to far larger issues. Quality cannot be analysed without also analysing early childhood and early childhood institutions, and all in turn need to be located within an analysis of the times in which we live.

The Times in which We Live

We are faced at the end of the twentieth century with a series of pronouncements and declarations that, taken either singly or together, amount to the claim that the western world is undergoing one of the most profound transformations of its existence. (Kumar, 1995: 152)

We are [at] a fundamental turning point in social thought, an epochal shift marked by thinking differently about how we think . . . We seem to be somewhere in the midst of a shift away from the concept of a found world, 'out there', objective, knowable, factual, towards a concept of constructed worlds. (Lather, 1991: 9, 86)

We have found it important to place our enquiry into the 'problem with quality' and into different understandings of early childhood and early childhood institutions in relation to the times in which we live and the great changes — politically, socially, culturally, economically and technologically — that characterize these times. Since the 1970s, a number of complex and interrelated economic and political developments have been occurring. We have witnessed the increasing dominance of a deregulated and increasingly volatile global capitalism,[6] prioritizing competition, markets and profitability, fuelled by growing inequalities between winners and losers in the market place (Marquand, 1998) and searching for profit without regard to national boundaries; this change has been characterized by Harvey (1989) as a transition from a Fordist capitalism to a capitalism of 'flexible accumulation'. At the same time there has occurred a weakening of the nation state. Unable to control the movement of capital and faced by ever more powerful transnational corporations, it has been left to adopt an increasingly managerial role to entice roving capital to invest by providing profitable conditions.

Capitalism and its changing forms are part of a larger picture of economic transformation in the Minority World. There is a change from production to consumption as the main focus of the economy. Goods are still manufactured, but the exchange of services and information, together with lifelong learning, become ever more important activities. Computers and telecommunications are the defining technologies. The composition and nature of employment is shifting; new types of work based on new skills emerge while others fade away, the information worker versed in new technology replacing the coal miner and steel worker; jobs for life are increasingly a thing of the past, but lifelong learning to reskill and maintain employability is offered as the way of the future; working practices become ever more flexible; the number of women workers increases, while the number of male workers decreases as the day of the male breadwinner passes.

Some consider that these and related changes constitute a shift from industrial to post-industrial or knowledge societies, and from Fordism to post-Fordism, in which diversity, differentiation and fragmentation replace homogeneity, standardization and the economies and organization of scale. Some have gone so far as to define these shifts as revolutionary in nature. Bell (1987) refers to a third industrial revolution, this one information-based compared to the first two energy-based revolutions of steam power and electricity. The concept of post-Fordism, it has been argued, transcends economic change: 'Just as Fordism represented not simply a form of economic organisation but a whole culture . . . so post-Fordism is also a shorthand for a much wider and deeper social and cultural development . . . The transition then is epochal' (Hall and Jacques, 1989: 12). Andersson and Sylwans (1997) have described current economic and technological changes as a transformatory process or 'logistic revolution', the fourth in a series of such revolutions beginning in the thirteenth century, each defined by profound changes in how production, services, capital and information are organized. The revolution we are living through today, they suggest, is characterized by an extreme complexity which requires non-hierarchical network relationships, new competencies and high levels of creativity, all in sharp contrast to the routinization, standardization, predictability and authoritarianism which marked the preceding Industrial Revolution.

Any analysis of the world in which we live also has to take account of other areas and the changes they are experiencing. Economic changes are paralleled by the fragmentation of social classes; individualistic modes of thought and behaviour and an entrepreneurial culture flourish; lifestyles proliferate, and domestic life and leisure are increasingly privatized (Kumar, 1995). The collapse of Communism has made the problems in contemporary liberal democracy all the more apparent, in particular widespread disengagement and disillusionment with traditional politics and political institutions and increasing cynicism about the elected representatives who populate these institutions. One response has been to reform these institutions, for example, through decentralization of power from the central institutions of the nation state; another has been to seek new institutions for the practice of democracy; yet another has been the rise of new social movements and networks based on region, race, gender or single-issue politics.

The welfare state has become one of the most important items on the political agenda in recent years. If there is widespread agreement that major change is needed, there is much disagreement about the reasons for wanting change and the proposed solutions. Some want a drastic reduction of the welfare state, with a fundamental shift from collective to private responsibility for welfare; others want to see a strong but reformed welfare state, less bureaucratic and more responsive to diversity and individual circumstance but still expressing an ideal of collective responsibility. For some, the welfare state both expresses and sustains social solidarity, viewed as an important value and as a necessary condition for the political and economic success of society. For others, the welfare state is primarily responsible for a perceived increase in dependency and passivity among the recipients of welfare, damaging both to them and the wider society.

Alongside and related to changes in our political, social, economic and technological conditions, another profound change is occurring — from modernity to postmodernity. This is a change no less than in how we understand our world, our lives and our selves. We devote particular attention to this change in Chapter 2, not only because of its scope and significance, but because it is a recurring theme in the rest of the book.

We realize that the issue of change — its scale and significance — is contested. There is a widespread feeling that the Minority World, perhaps the whole world, is undergoing fundamental changes, that we are living through more than the chronological end of an era and are in the midst of profound transformations. Patti Lather, in the quotation starting this section, captures that sense of being at a fundamental turning point, as does Benhabib: 'the many "postisms", like posthumanism, poststructuralism, postmodernism, postkeynesianism and posthistoire circulating in our intellectual and cultural lives, are at one level only expressions of a deeply shared sense that certain aspects of our social, symbolic and political universe have been profoundly and most likely irretrievably transformed' (1992: 1). Others, however, question whether we are living through such an epochal and fundamental transition, arguing that we are experiencing variations of existing conditions, not fundamentally new departures. Without taking one side or the other, it is still possible to conclude that 'there appears something genuinely at work here, something in the experience of contemporary modern societies that persistently provokes not just "the sense of ending" but also one of new beginnings' (Kumar, 1995: 5).

But what has this to do with early childhood? In our view, everything. Young children are of and in the world; their lives are constructed through interaction with many forces and in relationship to many people and institutions. We attempt throughout the book to relate our analyses of early childhood to social, political, economic and philosophical contexts. For example, we locate our discussion of early childhood institutions in relation to changes in capitalism and the nation state, and to concepts of the welfare state and democracy, while postmodern perspectives provide us with a theoretical framework for understanding early childhood and its institutions and the problem with quality. Indeed it seems to us that too much discussion of early childhood occurs in a social, political, economic and philosophical vacuum, as if young children exist apart from the world, as if concepts like quality and child development are ahistorical and free of value and context, and as if the needs and problems that early childhood institutions are so often asked to address (inequality, exclusion, dislocation) have fallen out of a clear blue sky. If we feel a need to apologize, it is not for bringing in the wider world, but for failing to do sufficient justice to the complexity of the times in which we live, the changes occurring in the world and their implications for early childhood and its institutions.

Why 'Early Childhood Institutions'?

We consider relationships to be the fundamental, organizing strategy of our educational system [for young children from 0 to 6] . . . and we consider small groups the most favourable type of classroom organization for an education based on relationships . . . The organization of small group work is much more than a simple functional tool; it is a cultural context that contains within itself a vitality and an infinite network of possibilities. In schools of young children, work in small groups encourages processes of change and development and is much desired by children . . . Interaction among children is a fundamental experience during the first years of life. Interaction is a need, a desire, a vital necessity that each child carries within. (Malaguzzi, 1993a: 11–12)

In our earlier book, *Valuing Quality*, we talked about *early childhood services*. Throughout this book we have used the term *early childhood institutions*. This change of language is deliberate. As we discuss in Chapter 4, the terms *services* and *institutions* reflect different understandings. The former is the language of provider and purchaser, giver and taker, producer and consumer. The latter is the language of public forums, plazas or arenas, bearing cultural and symbolic significance, located within and constituting civil society.

But we also use the term *institutions* because this book refers mainly to centre-based settings. An important feature of such settings is that they bring together sufficient children for them to be able to engage together on thematic work within small groups. Like Loris Malaguzzi (1993a), we believe in the importance of an education based on relationships. These relationships are diverse and complex, not only between children themselves and between children and adults, but also between adults. A distinctive feature of centre-based settings is that they offer possibilities for members of the staff to work together, as a group, providing mutual support and engaging with each other, as well as others, in the process of documentation and more general dialogue. A further feature of such centre-based settings is that they have the potential to become forums in civil society and, as such, contribute to a participant democracy and active citizenship.

Early childhood institutions come in various forms and under many labels: nursery, crèche, child care centre, *daghem, asilo nido*, nursery school, kindergarten, *école maternelle, scuola d'infanzia*, and so on. Some are 'age-integrated', taking children under and over 3 years of age, while others take narrower age groups, for example, only children under 3 or children from 3 to 6. The discussion in this book is intended to apply to all forms of institution and to the full age range of early childhood.

However, despite their range and variety we recognize that these early childhood institutions are not the only forms of provision for young children. For example, in many countries family day care plays a very significant role, in particular for children under 3 years of age, and this appears to reflect a preference among many parents for more domestic arrangements involving a single early childhood worker. It is not our intention to argue that there should be only one type of provision for young children; such an either/or position would be quite at odds with our whole approach, which recognizes diversity and multiple views. But it is our contention that early childhood institutions offer very different opportunities and possibilities compared to family day care, and that these opportunities and possibilities merit examination in their own right.

Meadow Lake, Reggio and Stockholm: Working the Tension between Theory and Practice

We asked what prompted the people of Reggio Emilia to design an early childhood education system founded on the perspective of the child. He [Bonacci, Mayor of Reggio Emilia in the 1960s] replied that the fascist experience had taught them that people who conformed and obeyed were dangerous, and that in building a new society it was imperative to safeguard and communicate that lesson and nurture and maintain a vision of children who can think and act for themselves . . . While enacting a broad social vision [in Reggio Emilia], it is quite obvious that this vision has not been framed within modernist concerns for progress and universal explanations. Like postmodernist and post-structuralist thinkers, the pedagogues of Reggio Emilia have not adhered to modernist claims of truth, but instead attempted to move away from the legacy of modernity with its universalism and binary oppositions between order and disorder, nature and culture, the rational and irrational, thinking and feeling . . . [Reggio Emilia] has been able to disrupt processes of normalization, standardization and neutralization and make way for and celebrate diversity, difference and pluralism. (Dahlberg, 1995: 8, 16)

Mention of theory can be a turn-off, to researchers as well as practitioners, and for understandable reasons. Too often, theory can be made so abstract as to appear meaningless or apparently irrelevant to practice; or it can become a straightjacket to creative thinking and practice by offering a foreclosed narrative of how the world should be understood, as such governing the practitioner. We believe that, on the contrary, theory can be of great help to practitioners, as a tool to help construct their understandings and enhance their practices; in turn practitioners can play an important part in the development of theory.

Theory should not be ignored for other reasons. In many ways, our lives are governed by theories, whether we recognize them as such or not. Theories shape our understandings and produce our practices. We 'embody' theories, often without realizing. In other words, we absorb theories into ourselves to such a degree that they govern our ideas and actions, although we may not recognize what is going on — even to the extent of confusing theory with truth. As such theories can become 'taken for granted', self-evident, unquestioned and seen as the only right way to think and act, rather than being understood as just one possible way of thinking and acting. What we hope will become more apparent during the course of this book is how theories can be not only methods of governing or controlling individuals, but also tools for challenging this governance and control through problematizing deeply embodied and taken-for-granted thinking. Theories, in short, are double-edged; they can function, for example, in pedagogical practice as a hindrance to change but also as a tool for change.

In Chapter 2 we introduce and discuss some theoretical perspectives that have been important to us. In Chapters 6, 7 and 8, we look in more detail at examples of practice which, so it seems to us, are working with these perspectives, in particular those that are related to what might be called postmodernity. We hope that these examples will help the reader to engage with our theoretical ideas and concepts. In looking for examples of practice related to postmodern theories and perspectives, we draw on diverse experiences including work in Stockholm (Chapter 6) and with First Nations, aboriginal peoples of Canada (Chapter 8). While at first sight the only thing they may seem to have in common is latitude, and while there are many differences, the reader will also see some important shared perspectives and understandings. In Chapter 7 we discuss the practice of 'pedagogical documentation', which we believe has great potential for applying the concept of 'meaning making' to pedagogical work, as such becoming an important part of our language about early childhood.

The other important example of practice, referred to throughout the book, is the Italian city of Reggio Emilia and its early childhood institutions. The city is situated in the northern region of Emilia-Romagna, 60 kilometres west of Bologna. Since the end of the Second World War, the commune (local authority) of Reggio has built up an extensive network of early childhood institutions for children from 0 to 6 (attended by 36 per cent of children aged 0 to 3 years and 98 per cent of children aged 3 to 6 years), at the same time working to develop pedagogical theory and practice. The results have been impressive. The pedagogical work in Reggio's early childhood institutions has become the subject of world-wide interest and admiration. This has been a collective achievement of the parents, politicians, practitioners and children of Reggio, but if one name should be singled out it is that of Loris Malaguzzi, the first head of the early childhood service, who died in 1993. His voice can be heard in many places in this book. Malaguzzi and the other early childhood pioneers in Reggio Emilia have already opened up many new spaces for different conversations about early childhood; we are aware of following behind and of finding those spaces a constant source of inspiration and wonder.

Three features of Reggio should be noted here: others will become apparent later. First, their conversation about early childhood contains little of the language with which we began this chapter (it has also been held in Italian). As we shall see, Reggio's vocabulary is quite different, and so are the consequences in terms of practice and relationships. Second, Reggio is a project which has run for nearly 30 years without the participants claiming that their understanding or work is complete. It has never been evaluated against its ability to deliver outcomes or meet predetermined criteria. It has never claimed that it offers a recipe or programme for export (as a speaker from Reggio put it at a conference in Britain 'our work is just one of the ways we have found to do things . . . it is not implementing a model but working together to find what could be the best we could offer to our children'). Yet despite this — or, perhaps, because of it — the early childhood institutions in Reggio offer thinking and practice of the greatest rigour, for example through the practice of 'pedagogical documentation', have sustained strong public and political support in their home city and have earned respect and acclaim for their pedagogical work far beyond their city limits.

Finally, while we focus on pedagogical philosophy and practice in this book, Loris Malaguzzi and his colleagues in Reggio have always recognized that these require a strong supporting organization in terms of administration, training and funding. Human agency has a vital role to play through pedagogical philosophy and practice, but structure can never be ignored (for a discussion of structural condi-tions to support early childhood institutions, see European Commission Childcare Network, 1996b); agency and structure are inseparable, each one a necessary but not sufficient condition. There is nothing in our postmodern perspective to justify poorly resourced and administratively fragmented early childhood institutions — nor indeed the horrifying social and economic inequalities among children and their families that have been allowed to occur in the Anglo-American world in recent years. From our perspective and understanding, working with postmodernism does not mean anything goes.

Minorities and Majorities

The developmental psychology we know is tied to the culture which produced it . . . In purveying what is advertised as a general, universalist model of develop-ment, developmental psychology is a vital ingredient in the 'globalization of childhood' . . . In general, the concept of childhood on offer is a Western construc-tion that is now being incorporated, as though it was universal, into aid and devel-opment policies . . . Anglo–US psychology extends its influence much further than its own domains through the dynamic of imperialism. Developmental psychology therefore functions as a tool of cultural imperialism through the reproduction of Western values and models within post-colonial societies. (Burman, 1994: 183–5)

It is more rewarding — and more difficult — to think concretely and sympathet-ically, contrapuntally, about others than only about 'us'. But this also means not trying to rule others, not trying to classify them or put them in hierarchies, above all, not constantly reiterating how 'our' country is number one (or not number one for that matter). (Said, 1993: 408)

Insisting on a common standard and common practices for educare [in South Africa] is highly problematic, not least for cultural reasons. As a number of com-mentators have pointed out, indigenous African cultures differ significantly from Anglo-American in their conceptions of child-rearing, and the enthusiastic trans-mission of 'developmentally appropriate practice' and Western models of nursery education or 'educare', far from enhancing competency in young children, may be damaging to those who use it. Put at its bleakest, it is a form of cultural intimida-tion. (Penn, 1997a: 106–7)

In the field of early childhood and early childhood institutions, and in particular with respect to research, measurement and discussion of quality, thinking and prac-tice originating in the United States are influential on an increasingly global scale, assuming almost hegemonic proportions — even though emerging from a very particular context and addressing a very particular agenda. Given the particular and rather problematic conditions of early childhood and early childhood institutions in the USA, already touched on earlier in this chapter and discussed further in Chapter 8, work in this field from the USA would be of only passing interest to the rest of the world (perhaps of less interest than, say, Italian or Swedish work on early childhood institutions) — if it were not that the USA is the world's most powerful country, and one of the wealthiest nations on earth. It has enormous influence, not only economically and militarily, but also academically, culturally and technologically. As Edward Said observes 'rarely before in human history has there been so massive an intervention of force and ideas from one culture to another as there is today from America to the rest of the world' (1993: 387).

The growing hegemony of the USA in this early childhood field projects understandings and approaches that are the products not only of a very particular economic, social and political context, but of one particular discipline within America. Developmental psychology has established a dominant position in the field of early childhood in America, including the search for quality in early childhood institutions; many researchers of quality in early childhood institutions have been developmental psychologists, developmental psychology has provided outcomes for quality work, and the two endeavours have shared assumptions, perspectives and methods. This disciplinary dominance is extremely significant. Developmental psychology adopts a highly positivistic, decontextualized and universalizing approach to children and their institutions (Kvale, 1992). As we discuss in Chapter 5, the questioning of quality as a universal and objective concept is paralleled by questioning — from within psychology itself, as well as from outside — of the discipline of developmental psychology, including its assumption of development as a linear movement along a biologically driven sequence of stages and its notion of the universal decontextualized child. Yet American literature on early childhood institutions, including the discourse of quality, gives little indication that the dominant discipline has been problematized.

An underlying theme of this book is to problematize the dominance of the USA and developmental psychology in the early childhood field. This does not mean ignoring or rejecting work from the United States. It does mean putting it in perspective, recognizing its specificity and its limitations, making visible its particular assumptions and understandings and questioning under what conditions, if any, it is appropriate to generalize from US research and experience and to export US 'solutions' to other societies. It is also important to recognize that, even in the early childhood field, the USA does not speak with only one voice and that there are other voices questioning the dominant language, seeking to reconceptualize the field of early childhood and exploring the implications of postmodernity (see Kessler and Swadener, 1992; Lubeck, 1996; Tobin, 1995, 1997).

As authors, we are aware that we too write from a very specific perspective, produced by very specific experiences and contexts. There are very considerable and important differences between our three countries — Canada, Sweden and the United Kingdom. Even after several years of collaboration, we still discover we have overlooked or not fully understood these differences. But our three countries share membership of the Minority World, with all that means in terms of important commonalities in demographic, economic, cultural, social, political and technological contexts. Yet even within the Minority World, we need to recognize that we write from a very particular position — as members of majority ethnic groups, but at a time of increasing ethnic diversity due to current or past immigration. Furthermore, within Canada and Sweden there are minority groups of indigenous peoples, the

Indian and Inuit who form the First Nation Peoples of Canada and the Sammi of Sweden.

The growing interest in early childhood institutions in the Majority World, and among indigenous groups in the Minority World, together with the growing economic, cultural and technological power of the Minority World, especially the United States, raises many questions about minority–majority relationships in the early childhood field. Is it possible to avoid dominating relationships and totalizing systems of knowledge in which the alterity, the otherness, of the other vanishes as part of a universal sameness? More specifically, is it possible to locate minority–majority relationships within a postmodern framework? If so, what would this look like? Is this framework, which foregrounds diversity, complexity and multiple perspectives, likely to be productive of more equal and dialogic relationships and of 'a form of knowledge that respects the other without absorbing it into the same' (Young, 1990: 9)? We seek some answers to these questions in Chapter 8, using the case of a particular collaborative relationship between a First Nations group and a university in Canada, entered into for the purpose of producing a curriculum for training early childhood workers. At the same time, we acknowledge that one chapter only begins to scratch the surface.

What Can We Do?

In this book we propose a way of understanding early childhood and its institutions, and an approach to pedagogical work itself, which is very different to that which is commonly found. Our examples are exceptional experiences. This way of understanding and working, with its possibilities and opportunities, excites and inspires us. We hope it will have the same effect on some of our readers. But what next, these readers may ask? What can we do?

We have puzzled over these questions. At times we have been tempted to offer an action plan, a blueprint that will transform, if only it is correctly followed. Such plans may have their time and place, for example, when applied to important technical issues such as administrative, legislative and financial reforms. But applied to issues of value and perspective, they seem both unrealistic and dangerous. The unreality comes because you cannot legislate for people's understanding. In any case what we are talking about is not the application of some finalized model, universal in scope and definitive in nature, but rather the adoption of a process of questioning, dialogue, reflection and meaning making which leads we know not where and has no obvious end point: it is work continuously in progress. The danger comes because of a lingering belief in the possibility of massive projects of social engineering, which seek progress through order and standardization. In a world of diversity and complexity, such engineering either leads to failure, when diversity and complexity prove resistant to control, or to repression, when that resistance is processed out of existence. Original and inspiring work, such as Reggio, comes about from a mix of structure and agency, but while structure can be legislated for, agency cannot be, coming instead from individual and collective commitment and struggle.

This does not mean that nothing can be done. Because we cannot do everything, because we cannot have (and perhaps do not want) a complete new system of thought or practice within short-term deadlines, it does not mean we can only settle for a resigned state of inaction. We have to accept temporal and spatial limitations — that there are no quick fixes and no universal projects. But there are possibilities for local knowledge and local action: the interested individual can read and reflect; the interested group, for example, the staff in an early childhood institution, can also discuss, but in addition can explore the possibilities of pedagogical documentation to deepen their understanding of pedagogical work and analyse their image of the child; while the interested community can take inspiration from (but not reproduce) the work in Reggio Emilia and Stockholm, and support committed staff and institutions. In each case — the individual, the group, the community — the possibility exists to create, then enlarge, a space for critical thinking, for meaning making, for making choices, for taking responsibility, for developing new types of conversations and practices.

This may seem rather modest and unambitious. It seems to us that it is far from being so. Creating such a space can help create a crisis in thinking and a struggle over meaning. Indeed, one of our purposes in writing this book is to contribute to bringing a crisis of thinking into the field of early childhood. We want to problematize the concept of quality and other dominant ideas, and we want to expose the field to the crisis in thinking in the world today, as the project of postmodernity questions the tenets of modernity. Some in the early childhood field may perceive this to be a cause for pessimism and despair. We do not. Rather than being a cause for cynicism and despair, crisis can offer new hope and optimism (a point we discuss further in Chapter 6). Creating a crisis in people's thinking may be creative, opening up new possibilities and expectations, alternative enquiries and solutions, opportunities for new understandings and new ways of seeing, visions of accessible futures which neither reflect a nostalgic longing for the past nor assume a pessimistic outlook. It holds out the prospect that we as human beings are not powerless. Through empowerment and democracy we recognize the agency, richness and power of each of us — child and adult alike — and question the legitimacy of authority.

But none of this can be done quickly. The work in Reggio has gone on for over 30 years, in Stockholm for more than 5 years, and neither are near completion — indeed, *completion* is not part of their vocabulary. We live in a world that is increasingly time-governed, driven by new technologies and demands for increasing productivity. We are saturated with information. We demand and expect instant answers and quick fixes. We do not make time for other things, not least reflection, dialogue, critical thinking, working the tensions between theory and practice. Perhaps one answer to 'what can we do?' is to say that we will struggle against the tyranny of time governance; we will risk crisis by choosing to work with complexity, finding ways to think critically and searching for new questions; by doing so, we will open up the possibility of new understandings and practices.

When asked once how the early childhood institutions in Reggio Emilia had time to work so rigorously with pedagogical documentation, Loris Malaguzzi answered, 'We prioritise'. When a colleague of Malaguzzi was asked how it comes about that early childhood institutions in Reggio have such a reflective and exciting atmosphere, she replied, 'We discuss, and we discuss, and we discuss and we discuss.' For the moment we can think of no better answers to the question 'what can we do?'.

Notes

1 We define *early childhood* as the period before compulsory schooling, which in most countries is the first six years of life. However, we recognize that it is problematic to focus exclusively on early childhood. The definition may make sense legally and administratively, but not from many other perspectives. Our analysis and discussion of early childhood and early childhood institutions could be applied to older children and compulsory school, indeed it implies rethinking school as well as pre-school and the relationship between them.

2 The dominance of one language has problematic consequences. Work in other languages becomes invisible, for example in literature reviews which often are, in effect, literature-in-English reviews. This in turn creates a distorted and limited view — a *partview* rather than an *overview* — and a misleading impression of uniformity and consensus in thought and practice. More fundamentally, given the importance of language for expressing and making meaning, there are problems involved in translating from one language to another without imposing meanings in the attempt to make one language fit with the other.

3 We use *dominant* throughout this book to denote ideas and practices, discourses and constructions which carry particular power and influence in governing thinking and action. It does not mean unanimously agreed and accepted.

4 We use the term *Minority World* to encompass those countries which are sometimes referred to as *developed* or of the North; while the term *Majority World* refers to the remaining countries of the world which account for most of the world's population and area.

5 Throughout the book we use the terms *pedagogy* and *pedagogical work*, which are commonly used in Scandinavian countries to refer to work in early childhood institutions. We understand these terms as a way of relating to the world and other human beings which is value-based and complex, and views knowledge as produced through co-construction. '[Pedagogy] denies the teacher as neutral transmitter, the student as passive and knowledge as immutable material to impart . . . [instead focusing] attention on the knowledge and means by which knowledge is produced' (Lather, 1991: 15). We have chosen these terms in preference to the term *education*, more commonly used in the Anglo-American countries, because we wish to problematize the transmission idea of knowledge with which it is often associated. Similarly, we prefer *pedagogue* to other terms widely used in the Anglo-American world for workers in early childhood institutions, such as *educator, teacher, nursery nurse*.

6 We use the term *capitalism* not as a political slogan, but to describe the system of economic relationships and means of production that holds sway over most of the world and is likely to do so for the foreseeable future. Within that broad system, however, exists the possibility of many variations and many relationships; capitalism is both dynamic and diverse (cf. Harvey, 1989; Hutton, 1995).

Chapter 2

Theoretical Perspectives: Modernity and Postmodernity, Power and Ethics

The Project of Modernity

The project of Modernity came into focus during the eighteenth century. That project amounted to an extraordinary intellectual effort on the part of Enlightenment thinkers to develop objective science, universal morality and law and autonomous art . . . The idea was to use the accumulation of knowledge generated by many individuals working freely and creatively for the pursuit of human emancipation and the enrichment of human life. The scientific domination of nature promised freedom from scarcity . . . The development of rational forms of social organisation and rational modes of thought promised liberation from the irrationalities of myth, religion, superstition, release from the arbitrary use of power as well as from the dark side of human natures. Only through such a project could the universal, eternal and immutable qualities of all humanity be revealed . . . The Enlightenment project took it as axiomatic that there was only one answer to any one question. (Harvey, 1989: 12, 27)

'Modernity' is both an historical period and a project that held sway during that period. Bauman (1993) defines the historical period of modernity as beginning in Western Europe in the seventeenth century with a series of profound social and intellectual transformations. It achieved its maturity as a cultural project in the growth of the eighteenth-century Enlightenment, and as a 'socially accomplished form of life' with the growth of industrial society. What Habermas (1983) calls the *project* of modernity had ambitious goals: progress, linear and continuous; truth, as the revelation of a 'knowable' world; and emancipation and freedom for the individual, socially, politically and culturally.

If the ambitions of the Age of the Enlightenment were high, this was because the means appeared to be at hand: the power of human reason and the application of uniquely rational procedures, in particular objective empirical scientific method, and the enormous potentials of technology and industrialization. It was these means that gave moderns the confidence that they could progress. With the help of these powerful tools, modernity has sought to transcend place, culture and particular historical experience, and abstract the individual from his or her context. The search has been certainty secured on the foundations of universal and knowable essences, properties, laws and explanations, foundations for an ordered world that were general, timeless, decontextualized, and constituted 'a universal canon of rationality through which human nature could be known, as well as unconditional universal truth' (Mouffe, 1996b: 245).

Central to modernity has been a view of the world as knowable and ordered, and of the individual as an autonomous, stable, centred subjects. Just as there is a 'real' world to be revealed, so too there is an inherent and preordained human nature, existing independently of context and relationships, that can be fully realized through the transmission of a pre-constituted body of knowledge, assumed to be value-free, universal and offering a true account of the world and ourselves. To be fully realized is to be mature and adult, independent and autonomous, free and self-sufficient, and above all rational, an individual whose other qualities all serve reason. The closer individuals come to reason the closer they come to themselves, to their true nature or essence. Realized individuals can reflect on themselves and the world, arriving at true understanding by the personal application of reason, knowledge and self-consciousness.

The ambition and optimism of the Enlightenment are captured in a famous sentence from Jean Antoine de Condorcet's book *Esquisse d' un tableau historique des progrès de l'esprit humain* about the progress of man: 'One day the moment will come when the sun only shines over free human beings who do not acknowledge any other master than their own reason.' In the book, Condorcet portrays how humanity slowly leaves ignorance and prejudices behind, and turns its gaze towards a brighter future, a society where equality between human beings prevails irrespective of descent, race and gender. This is a society where knowledge prospers and where science is the motor both of economic equality and for accomplishing an ethic that will make us act in the right way (Liedman, 1997).

The Enlightenment's confidence in science and human reasoning as a possibility to free human beings socially, politically and culturally still holds powerful sway. The present-day supporters of Enlightenment (or, more generally, the project of modernity) argue that it has become the preferred mode of thought of most educated people in the world and has conferred enormous economic and political power on those who have adopted it (Gellner, 1992). However, it has not gone unchallenged. The Enlightenment project of combining freedom and happiness through progress based on science and technology has more and more lost credibility. *Modernity* has been under attack, increasingly since the late nineteenth century when the movement of *modernism* in the arts offered a cultural critique, while modernist assumptions in political and economic theory that people were simply self-interested, utility-seeking and rational were queried. What all these criticisms had in common was a questioning of reason — one of the central beliefs of the project of modernity — and scientific method, and the pervasive belief that through their application it was possible to establish reliable, value-neutral truths about a supposedly objective, *real* world.

The twentieth century has shattered the optimism of modernity (Harvey, 1989). The century's terrible history led Theodore Adorno and Max Horkheimer, the founders of critical theory and the Frankfurt School, to question 'why mankind, instead of entering into a truly human condition, is sinking into a new kind of barbarism' (1944: xi). They directed major criticisms towards the project of the

Enlightenment. In *Dialectic of Enlightenment* they argued that the logic behind Enlightenment rationality is a logic of domination and oppression, by instrumental reason over culture and personality. They spoke of the 'indefatigable self-destructiveness of enlightenment', arising from a senseless instrumentalization of science, through positivism and technical rationality:

> On the road to modern science, men renounce any claim to meaning. They substitute formula for concept, rule and probability for cause and motive . . . For the Enlightenment, whatever does not conform to the rule of computation and utility is suspect . . . [T]he Enlightenment recognizes as being and occurrence only what can be apprehended in unity: its ideal is the system from which all and everything follows . . . It makes the dissimilar comparable by reducing it to abstract numbers. To the Enlightenment, that which does not reduce to numbers and ultimately to the one becomes illusion . . . it excises the incommensurable. Not only are qualities dissolved in thought, but men are brought to actual conformity . . . Nature, before and after quantum theory, is that which is to be comprehended mathematically; even what cannot be made to agree, indissolubility and irrationality, is converted by means of mathematical theorems . . . [Enlightenment] confounds thought and mathematics. (1944, 1997 edn: 5, 6, 7, 12, 24–5)

At the heart of this analysis is a criticism not only of scientific method but of an accompanying lack of reflection and theoretical understanding. The weakening of the modern theoretical faculty paves the way for error and madness and for the 'technically educated masses to fall under the sway of despotism' (p. xiii). Without critical, reflexive thought, Adorno and Horkheimer argued, the Enlightenment and its project of emancipation is reduced to a solely instrumental, calculative concept of reason, which leads to domination and exploitation of nature and humanity through social engineering and rationalist planning.

Zygmunt Bauman concludes that modernity set itself unattainable tasks — absolute truth, pure art, humanity as such, order, certainty, harmony and the end of history — but that from amongst these tasks *order* stands out. Modern states are governed by the ideal of order, 'born as a crusading, missionary, proselytizing force, bent on subjecting the dominated populations to a thorough once-over in order to transform them into an orderly society, akin to the precepts of reason' (1991: 20). Bauman argues that the Holocaust and other recent horrors are not outbursts of pre-modern barbarism but the products of this permeation of the nation state with the ideals of modernity:

> [The actions presided over by Hitler and Stalin] were legitimate offspring of the modern age — of that optimistic view, that scientific and industrial progress in principle removed all restrictions on the possible application of planning, education and social reform in everyday life, of that belief that social problems can be finally solved. The Nazi vision of a harmonious, orderly, deviation-free society drew its legitimacy and attractiveness from such views and beliefs already firmly entrenched in the public mind through the century and a half of post-Enlightenment history, filled with scientific propaganda and the visual display of the wondrous

potency of modern technology. Neither the Nazi nor the communist vision jarred with the audacious self-confidence and the hubris of modernity. (1991: 29)

Underlying the growing scepticism about modernity and its claims is a growing disillusionment with its inability to comprehend and accommodate human diversity, complexity and contingency and its reaction of trying to order them out of existence. Modernity's project of control via knowledge, the 'lust for certainty', has imploded. But this is not to say that the dreams of modernity are unworthy: 'it is what they render absent and their conflictual and confusing outcomes that underscore the limits of reason and the obsolescence of modernist categories and institutions' (Lather, 1991: 88).

The Project of Postmodernity

What the inherently polysemic and controversial idea of postmodernity most often refers to (even if only tacitly) is first and foremost an acceptance of ineradicable plurality of the world; plurality which is not a temporary station on the road to the not-yet attained perfection . . . but the constitutive element of existence. By the same token, postmodernity means a resolute emancipation from the characteristically modern urge to overcome ambivalence and promote the monosemic clarity of the sameness. Indeed, postmodernity reverses the signs of the values central to modernity, such as uniformity and universalism . . . Liberty, equality, brotherhood was the war cry of modernity. Liberty, diversity, tolerance is the armistice formula of postmodernity. (Bauman, 1991: 98)

The stage in Western culture and society that we are now entering — whether we see it as the third phase of Modernity, or as a new and distinctive 'post-modern' phase — obliges us to reappropriate values from Renaissance humanism which were lost in the heyday of Modernity . . . Looking back at the intellectually challenging years between 1650 and 1950, from a position of lesser confidence but greater modesty, we can appreciate why the projects of Modernity carried the conviction they did. Not the least of these charms was an oversimplification that, in retrospect, was unrealistic . . . The seduction of High Modernity lay in its abstract neatness and theoretical simplicity: both of these features blinded the successors of Descartes to the unavoidable complexities of concrete human experience. (Toulmin, 1990: 200–1)

It is in this context of growing scepticism about modernity and its consequences, but also in relationship to other developments in capitalism and society (Harvey, 1989), that the most sustained challenge to modernity and the Enlightenment project has arisen since the 1960s, embodied in what has been called the *project of postmodernity*. This project recognizes, even welcomes, uncertainty, complexity, diversity, non-linearity, subjectivity, multiple perspectives and temporal and spatial specificities. Where the project of modernity offered progress through the expert application of scientific knowledge, the project of postmodernity offers opportunities to appreciate social and individual diversity as a source of creative adaptation:

'philosophically speaking, the essence of the postmodern argument is that the dualisms which continue to dominate Western thought are inadequate for understanding a world of multiple causes and effects interacting in complex and non-linear ways, all of which are rooted in a limitless array of historical and cultural specificities' (Lather, 1991: 21).

From a postmodern perspective, there is no absolute knowledge, no absolute reality waiting 'out there' to be discovered. There is no external position of certainty, no universal understanding that exists outside history or society that can provide foundations for truth, knowledge and ethics. Instead, the world and our knowledge of it are seen as *socially constructed* and all of us, as human beings, are active participants in this process (Berger and Luckman, 1966), engaged in relationship with others in meaning making rather than truth finding; the facts of knowledge are 'textual and social constructions created by us in our efforts to understand our situations' (Lather, 1991: 99). Social construction is a social process, and in no way existent apart from our own involvement in the world — the world is always *our* world, understood or constructed by ourselves, not in isolation but as part of a community of human agents, and through our active interaction and participation with other people in that community. For these reasons, knowledge and its construction is always context-specific and value-laden, challenging the modernist belief in universal truths and scientific neutrality.

The postmodern world therefore consists of many 'perspectival realities' (Gergen, 1992), with knowledge of the world understood to be 'socially constituted, historically embedded and valuationally based' (Lather, 1991: 52) — and, consequently, unavoidably provisional and open-ended. Nor is there a centred, autonomous, unified, stable subject, an 'essential' human nature, independent of context, struggling to be realized and described. In postmodernity, the self is constituted and reconstituted relationally and historically, in the jargon 'decentred', 'a shifting self in contrast to the static and essentialised self inherent in the (modernist) concept of free and self-determining individuals' (Lather, 1991: 118). If the subject is said to be 'dead' in postmodernity, what has died is 'the unified, monolithic, reified, essentialized subject capable of fully conscious, fully rational action . . . replaced by a provisional, contingent, constructed subject which must be engaged in processes of meaning-making' (1991: 120). Rather than being a unitary individual — coherent and integrated — we are collections of subindividuals, influenced by different drives and motivations, the relationships between these different subjectivities being unstable and never finalized (Ransom, 1997).

This idea of the individual as decentred, contingent, heterogeneous and fluid is captured by the term *singularity* used by Deleuze and Guattari, with its implication that there is nothing that one can be presumed in advance to share with someone else.

> There are no shared subjectivities that would make them transparent to each other in discussion . . . Rather, singularities *negotiate*, and the structure of singularity is very odd, since it is not repeatable. Hence a singularity cannot achieve total self-consciousness, since if it did know itself, the self that it knew would not be

the same self as the self that did the knowing . . . To speak of the 'peripheral singularity' is to insist that there is no ideal individual that might achieve either total self-consciousness or a harmonious, balanced relation to others in the world . . . The advantage of speaking in terms of singularities is that it offers us a way of discussing the contradictory and multiple ways in which relations of desire (for commodities and other things), power, and knowledge flow among individuals, without having to presume that there is a stable, natural, or logical order of such relations that we have lost and to which we should return. (quoted in Readings, 1996: 115–6, original emphasis)

Or, as the philosopher Herakleitos once said, the second time that you jump into the water you do not jump into the same water.

Linear Progress, Legitimation and Representation

Although the postmodern discourse cannot be seen as a unified body there are some themes that are particularly important to postmodern thinking. The first theme is associated with the writing of Jean-François Lyotard, a critic of the Enlightenment project who argued in *The Postmodern Condition* (1984) that it is now time to re-examine the 'modern' idea of history as a story of linear progress, moving purposively towards a predetermined culmination, and as a universal model of reason for the whole of humanity. Lyotard talks of 'metanarratives' or 'grand narratives', all-encompassing historical and philosophical theories of universal progress and perfectibility produced within the Project of Modernity, such as Marxism or liberalism or the ideology of progress through modernization and industrialization. Lyotard applies the concept 'modern' to any science that legitimates itself with reference to a grand narrative such as 'the dialectics of spirit, the hermeneutics of meaning, the emancipation of the rational or working subject or the creation of wealth' (1984: xxiii). Every human destiny and every event has been given meaning through these grand narratives — but postmodernity is characterized by a loss of faith in them, an incredulity. The abandonment of these grand narratives, Lyotard argues, leaves the way open for 'little narratives', forms of local knowledge, which are internal to the communities within which they occur, self-legitimating in that they determine their own criteria of competence, sensitive to difference and tolerant of incommensurability.

Second, postmodernity brings a crisis of legitimation, which questions the modernist idea of knowledge as objective truth, the claim to which is legitimated or validated on account of being the product of abstract and disinterested scientific enquiry — giving science in effect a monopoly on truth.[1] Rather, from a postmodern perspective, knowledge is seen as inscribed in power relations, which determine what is considered as truth or falsity: in short, knowledge is the effect of power and cannot be separated from power. In a socially constructed world, there can be no external position of certainty, no universal understanding that is beyond history or society, no metanarrative to offer external legitimation. We return to this theme, the relationship between knowledge, truth and power, later in the chapter when we discuss the theories of Michel Foucault.

Third, postmodernism creates another crisis — of representation, 'a profound uncertainty about what constitutes an adequate depiction of social "reality"' (Lather, 1991: 21). Modernity holds to the belief that, through language and other means, it is possible to represent an objective reality accurately; the issue is how best to describe, mirror or reproduce the truth. The 'real', therefore, becomes something which has existence independent of the knower and the process of knowing. Indeed, this belief predates the project of modernity:

> Western philosophy has been under the spell of 'the metaphysics of presence' at least since Plato. Most Western philosophers took as their task the construction of a philosophic system in which something Real would and could be represented through thought. This Real is understood to be an external or universal subject or substance, existing 'out there' independent of the knower. The philosopher's desire is to 'mirror', register, mimic, or make present the Real. Truth is understood as correspondence to it. (Flax, 1990: 34)

But if, viewed from a postmodern perspective, there is no single reality, only many perspectival realities, then construction replaces representation. Claims to represent can be understood as tools that project power by privileging one particular construction or perspective over others, and as forms of normalization by constructing standardized categories and criteria against which people and things are judged. Seen in this way, language does not copy or represent reality — it constitutes reality. From the postmodern perspective, the world is infinitely more complex than the maps we draw, the descriptions we make and the categories we use. From this follows that concepts never can be neutral or innocent.

Postmodern thinkers, therefore, take a sceptical attitude towards the idea that a world can be known objectively, discounting, that is, the knowing activity of the individual. Man must be seen as a social, historical, or linguistic artefact, not a transcendental being who is able to stand outside time, place or relationships to produce true representations of what is real. There is, and can be, 'no Archimedes point — no moment of autonomy, no pure reason or constituting consciousness with independent, non-linguistic, or non-historical access to the Real or being of the World' (Flax 1990: 32).

None of these themes in postmodern thinking means dismissing science. Indeed, the postmodern view of science treats it very seriously, recognizing that science and scientific rationality have been very influential on our lives. But through the crises of legitimation and representation, postmodernity problematizes science and its claims to hold a monopoly of the truth. Modern science is not rejected out of hand, but it is no longer understood as the only source of knowledge, and as capable of comprehending the complexity of the world and the multiplicity, ambivalence and uncertainty of life, which are seen as sources of rich possibilities rather than obstacles to be overcome to arrive at the truth.

Postmodernism also problematizes dualistic thinking ('binary oppositions between order and disorder, nature and culture, the rational and irrational, thinking and feeling'), 'both/and' being preferred to 'either/or'. Cut and dried boundaries and total discontinuity are as suspect as linear progress and development of thought. It is not an either/or choice between science, which foregrounds abstract, timeless, universal and context-free questions and starting points, and the more practical, situated and local questions and starting points of postmodernity. The same goes for the relationship between modernity and postmodernity.

Both Modernity and Postmodernity

> Postmodernity is modernity that has admitted the non-feasibility of its original project. Postmodernity is modernity reconciled to its own impossibility — and determined, for better or worse, to live with it. (Bauman, 1993: 98)

As Bauman observes, postmodernity reverses the signs of the values central to modernity: singularity is preferred to universality; local knowledge to metanarratives; multiple perspectives and complexity to unity and coherence; diversity to consensus; ambivalence to certainty; meaning making to truth; the possibility of chance in history to natural progress to a preordained end. Yet despite these very different perspectives and values, it would be misleading to imply a complete opposition or rupture between modernity and postmodernity, or to see them as two warring camps with nothing in common demanding the undecided onlooker make an either/or choice. The situation and the relationship is much more complex than that.

For a start, some take the view that we live in a period of 'late' or 'reflexive' modernity, rather than postmodernity (Beck, 1992; Giddens, 1990, 1991). Despite their fierce attack on the Enlightenment, Adorno and Horkheimer (1997) argue that social freedom is inseparable from enlightened thought and that the Enlightenment always had as its purpose to free human beings from fear and make them into their own masters — but to avoid its self-destruction, its deterioration into the blind exercise of power, Enlightenment must accommodate reflection, the willingness to think critically about itself.

The German critical theory philosopher Jürgen Habermas also sees the Project of Modernity as unfinished, retaining a belief in the emancipatory potential of reason and science, but reconstructed and reformulated (Habermas, 1983). He argues that the Enlightenment has already provided its own antidote to the criticisms made of it by Adorno and Horkheimer, and others. Habermas claims that it is possible to determine what social rules are right or wrong, and therefore to arrive at universal foundations — but not through 'subject-centred reason', applied autonomously by the mature and self-sufficient individual to the identification of value-free and universal criteria. Habermas looks instead to communication between individuals through discourse producing 'communicative reason': 'the perspective of the all-knowing individual subject is subordinated to the consensual agreement that is reached through communicative action between equals . . . our problem is not, [as postmodernists] assert, reason itself, but the dominance of a particular, one-sided version' (Kumar, 1995: 174). Habermas therefore looks to interaction and cooperation, reflection and discourse, based on procedural rules, as the means to construct foundations. Intersubjective agreement is achieved through argumentation, and what is true and normatively right can be judged through such argumentative discourse: '[communicative rationality] is judged in relation to its degree and form of consensus. The better argument does not persuade through casual force but through insight' (Carleheden, 1996: 15). This communicative action and argument are seen by Habermas as mechanisms which are able to integrate individuals into society on the basis of recognizing and valuing diversity, so constructing collective identity without subordination and the negation of individuality.

Taking a historical perspective, but not a view of history as linear progress, important features of postmodernity do not appear to be particularly new and original. Spanos suggests that 'the impulse informing the postmodern occasion is not fundamentally a chronological event in a developing plot but rather an inherent mode of human understanding that has become prominent in the present (decentred) historical conjuncture' (1987: 194). Toulmin argues that the origins of modernity lie in the Renaissance of the sixteenth century, earlier than is often suggested, and that in these early stages modernity was characterized by a respect for diversity and complexity, a tolerant skepticism which has something in common with today's project of postmodernity:

> In writing about ethics and poetics, Aristotle exhorted us not to aim at certainty, necessity, or generality beyond 'the nature of the case'. The [sixteenth-century humanist] skeptics placed similar limits to appeals to experience. We need not be ashamed to limit our ambitions to the reach of humanity: such modesty does us credit . . . There may be no rational way to convert to our point of view people who honestly hold other positions, but we cannot short-circuit such disagreements. Instead, we should live with them, as further evidence of the diversity of human life. Later on, these differences may be resolved by further shared experience, which allows different schools to emerge. In advance of this experience, we must accept this diversity of views in a spirit of toleration. Tolerating the resulting plurality, ambiguity, or the lack of certainty is no error, let alone a sin. Honest reflection shows that it is part of the price we inevitably pay for being human beings, and not gods. (Toulmin 1990: 29–30)

So, although we are using the concept of postmodernism we have some doubts about its use. We agree with Jane Flax (1990: 188) when she says that 'by even speaking of "postmodernism", I run the risk of violating some of its central values — heterogeneity, multiplicity of rules and difference.' Readings prefers to use the concept 'post-historical' instead of postmodern: 'since the postmodern has by and large ceased to function as a question and has become another alibi in the name of which intellectuals denounce the world for failing to live up to their expectations, I prefer to drop the term' (1996: 6). We are therefore sympathetic to Tom Popkewitz (1998a) when he refers to his 'postmodern sensibility', which we take as a request to be more sensitive to the importance of focusing on questions.

Even if we have started on a journey to deconstruct the field of early childhood pedagogy and its social practices, and tried to be open for tensions in these practices by being sceptical to natural categories, essentialist oppositions and representational claims, we are fully aware that we are all inscribed in modernist discourses. We, as authors of this book, have all been brought up in this tradition, which means that it has got a strong hold on us. We are always inside the concepts we wish to critique. Or, as Docker says in his provocative book on postmodernism and popular culture:

> I am sure that my own debt to modernism, to its great literature and its critical theories, concepts, and methods, will be more than I know myself. I suspect too that while I have tried to present cultural history as replete with heterogeneous fragmentation, discontinuity, multiple and conflicting and contesting meanings and values, history as finally undecidable textuality, my argument probably keeps re-introducing the very notions I'm trying to oppose. (1994: xiv)

Operating within postmodernity, therefore, does not mean rejecting everything that the project of modernity and the Enlightenment stand for, dismissing all the work that has been undertaken within that project, ignoring the possibility of continuities or shared concerns. Methods of work adopted within the project of postmodernity may be just as concerned with rigour, openness and fairness, as methods adopted within the project of modernity. We agree with Stephen Toulmin when he argues that we need to try and combine the abstract strictness of modern philosophy and science with a practical love of the concrete details of human life, and by so doing 'regain the humane wisdom of the Renaissance, without in turn losing the advantages we won during the three hundred years in which intellectual life was dominated by Cartesian philosophy and the exact sciences' (1990: 174).

Foucault, Discipline and Power

> Maybe the target nowadays is not to discover what we are, but to refuse what we are . . . The political, ethical, social, philosophical problem of our days is not to try and liberate the individual from the state, and from the state's institutions, but to liberate us both from the state and from the type of individualization which is linked to the state. We have to promote new forms of subjectivity through refusal of this kind of individuality which has been imposed on us. (Foucault, 1980c: 216)

Michel Foucault, the French philosopher, has an important role in the development of postmodern thinking. We focus here on his ideas about power and its workings, which we have found very helpful to our thinking. Foucault criticized reliance on one concept of power, sovereignty, with its model of power as a simple dualism of ruler and ruled, master and slave, colonizer and colonized, and its debates about consent and coercion, legitimacy and acceptability:

> Power in this landscape is 'something' that people own, and that ownership can be re-distributed among groups to challenge inequities — hence the use of the term 'sovereignty' . . . Power as sovereignty often creates a dichotomous world in which there is oppressor and oppressed, thus producing a dualism whose effect is to define particular social groups as monolithic entities. (Popkewitz and Brennan, 1998: 18)

Foucault argued that from the sixteenth century, new opportunities arose to those exercising power:

> A new kind of power arose with novel tactics and new strategic objectives. At the heart of this change was a displacement in the theory and practice of statecraft away from the sovereignty of the monarch and towards a concern for 'government', where the latter refers not only to the person governing but also to a wide variety of efforts in both the 'public' and 'private' spheres *to shape the human material at one's disposal* . . . Governance, as it turned out, had less to do with forcing people to do what the sovereign wanted and more to do with *steering them in the desired direction* without coercion. (Ransom, 1997: 28, 29, emphasis added)

Power in modern societies has subsequently become far more diverse and pervasive. It is exercised not only by the sovereign but by many others, for a wide variety of purposes. Everyone is not only affected by power, but also to some extent exercises it; we are governed, but also govern ourselves and may govern others, to a greater or lesser extent. Power operates through many devices which do not rely solely on rational discourse or overt coercion. In particular, Foucault identified 'disciplinary power':

> . . . *it shapes individuals* — neither with or without their consent. It does not use violence. Instead individuals are trained or moulded to serve the needs of power. In addition, this method of training — its originators and practitioners hope — will not only impart skills but will do so while reducing the political efficacy of the individuals involved. (Ransom, 1998: 37, emphasis added)

Disciplinary power does not coerce in a straightforward sense, but achieves its goals through the constraint of a conformity that must be achieved. In short, it normalizes, that is it shapes individuals towards a particular norm, a norm being a standard of some kind. Disciplines determine what is normal, then develop measures and other practices to assess if individuals are normal and to shape them towards a norm. This form of disciplinary power is not a confrontation between two adversaries involving direct force, but is a matter of steering or guiding the subject to a desired end preferably without their awareness of what is happening: 'with both governance and disciplines, the goal is to persuade groups of individuals to behave in a certain way *without provoking them into thinking critically about what they are being asked to do*' (emphasis added) (Ransom, 1997: 30–1). Power associated with disciplines is dangerous in its own way, because it is difficult to see, unlike power in the sovereign model, which is dangerous but up front and clearly visible. Disciplinary power often achieves its effect by the subject embodying disciplinary power and through doing so, governing him or herself.

Foucault does not believe in an essential human nature, to be emancipated through the removal of social constraints (including oppressive sovereign power). He thinks that the subject is constructed or constituted through power relations, by specific technologies of power or disciplinary mechanisms. 'Discipline "makes" individuals; it is the specific technique of power that regards individuals both as objects and instruments of its exercise' (Foucault, 1977: 170). Processes of self-formation entail processes of self-reflexivity built on scientific classifications and dividing practices (Foucault, 1980a).

Disciplinary power works through various means and technologies, and knowledge, truth and discourse play a central and related role. Foucault does not understand truth and knowledge in essential or foundational terms, but rather as what comes to be defined or accepted as 'true' or as 'knowledge'. The issue is not the essential truth or falseness of a claim, whether it is right or wrong in some absolute and objective sense; rather, the issue is how particular claims come to be treated in a particular time and place *as if* they were true knowledge. Truth is not 'the ensemble of truths which are to be discovered' but rather 'the ensemble of rules according to which the true and the false are separated and specific effects of power attached to the true' (Foucault, 1980a: 132). Hence, systems of ideas are also systems of action and are related to power; just as individuals are constituted by power, so too is truth and knowledge.

Foucault therefore challenges the Enlightenment belief that power crushes individuals, while knowledge sets them free. Instead the two are closely implicated. Knowledge, or what is defined as legitimate knowledge, is a product of power, but in turn acts as an instrument of power, playing a key role in the formation and constitution of disciplines.

> Because knowledge is assumed to be innocent of power, we believe that knowledge is disinterested . . . [However] knowledge can never be of an absolute or final nature but is instead a selecting out, among the many readings and possibilities present in a concrete instance, of those characteristics and aspects that will promote the goals of the individual or group doing the selecting . . . By picking out what to emphasize and what to present positively or negatively, knowledge shapes the world it 'describes'. (Ransom, 1997: 19)

Knowledge not only shapes our understanding of the world by offering descriptions that we understand to be true. It also provides techniques of normalization, such as surveillance, measurement, categorization, regulation and evaluation. In the operation of disciplinary power, knowledge of what makes up individuals and characterizes populations shapes them in essential ways; the social sciences have played a particularly important role in this respect by making objectivist knowledge the classificatory criteria through which individuals are disciplined and self-regulated.

Discourses are strongly implicated with the constitution of truth:

> each society has its regime of truth, its 'general politics' of truth: that is the types of discourse which it accepts and makes function as true; the mechanisms and instances which enable one to distinguish true and false statements, the means by which each is sanctioned; the techniques and procedures accorded value in the acquisition of truth; the status of those who are charged with saying what counts as true. (Foucault, 1980a: 131)

As this quotation suggests, *discourses* transmit and produce power and as such are an important instrument of power. The importance of discourse comes from the decisive role of language in the process of constructing the world, rather than being simply a means of representing or copying reality. The language we use shapes and directs our way of looking at and understanding the world, and the way we name different phenomena and objects becomes a form of convention. Foucault calls such conventions — our way of naming things and talking about them — *discourses*, and those discourses that exercise a decisive influence on a specific practice can, in his view, be seen as *dominant discursive regimes*, or *regimes of truth*. Such discursive regimes serve a regulatory function; they organize our everyday experience of the world. They influence, or govern, our ideas, thoughts and actions in a specific direction. But they also constitute boundaries, through processes of inclusion and exclusion, for what during a specific time epoch and in a specific culture is seen as 'the truth', and 'the right thing to do' (Foucault, 1980a). They exercise power over our thought by directing or governing what we see as the 'truth' and how we construct the world, and hence our acting and doing; as such discourse provides the mechanism for rendering reality amenable to certain kinds of actions (Miller and Rose, 1993). By so doing, they also exclude alternative ways of understanding and interpreting the world.

These processes are captured in Hans Christian Anderson's story of the *Emperor's New Clothes*. The little boy who comments on the king's nakedness is alone in questioning the regal regime of truth which, by asserting that the monarch is actually wearing magnificent apparel, governs the way his subjects view the world. It is only the child who dares to think the unthinkable, and by so doing calls on others to understand the world in a different way and adopt a 'counter-discourse'.

Dominant discursive regimes work through the concepts, conventions, classifications and categories that we use to analyse, construct and describe reality; through them we acknowledge what is seen as true or false, normal or abnormal, right or wrong. For example, the concepts and categories we use to talk about the child, such as child development and developmental stages, become productive themselves of how we construct or understand the child. We develop this example in the next section. Concepts and classifications become a framework bounding and shaping our thinking, more or less unconsciously governing our thoughts and actions — but we also govern ourselves through embodying them and using them. They shape our understanding of what is possible and what is desirable, for example, in early childhood institutions. They are expressions of the power exercised by discursive regimes — but they also become means of exercising power, as we use them (for example, concepts of child development) to shape policies, practices and relationships.

Discourses are also not just linguistic, but are expressed and produced in our actions and practices, as well as in the environments we create. All bear meanings, in the same way as language. One example given by Foucault of the environment as discourse is the invention of the nineteenth-century classroom:

> Rectangular desks arranged in a rectangle allow for the formation of 'a single great table, with many different entries, under the scrupulously "classificatory" eye of

the master'. The student's 'progress, worth, character . . . application, cleanliness and parents' fortune' would all be reflected in the pupil's position on the table. As a result, a mass of individuals is dispersed, individualised, and organised. The goal however is not to maintain a static distribution. Instead a standard of performance is set. Individuals are evaluated and organised according to that standard but also subjected to exercises that will move them closer to the norm. As students' performances improve or decline, their position on the table changes accordingly. (Ransom, 1997: 16–17)

Power is pervasive and complex. It is also, Foucault proposes, a productive force, rather than being solely or even primarily repressive: 'if power was never anything but repressive, if it never did anything but say no, do you really think one would be brought to obey it? What makes power hold good, what makes it accepted, is simply the fact that it traverses and produces things, it induces pleasure, forms knowledge, produces discourse' (Foucault, 1972, quoted in Rabinow, 1984: 61).[2] Nor does he view disciplinary power as inherently bad or immoral, recognizing that all experience involves a certain shaping of the individual. Power relations are multiple, and involve each of us as vehicles of power, as well as the effects of power.

Foucault's theories challenge many ideas of change, for example, the Enlightenment idea that the subject could direct social action and guarantee future betterment through the application of reason and systematic knowledge:

> . . . dominant and liberal educational reform discourses tend to instrumentally organize change as logical and sequential . . . the agents of redemption (being) the State and educational researchers, (while) the agents of change are teachers as 'self'-motivated professionals. Critical traditions, particularly those related to Marxism, also maintain commitments to progress through philosophical assumptions about agents. With some hesitation and some dissent, contemporary critical traditions continue a nineteenth-century view of redemption through schooling. Intellectual work is to provide universal norms and direction for social change. (Popkewitz and Brennan, 1998: 7)

But Foucault's work questions whether ideas of autonomous actors, applying reason and knowledge to bring about progress, can be regarded as an adequate theory of change if the individual is understood no longer as an agent able to stand outside power but rather as constituted through power relations; and if knowledge is similarly understood no longer as some objective and 'innocent' body of truth but in relation to power, and productive through its capacity to shape us, to construct and normalize individuality to the point that 'thinking of our "selves" through such (expert systems of knowledge) seems natural' (Popkewitz and Brennan, 1998: 13). Indeed, Foucault argues that one feature of power relations is that they cannot be based on permanent physical coercion if they are to be productive and efficient, with modern societies having the capacity to shape subjective experiences that we believe to be uniquely our own.

Similarly, Foucault dismisses revolution as a workable critical paradigm, recognizing the disappointments, and often the perverse and disastrous consequences, that have followed the revolutionary utopias of the last two centuries. He does not believe in an essential human nature that is covered over by social constraints whose removal through revolutionary action will set us free, any more than in the possibility of autonomous human agents acting outside power to bring about reform and progress. He recognizes some value in rights, but believes they produce a false sense of security, providing no defence against the dispersed nature of disciplinary power and its ability to create and normalize the individual.

This has led some people to believe that Foucault's theories offer no possibility of agency and change. But what he is seeking to achieve is 'both a reconceptualization of human freedom and a successful separation from the means used to achieve it until now . . . he wants to develop a postrevolutionary ethos that does not degenerate into apathy or, implicitly, into an accommodationist reformism' (Ransom, 1997: 105).

Foucault argues that we have lacked the conceptual tools for opposing the operation of power because of the failure to develop a clear picture of how power operates outside the conventional sovereignty model. Because we are inscribed in power, because we are constituted by power relations, we cannot challenge power from outside, pretending that we are acting upon power. But power can be opposed because despite its apparently pervasive and hegemonic nature, it is in fact neither monolithic nor total, but fragile and open to challenge; moreover, to talk of constructed individuals is not the same as to talk of determined individuals. There is a possibility of choice and refusal in power relations; individuals can learn how not to be governed so much. And if individuals cannot discover who they are, through finding their 'true selves', which are waiting to be discovered, they can participate in the process of constituting their own make-up, including subjectivity, a process of becoming mature:

> Disciplinary power is to be resisted because it impedes one's ability to form oneself as a subject of one's own activity . . . Foucault complains, in a manner similar to Kant, that we are not yet 'mature'. For Kant this meant that we did not use the reason present in all of us to order our lives and societies but instead relied on external authorities such as priests and royalty. For Foucault our immaturity consists in our inability to shape our own subjectivities in the face of the silent and invisible work of the disciplines. Indeed, the assumption that subjectivity is a universal birthright bars the insight that the attainment of subjectivity is a task at all and effectively gives rein to those forces that would shape it in one way or another . . . (But) by entering into the activity of shaping our own subjectivity, each of us can potentially thwart, challenge or at least question the ways in which we have been made. (Ransom, 1997: 143, 152)

Foucault refers to this 'activity of shaping our own subjectivity' as 'care of the self', which means not only examining the various things that present themselves for admission to the soul or mind of the individual, but the individual seeing to his or her own constitution by consciously deciding on his or her character and direction of existence, to the extent that such is under the individual's control (this concept of 'care of the self' is further discussed in Chapter 7, in relation to pedagogical documentation). The means to practice 'care of the self' are 'technologies of the self', and the role of thought is centrally important. Thought — in the sense Foucault wishes to use the term — both makes it possible to criticize and free ourselves from embodied concepts and produce new concepts. Seen from this perspective

> . . . thought . . . is what allows one to step back from [a] way of acting or reacting, to present it to oneself as an object of thought and question it as to its meaning, its conditions and its goals. Thought is freedom in relation to what one does, the notion by which one detaches oneself from it, establishing it as an object, and reflects on it as a problem. (Ransom, 1997: 129)

'Thought' in this context refers to a form of criticism which enables us to question, or deconstruct, the way we view the world and our relation to it. The focus is on specific events and practices rather than seeking to identify some foundational ethic, knowledge or set of norms. These specific events or practices 'can be reflected on and the constitutions of ourselves resulting from them considered, rejected or even affirmed' (Ransom, 1997: 129).

As part of the exercise of thought, dominant discourses and the constructions and practices that they produce can be challenged, and spaces can be created within which alternative discourses and constructions can be produced and new boundaries created. It may not be easy to distance ourselves from social conventions and social representations embedded in metanarratives and discursive practices, as they place boundaries on our knowledge and our critical abilities, but it can be done. To do so, as pedagogues and researchers, we must first make visible — unmask — and problematize prevailing (and therefore usually taken-for-granted) discourses, and the constructions, practices and boundaries they produce (in Foucault's words 'regimes of knowledge' (1980c: 212)).

> We grow up in a mostly unreflective state with regard to the influences that shape us. [Foucault] wants to give us an experience of a certain kind of rationality that could help change our relationships with ourselves — our relations with ourselves will change when powers that have worked secretly are revealed. (Ransom, 1997: 57)

This unmasking requires us to enhance our reflexivity, to become more aware and critical, a recurring theme of the book.

In his reformulation of freedom and the means to achieve it, he turns away from projects that claim to be global and radical, not as an unavoidable retreat from real solutions to an ineffective localism, but because he disdains projects of transformation of 'society' for their impotence, being convinced that local actions are the best way to introduce changes into larger structures of power (what might be termed a bottom-up rather than a top-down approach to change). Foucault is not advocating minor cosmetic change in the face of unchallengeable power, but a project of major political impact, for 'in a society that relies on the unrecognized permeability of subjective states, the spread of technologies of the self will result in so many newly resistant points' (Ransom, 1997: 152). What he is proposing is that in the 'discursive struggle for our subjectivity' we can be active if not sovereign (Lather, 1991).

One direction in which Foucault's thinking leads him is to identify truly productive sites for the creation and application of the disciplines as local settings, and that oppositional interests should focus on these narrowly defined areas. Local settings include schools, and 'institutions of formal education . . . have become central to the "disciplining" in most if not all fields' (Popkewitz and Brennan, 1998: 22); but they also include many other local institutions, such as clinics and early childhood institutions. One way in which they apply disciplines, shaping people and their subjectivity, is through the application of disciplinary knowledge. We turn now to consider one of these areas of knowledge, which has been very productive in the early childhood field.

The Powerful Role of Developmental Psychology

The emergence of developmental psychology was prompted by concerns to classify, measure and regulate . . . In general, developmental psychology is a paradigmatically modern discipline arising at a time of commitment to narratives of truth, objectivity, science and reason. (Burman, 1994: 18)

Since the Enlightenment, science, and especially the 'truth-seeking' scientific discourse, has been a *dominant discursive regime*, with a profound influence on the development of Minority World societies. As a dominant discursive regime, science has been powerful in the construction of knowledge, through providing rules for separating true and false and thus determining how truth is recognized. Within the field of early childhood, the professions — the experts — have been very significant in this process of constructing knowledge, through the identification of new problems and the construction of means to solve them as well as staffing the organizations to cope with them. Developmental psychology and the experts within this field have played a particularly important role in power relations through a governing system of concepts and classifications, which have been extremely productive, for example constructions of the young child and the early childhood institution.

Following Foucault's analysis, concepts and classifications in developmental psychology, such as universal stages of development, can be seen as a type of language which has constructed the child in the project of modernity. We can talk of a *scientific child*, constructed mainly through developmental psychology, and we discuss this construction further in the next chapter. Furthermore, developmental psychology, with its metaphors such as 'developmental stages', has been productive of pedagogical practice. Through drawing abstract maps — for example, by using theories which say that children of a particular age are egocentric and cannot take the perspective of the other, or that children of another age cannot concentrate longer than 20 minutes — we construct classifications that start living their own life by processes of normalization, hence also constructing teachers and children and their respective expectations and social practices.

As Valerie Walkerdine argues,

> the understanding of the 'real' of child development is not a matter of uncovering a set of empirical facts or epistemological truths which stand outside, or prior to, the conditions of their production. In this sense developmental (as other) psychology is productive; its positive effects lie in its production of practices of science and pedagogy. (1984: 163)

Viewed from this perspective, developmental psychology can be seen as a discourse which not only contributes to the construction of our images of children and our understanding of children's needs, but also to the construction and constitution of the whole childhood landscape.

In pedagogical practice developmental psychology has come to play a dominant role, something which can be understood in relation to our earlier discussions about the importance attached to science in the project of modernity, both for legitimating truth and knowledge and for producing progress. Popkewitz (1994) writes that psychology was expected to answer questions about how individuals were to be self-regulating within the roles fixed in the new institutions of modernity, referring to this process as a form of social engineering that would spread the reasoning and rationalities of modernity. In this context, psychology has, since the beginning of this century, been very influential in answering the question of what is of value for pedagogical practice.

But this has been problematic in a number of ways. Making pedagogical questions scientific, mainly with psychology, has meant not only that pedagogy has to a large extent become synonymous with psychology, but also that pedagogy has been cast adrift from societal and value-based considerations. Theories used to describe children's development have a tendency to start functioning as if they were 'true' models of reality, becoming a kind of abstract map spread over the actual territory of children's development and upbringing. Instead of being seen as socially constructed representations of a complex reality, one selected way of how to describe the world, these theories seem to become the territory itself. By drawing and relying on these abstract maps of children's lives, and thus decontextualizing the child, we loose sight of children and their lives: their concrete experiences, their actual capabilities, their theories, feelings and hopes.

As a consequence, all we know is how far this or that child conforms to certain norms inscribed on the maps we use. Instead of concrete descriptions and reflections on children's doings and thinking, on their hypotheses and theories of the world, we easily end up with simple mappings of children's lives, general classifications of the child of the kind that say 'children of such and such an age are like that'. The maps, the classifications and the ready-made categories end up replacing the richness of children's lived lives and the inescapable complexity of concrete experience.

Gregory Bateson (1988) warns that we live with the illusion that the map is the territory, or the landscape, and the name is the same as the named. The following quotation from Lewis Carroll's book *Sylvie and Bruno Concluded*, suggests the dangers of this kind of mapping:

> Mein Herr looked so thoroughly bewildered that I thought it best to change subject. 'What a useful thing a pocket map is!' I remarked.
>
> 'That's another thing we've learned from *your* Nation,' said Mein Herr, 'map-making. But we've carried it much further than *you*. What do you consider the *largest* map that would be really useful?'
>
> 'About six inches to the mile.'
>
> 'Only *six inches*!' exclaimed Mein Herr. 'We very soon got to six *yards* to the mile. Then we tried a *hundred* yards to the mile. And then came the grandest idea of all! We actually made a map of the country, on the scale of *a mile to the mile*!'
>
> 'Have you used it much?' I enquired.
>
> 'It has never been spread out, yet,' said Mein Herr: 'the farmers objected: they said it would cover the whole country, and shut out sunlight! So we now use the country itself, as its own map, and I assure you it does nearly as well.' (Carroll, 1893, 1973 edition: 556–7)

Not only do these abstract maps drawn from theories of child development make us loose sight of what is really taking place in the everyday lives of children and pedagogues, since reality is more complex, contextualized and perspectival than the maps we draw, the descriptions we make and the categories we use (hence the 'crisis of representation'), but they can easily objectify children and ourselves as pedagogues and researchers. The child becomes an object of normalization, via the child-centred pedagogy that has grown out from developmental psychology, with developmental assessments acting as a technology of normalization determining how children should be. In these processes power enters through the creation of a type of hierarchy among children according to whether or not they have reached a specific stage, and achieving the norm and preventing or correcting deviations from the norm take over the pedagogical practice. Such classificatory practices can be seen as a form of manipulation through which the child is given both a social and a personal identity (Popkewitz, 1993).

They can also be seen as examples of what Foucault (1977) calls dividing practices, methods of manipulation that combine the mediation of a science and the practice of exclusion. Dividing practices and the related methods of scientific classification are closely connected with the growth of the social sciences which, like other sciences, have come to be a form of language that serves both to include and exclude through claiming to measure what is good and bad, normal and non-normal. Through this scientific mediation the individual child is placed within normalizing systems of classification that assign and measure children and their skills. By dividing children from each other, but also dividing children within themselves, these dividing practices distribute, manipulate and control children, leading to a diagnostic, assessment and therapeutic culture where normative judgments about the child enter in and take over (Dahlberg and Lenz Taguchi, 1994).

The classification of children at risk or children in need are very obvious examples of such normalizing and dividing practices which occupy an important place in many countries. To problematize these classifications of children in need and children at risk does not mean that we think there are no children who would benefit from additional support or who live in poor environments or suffer abuse from adults or other children. All of these are important issues that need to be addressed. However, this terminology is problematic because it is not neutral. It is produced by 'historically constructed ways of reasoning that are the effects of power' (Popkewitz and Brennan, 1998: 9). It contributes to a construction of the 'poor' child — weak, incompetent, dependent and privatized — and of the relationship between young children and society as abnormal, only legitimated in such diagnostic and therapeutic terms as 'compensation' and 'intervention' when the family, the 'natural' place for the child, is in some way deemed to have failed the child. In this way, the classification exercises power over how we think and act (Popkewitz, 1998a).

An Ethics of an Encounter

> The concept of Totality has dominated Western philosophy in its long history of desire for unity and the One. In Western philosophy, when knowledge or theory comprehends the Other, the alterity of the latter vanishes as it becomes part of the same. (Young, 1990: 13)

Postmodernity may doubt the concept of grand narratives with their universal claims. However, this does not mean that anything goes in conditions of post-modernity (an issue we shall return to in relation to early childhood institutions and pedagogical work in Chapter 5). In his book on *Postmodern Ethics*, Bauman (1993) argues that the demise of the universal rules and absolute truths that have been an integral part of the project of modernity has made the responsibilities of the individual greater and more profound. Postmodern ethics means that the individual has to take responsibility for making very difficult decisions, without being able to fall back on rules and codes, purporting to be universal and unshakeably founded, which tell what choices to take. We must instead repersonalize morality, become our own moral agents, recognizing that we bear responsibility for making moral choices for which there are no foolproof guidelines offering unambiguously good solutions. Far from finding this a cause for pessimism, Bauman argues that 'personal responsibility is morality's last hold and hope' (1993: 34). According to this view, therefore, we bear moral responsibilities, whether we choose to or not, and confront the world as a moral problem and our life choices as moral dilemmas; 'taking responsibility for one's own responsibility is the meaning of being moral' (1993: 56).

For Bauman, responsibility for the Other is the central feature of postmodern morality: 'to take a moral stance means to assume responsibility for the Other. We are, so to speak, ineluctably — existentially — moral beings: that is we are faced with the challenge of the Other, which is the challenge of responsibility for the Other' (1993: 1). In taking this perspective, Bauman, like many philosophers and postmodern thinkers today, has taken inspiration from the Lithuanian thinker, Emmanuel Levinas. Levinas troubled the logocentrism of the modern project and philosophy's 'horror of the other as other', distrusting totalizing systems of know-ledge which assimilated the Other into being the same (Kemp, 1992). Levinas attempts to shift the relation to otherness ('alterity') from an appropriation by the same into its totality to a respect for the other's heterogeneity, a shift from grasping the other to respecting the other. To trouble the 'logos' of the modernist project and to transgress unity and homogeneity towards difference and heterogeneity Levinas proposes ethics in the place of philosophy, in particular the ethical as the injunction of responsibility for the other. He argues that philosophy has been so bound to the rational project of seeking justice in terms of regimes of truth or self-knowledge that it has become incapable of respecting the being and meaning of the other to the extent that philosophical tradition makes 'common cause with oppression and with the totalitarianism of the same'.

Others too have addressed the same issue. Derrida's reading of Western philo-sophical tradition is that it is marked by a foundational violence which seeks to reduce the Other to the status of the addressee. Butler has expressed something similar in relation to the modernist project: 'in order to make the whole appear Rational, the contradictory stories of others must be erased, devalued, suppressed. Any appearance of unity presupposes and requires a prior act of violence' (Butler, 1993: 37).

How to establish forms of knowledge and types of relationship that do not simply turn the Other into the same? Bauman says that taking responsibility for the Other means *not* treating the Other as the same as us or as having some universal or generalized character; rather the Other must be recognized as unique and unexchangeable, and the relationship must be to this 'concrete Other'. Levinas argues that what the Other is we discover only in the encounter with the Other, and in particular in the face of the Other; for it is in the face that we discover what the Other is, and it is the gaze that problematizes all attempts to oppress the Other. A relationship to the Other through dialogue is a necessary part of encounters, as is the art of listening — listening to the Other, from their own position and experi-ence, not putting my understanding onto them. The encounter must be character-ized by the alterity of the Other.

The relationship with the Other is also characterized by a rejection of instru-mentality. The emphasis is placed on obligation to the Other, without expectation of recompense or exchange:

> Morality is the encounter with the Other as face. Moral stance begets an essentially unequal relationship; thus inequality, non-equity, this not-asking-for-reciprocation, this disinterest in mutuality, this indifference to the 'balancing up' of gains or rewards — in short, this organically 'unbalanced' and hence non-reversible char-acter of 'I versus the Other' relationship is what makes the encounter a moral event. (Bauman, 1993: 48–9)

Instead of autonomy, Levinas in his writings refers to the idea of heteronomy, which means a community that has to be understood in terms of *dependency* rather than emancipation. This is *not* the logic of exchange as understood in capitalism, in which obligations must have monetary value to be real and to be potentially the object of an agreed settlement; this idea of substitutability (the cash-nexus) presumes that all obligations are finite and expressible in financial terms, capable of being turned into monetary value (Readings, 1996). Rather, it has more in common with Lyotard's account of a *dissensual community*, where the social is the fact of an obligation to others that we cannot finally understand.

> We are obligated to them without being able to say exactly why. For if we could say why, if the social bond could be made an object of cognition, then we would not really be dealing with an obligation at all but with a ration of exchange. If we knew what our obligations were, then we could settle them, compensate them, and be freed from them in return for payment. (Readings, 1996: 227)

This ethical perspective not only contests universalism, but also consensus, and instead foregrounds not knowing for certain, or undecidability. Mouffe (1996a) argues that without taking rigorous account of undecidability, it is impossible to think the concepts of political decision and ethical responsibility. Undecidability, therefore, is not a moment to be traversed or overcome; I can never be satisfied that I have made a good choice since a decision in favour of one alternative is always to the detriment of another one. Politicization never ceases because undecidability continues to inhabit the decision. Every consensus appears as a stabilization of something essentially unstable and chaotic. Chaos and instability are irreducible, but as Derrida indicates, this is at once a risk and a chance, since continual stability would mean the end of politics and ethics. Mouffe (1996a) states that this is why, in Derrida's words, democracy will always be 'to come', traversed by undecidability and for ever keeping open its element of promise.

This ethical perspective, with its emphasis on the Other and respecting Otherness, has major implications for knowledge and pedagogy. Imbued with Enlightenment claims to the universality of its values and its truth claims, knowledge has often been constituted through comprehension and incorporation of the Other (Young, 1990) — which returns us to the earlier discussion of the close relationship between knowledge and power, for example 'the link between the structures of knowledge and the forms of oppression of the last 200 years, a phenomenon that has become known as Eurocentrism' and the way that 'the appropriation of the other as a form of knowledge within a totalising system can be set alongside the history of European imperialism' (1990: 2, 4). Distrusting such totalizing, both Lyotard and Foucault were concerned to foreground singularity as opposed to universality, while Said has argued the need for a new type of knowledge that can analyse plural objects as such rather than offering forms of integrated understanding that simply comprehend them within totalizing schemes. The theoretical issues are how the other can be articulated as such, and how other cultures can be articulated — how can we know and respect the Other?

This perspective problematizes the idea of pedagogy as transmission of pre-determined knowledge, producing an autonomous subject freed of obligations. It implies instead a pedagogic relationship that compels an obligation to the existence of Otherness, in Blanchot's words 'an infinite attention to the other' (quoted in Readings, 1996: 161). Readings talks of 'the pedagogical relation as dissymmetrical and endless', with the parties caught in a 'dialogic web of obligations to thought . . . (which appears as) the voice of the other' (1996: 145). Pedagogy is 'the listening to thought' which is not

> the spending of time in the production of an autonomous subject on an autonomous body of knowledge [but rather] to think beside each other and ourselves to explore an open network of obligation that keeps the question of meaning open as a locus of debate . . . Doing justice to thought means trying to hear that which cannot be said but which tries to make itself heard — and this is a process incompatible with the production of stable and exchangeable knowledge. (Readings, 1996: 165)

Readings speaks of pedagogy in the university. But it seems to us that his themes are relevant to early childhood institutions: pedagogy as a relation, a network of obligation, a radical form of dialogue with the Other; and institutions for pedagogical work as sites of obligation and loci for ethical practices, whose purpose is not to make the Other into the same but to work alongside the Other in a relationship where neither is the master and each listens to the thought of the Other.

It is impossible to do justice to such complex and diverse theories, and the debates that surround them, in a few pages. Many books could be, and have been, written about each one. Furthermore each of the subjects on which we have touched attracts controversies and counter-arguments that we have no space to go into in this book. Rather than apologize for complicating the discussion of young children with so much 'theory', we would criticize our own efforts for not offering wider and more complex analyses. It seems to us that the real danger resides in treating young children, early childhood institutions and the many people associated with them as if they exist in a cosy world of their own, in which every matter can be reduced to value-free technical inputs and measurable outputs, and the only question is 'what works?'

What we have tried to do, albeit sketchily, is to point to a number of theories that we find useful in trying to understand early childhood and its pedagogy and institutions, as well as the problem with quality. We have already touched on a few examples of how these theories can throw light on practice in this field, and we will make further connections in the chapters that follow. We will discuss some different constructions of early childhood and its institutions, and how these constructions produce different practices. We will propose that the problem with quality can be understood in terms of the location of the 'discourse of quality' within the project of modernity, and that postmodernity suggests alternative ways of understanding and evaluating pedagogical work that accommodates diversity and multiple perspectives within a 'discourse of meaning making'. We will discuss pedagogical documentation as an example of how critical thinking and reflection can be brought to bear in the field of early childhood, to enable dominant discourses to be made visible and problematized, and the production of alternative discourses including pedagogical practice. We will suggest that the pedagogical philosophy and practice of Reggio can, in many respects, be understood as postmodern, and show how the Stockholm Project has started out from postmodern conditions and their meaning for young children and for early childhood institutions, and developed its work quite explicitly within a postmodern and social constructionist perspective. We will argue that the increasingly hegemonic relationship between Minority and Majority Worlds, in early childhood amongst other subjects, has been produced, in part at least, from modernity's aspiration to universal laws and totalizing systems. The ethics of an encounter, addressing as it does relationships with the Other, provides one ethical perspective for relationships throughout the early childhood field, whether between practitioners and other adults, children and adults, different disciplines, different social groups or different societies.

Of course to bring theory into early childhood is not at all unusual. What is perhaps less common is to bring in the theories that we have done, whose theorists have generally ignored early childhood and its institutions (even though, as already noted, Foucault believed that such local sites were very productive for analysing theories of power). Furthermore, we have problematized, and will do so further, the area of theory most commonly referred to in early childhood — child development.

Early childhood institutions and pedagogy are often seen as neutral phenomena, subject to the technical application of value-free and universally true knowledge produced through scientific method. But according to a postmodern perspective outlined in this chapter, there can never be any knowledge that is objective or independent of context and power. Absolute certainty based on universal truths is an illusion. This means that, from our view, what 'good' and 'bad' pedagogical practice in institutions for young children can only be answered in a communicative context, in encounter and dialogue with others. Furthermore, early childhood institutions and the pedagogical work in which they engage are arbitrary and socially constructed; from possible alternative constructions, we always have to make choices which are both produced by constructions of the young child and are productive in turn of these constructions. We expand these statements in the next three chapters.

Notes

1 Young (1990) suggests that while the difference between twentieth-century Anglo-American positivism and European theory has been expressed in terms of contending models of explanation and interpretation, another distinction concerns ideas about objectivity. Positivist assumptions that persist in Anglo-American theory mean that the position of the investigator often remains unquestioned.

2 It is in this sense that we use the term 'productive' throughout the book, to indicate how power (and the means of exercising power such as knowledge and concepts) 'produces things', that is it shapes, forms, constitutes the social world and our understanding of it.

Chapter 3

Constructing Early Childhood:
What Do We Think It Is?

Introduction

> Children's lives are lived through childhoods constructed for them by adult under-
> standings of childhood and what children are and should be. (Mayall, 1996: 1)

In early childhood institutions, we often say that we are taking the perspective of
the child and that our pedagogical practice is *child-centred*. What do we mean by
that? Child-centredness seems to be such a concrete and unproblematic concept.
But in practice it is very abstract and rather problematic. The very term child-
centred might be thought to embody a particular modernist understanding of the
child, as a unified, reified and essentialized subject — at the centre of the world —
that can be viewed and treated apart from relationships and context. The postmodern
perspective, in contrast, would *decentre* the child, viewing the child as existing
through its relations with others and always in a particular context.

Furthermore, what the term might mean depends on what we understand the
young child is and might be — who is the child on whom practice is centred? From
our postmodern perspective, there is no such thing as 'the child' or 'childhood', an
essential being and state waiting to be discovered, defined and realized, so that we
can say to ourselves and others 'that is how children are, that is what childhood is'.
Instead, there are many children and many childhoods, each constructed by our
'understandings of childhood and what children are and should be'. Instead of
waiting upon scientific knowledge to tell us who the child is, we have choices to
make about who we think the child is, and these choices have enormous significance since our construction of the child and early childhood are *productive*, by
which we mean that they determine the institutions we provide for children and the
pedagogical work that adults and children undertake in these institutions.

This chapter is an extended discussion of this statement of our perspective.
We enquire critically into some interrelated constructions of the young child —
how he or she has been understood and conceptualized — which we believe to
be influential in much public debate about early childhood, as well as much policy
and practice in this field, including discussions about quality in early childhood
institutions. These constructions are themselves produced within dominant discourses, which are located within the project of modernity, and which we as parents, practitioners, researchers or politicians have embodied. From our perspective

these dominant discourses, through being embodied, influence the whole 'childhood landscape' — relations between children and pedagogues, children and parents and between children themselves, the organization of early childhood pedagogical institutions, as well as how these institutions are ordered and designed in time and space, and what kind of meaning we give to them. They have consequences for the whole ecology of the system of early childhood pedagogy. But as we shall see later in the chapter, these are not the only constructions to be found; with the inspiration of Reggio, we can find other ways of understanding who the young child is and might be.

The Child as Knowledge, Identity and Culture Reproducer

As the global economy takes hold, politicians and business leaders — heretofore largely uninterested in young children — are voicing concern and demonstrating readiness for action. Facing an increasingly competitive global economic market, they are worried about economic productivity . . . Given this climate, quality early care and education services have been advocated as a cost-effective approach to maintaining a stable, well-prepared workforce today [through providing care for workers' children] — and preparing such a workforce for the future . . .

Fuelled by the concerns of the business and political communities, national education reform [in the United States] now includes a focus on the early years. The first National Education Goal, that all children will start school ready to learn, which has been endorsed by all the governors and two presidents, has highlighted the important relationship between early care and education and later educational achievement. (Kagan, Cohen and Neuman, 1996: 12–13)

Investment in learning in the 21st century is the equivalent of investment in the machinery and technical innovation that was essential in the first great industrial revolution. Then it was physical capital; now it is human capital . . . We know that children who benefit from nursery education — especially from disadvantaged backgrounds — are more likely to succeed in primary school. And we know that children who benefit from a good primary education are more likely to succeed in secondary school . . .

Our aim is that all children should begin school with a head start in literacy, numeracy and behaviour, ready to learn and make the most of primary education. (Department for Education and Employment (DfEE), 1997: 14–16)

In the construction of *the child as a knowledge, identity and culture reproducer*, the young child is understood as starting life with and from nothing — as an empty vessel or *tabula rasa*. One can say that this is *Locke's child*. The challenge is to have him or her 'ready to learn' and 'ready for school' by the age of compulsory schooling. During early childhood, therefore, the young child needs to be filled with knowledge, skills and dominant cultural values which are already determined, socially sanctioned and ready to administer — a process of reproduction or transmission — and to be trained to conform to the fixed demands of compulsory schooling.

Viewed from this perspective, early childhood is the foundation for successful progress through later life. It is the start of a journey of realization, from the incompleteness of childhood to the maturity and full human status that is adulthood, from unfulfilled potential to an economically productive human resource. The child is in the process of becoming an adult, and represents potential human capital awaiting realization through investment; he or she is that which is yet to be, a 'structured becoming' (Jenks, 1982). Progress on the journey of realization is denoted by the acquisition of appropriate skills, the accomplishment of successive stages or milestones and increasing autonomy: the metaphor is climbing the ladder. Each stage of childhood, therefore, is preparation, or readying, for the next and more important, with early childhood the first rung of the ladder and a period of preparation for school and the learning that starts there.

This construction is arousing interest in early childhood among 'politicians and business leaders, heretofore largely uninterested'. To these powerful people, early childhood is coming to be seen as the first stage in the process of producing a 'stable, well-prepared' workforce for the future, and thus as a foundation for long-term success in an increasingly competitive global market. As well as reproducing knowledge and skills, that foundation entails reproduction of the dominant values of today's capitalism, including individualism, competitiveness, flexibility and the importance of paid work and consumption.

The Child as an Innocent, in the Golden Age of Life

The image of the child as innocent and even a bit primitive has been intriguing for many centuries. It is a construction which contains both fear of the unknown — the chaotic and uncontrollable — and a form of sentimentalization, almost a utopian vision, where childhood is seen as the golden age. This is *Rousseau's child*, reflecting his idea of childhood as the innocent period of a person's life — the golden age — and the belief in the child's capacity for self-regulation and innate will to seek out Virtue, Truth and Beauty; it is society which corrupts the goodness with which all children are born. Learning to know yourself — your inner nature and essential self — through transparency and introspection has been an important idea. Psychology has legitimated this construction of the young child, especially experts of young children who have placed the child's expression in free play and free creative work at the centre of pedagogical activity.

This image of the child generates in adults a desire to shelter children from the corrupt surrounding world — violent, oppressive, commercialized and exploitative — by constructing a form of environment in which the young child will be offered protection, continuity and security. From our experience, however, we become more and more aware that if we hide children away from a world of which they are already a part, then we not only deceive ourselves but do not take children seriously and respect them.

*The Young Child as Nature . . . or as the Scientific Child
of Biological Stages*

The third dominant construction, closely related to the previous two, produces an understanding of the young child as nature, an essential being of universal properties and inherent capabilities whose development is viewed as an innate process — biologically determined, following general laws — unless, of course, the child has some abnormality. That, we say, is the way children of that age are, that is their nature, that is what they can and cannot do if they are 'normal'. Albeit simplified, one could say that this is *Piaget's child*, since Piaget's theory of stages has surely been very influential for this construction, even through Piaget himself never put much stress on stages (Dahlberg, 1985).

This construction produces a young child who is a natural, rather than a social, phenomenon, abstracted and decontextualized, essentialized and normalized, defined either through abstract notions of maturity (Gesell and Ilg, 1946) or through stages of development. The influence of culture and the agency of children themselves are equally discounted, leaving 'the decontextualised individual who develops through natural and autonomous processes' (Vadeboncoeur, 1997: 33–4). In this construction, 'the psychological classifications assigned to children have no particular time or space continuum — self-esteem, competence and creativity seem to exist outside history and social contexts' (Popkewitz, 1997: 33).

The focus is on the individual child who, irrespective of context, follows a standard sequence of biological stages that constitute a path to full realization or a ladder-like progression to maturity. Although we have used the term 'the child as nature', we might also talk of the *scientific child*, as it is a biologically based construction much favoured by medicine and, as discussed in the last chapter, developmental psychology: 'the dominant developmental approach to childhood, provided by psychology, is based on the idea of natural growth . . . childhood therefore is a biologically determined stage on the path to full human status' (Prout and James, 1990: 10). Despite frequent talk about a holistic perspective, in this construction the child is frequently reduced to separate and measurable categories, such as social development, intellectual development, motor development. Consequently, processes which are very complex and interrelated in everyday life are isolated from one another and viewed dichotomously, instead of viewing them as intrinsically interrelated functions that all work together in the production of change.

The Child as Labour Market Supply Factor

During the course of the present century, a construction of motherhood has become increasingly influential in the Minority World: the mother, like the child, as nature. The young child is biologically determined to need exclusive maternal care, certainly in the earliest years (up to around the age of 3 years), with a gradual introduction thereafter into the company of other children and adults. The mother is biologically determined to provide such care. Not to receive or to give this exclusive care is unnatural and harmful, undermining the young child's attachment to his or her mother and exposing the young child to relationships with other adults and children for which he or she is unready (Bowlby, 1969).

A large survey undertaken in the European Union in 1993 reported that more than three-quarters of all respondents thought that mothers should stay at home when children are young, although the proportion was lower in Denmark, the one Scandinavian country included (Malpas and Lambert, 1993). In a 1994 British survey of social attitudes, 62 per cent of respondents stating an opinion thought that women with a child under school age should stay at home. Of those who thought women should work, the great majority (31 per cent) said they should work only part-time rather than full-time (7 per cent) (compared to 88 per cent who thought married women who had not yet had any children should work full-time) (Jowell et al., 1995).

In fact, the empirical evidence does not support this view. There is no convincing evidence that young children necessarily suffer harm or that their relationship with their mother is inevitably undermined if care is shared (McGurk et al., 1993; Mooney and Munton, 1997). This is hardly surprising since exclusive maternal care is uncommon viewed either culturally or historically (Weisner and Gallimore, 1977); it is a construction of motherhood produced in particular societies at a particular stage in their histories. Yet despite the evidence, this construction remains pervasive and influential, with all its implications for the construction of early childhood.

But times change. Since the 1960s, the labour market in Minority World countries has *increasingly* needed the labour of women, as well as men, in their prime working years, and women as well as men, in general, wish to sell their labour at this stage (during the same period, capitalism has had *decreasing* need of the labour of other groups, such as young people under 25 and men over the age of 50; for a discussion of these trends in Western Europe, see Deven et al., 1998). Consequently, increasing numbers of mothers are joining fathers in the labour market. The number of 'traditional' two parent families, in which the mother cares for the children at home while the father acts as breadwinner, is diminishing. Increasing numbers of young children, under as well as over 3, are not cared for exclusively by their mothers.

In these circumstances, young children acquire a further construction: *as a labour market supply factor* which must be addressed to ensure an adequate labour supply and the efficient use of human resources. Alternative, non-maternal care must be arranged for young children if their mothers are to be employable (not, it should be noted, for their 'parents' to be employable, since the dominant discourse about gender governs ideas about roles and relationships, producing a taken-for-granted assumption that fathers go out to work and that mothers are primarily responsible for ensuring child care). In Britain and the United States, government, advocacy groups and others speak openly about the business case for employers to invest in child care, 'as a cost-effective approach to maintaining a stable, well-prepared workforce today'. This is matched by an increasing and diverse involvement — from direct provision of 'child care' to funding child care information and referral services — of individual employers and economic agencies in early child-hood institutions and other forms of child care, alongside a range of other occupa-tional benefits, all intended to attract and retain labour — until such time may come that labour is no longer required.

The Child as a Co-constructer of Knowledge, Identity and Culture

> Our image of children no longer considers them as isolated and egocentric, does not see them only engaged in action with objects, does not emphasize only the cognitive aspects, does not belittle feelings or what is not logical and does not consider with ambiguity the role of the affective domain. Instead our image of the child is rich in potential, strong, powerful, competent and, most of all, connected to adults and other children. (Loris Malaguzzi, 1993a: 10)

The constructions of the young child that we have considered so far have in com-mon that they can be understood as produced within the project of modernity, sharing modernity's belief in the autonomous, stable, centred subject, whose inher-ent and preordained human nature is revealed through processes of development and maturity and who can be described in terms of scientific concepts and classifica-tions. These constructions also have something else in common. They produce a 'poor' child, weak and passive, incapable and under-developed, dependent and isolated.

But new constructions productive of a very different child have been emerg-ing, as the result of a number of interrelated developments (Mayall, 1996): social constructionist and postmodernist perspectives within philosophy, sociology and psychology; the problematizing of developmental psychology, and the increasing influence of the comparative movement within psychology; and the work of indi-vidual researchers, and of a number of specific projects, notably the Childhood as a Social Phenomenon Project begun in 1987 under the auspices of the European Centre in Vienna (Qvortrup et al., 1994) and the BASUN (Childhood, Society and Development) Project undertaken in the late 1980s for the Nordic Council as a study of the everyday lives of young children (Dencik, 1989). This process of rethinking children and childhood[1] has mainly taken place in Europe, rather than the US, with the lead taken in many respects by Scandinavia. One reason for this rethinking may be that children's daily lives in this part of northern Europe have been transformed in recent decades due both to social and economic change and to government policy initiatives which have led, *inter alia*, to an extensive network of public-funded early childhood institutions:

> Most children now spend many hours a day in group care . . . The dramatic Scandinavian experiment in changing children's childhoods has promoted rethink-ing about inter-relationships between the triangle of parents, children and the state. Traditional formulations have thought of children mainly in relation to parents, with the state as a back-up; but Scandinavian policy now has an altered focus: children are a shared responsibility of the state and parents. Under these circumstances, it

is appropriate to think of children's own direct relationships with the state, its policies and goals. In addition, concern for social justice and the rights of the individuals in these countries has led to a movement to regard children and parents as independent subjects with separate legal status. Thus the stage has been set for extracting children out from under the family, conceptually, and thinking about them, not only as individuals, but also, more widely, as a social group. (Mayall, 1996: 56)

In this passage we can see some of the main features of a new understanding of childhood and children, also referred to as a 'new paradigm of the sociology of childhood' (Prout and James, 1990). Children are both part of, but also separate from, the family, with their own interests that may not always coincide with those of parents and other adults. Children have a recognized and independent place in society, with their own rights as individual human beings and full members of society. Children are considered to be a social group: 'psychological individualisation of children gives way to sociological consideration of how as a group their lives are affected by large-scale socioeconomic factors' (Mayall, 1996: 61). Childhood is understood not as a preparatory or marginal stage, but as a component of the structure of society — a social institution — and important in its own right as one stage of the life course, no more nor less important than other stages.

Other features of this new paradigm include recognition that:

- childhood is a social construction, constructed both for and by children, within an actively negotiated set of social relations. While childhood is a biological fact, the way in which it is understood is socially determined;
- childhood, as a social construction, is always contextualized in relation to time, place and culture, and varies according to class, gender and other socioeconomic conditions. There is, therefore, neither a natural nor universal childhood, nor indeed a natural or universal child, but many childhoods and children;
- children are social actors, participating in constructing and determining their own lives, but also the lives of those around them and the societies in which they live, and contributing to learning as agents building on experiential knowledge. In short, they have agency;
- children's social relationships and cultures are worthy of study in their own right;
- children have a voice of their own, and should be listened to as a means of taking them seriously, involving them in democratic dialogue and decision-making and understanding childhood;
- children contribute to social resources and production and are not simply a cost and burden;
- relationships between adults and children involve the exercise of power (as well as the expression of love). It is necessary to take account of the way in which adult power is maintained and used, as well as of children's resilience and resistance to that power.

Within this framework, a construction of early childhood and of the young child is produced that is very different to the modernist constructions described above. The young child emerges as *co-constructor*, from the very start of life, of knowledge, of culture, of his or her own identity. Rather than an object that can be reduced to separate and measurable categories (for example, social development, cognitive development, motor development and so on), through isolating from one another processes which are very complex and interrelated, the young child is understood as a unique, complex and individual subject. This construction produces a child who, in Malaguzzi's words is 'rich in potential, strong, powerful, competent'.

In Reggio Emilia they always say that they have dared to take, as the starting point for their pedagogical practice, the idea of 'the rich child' and that 'all children are intelligent'. Having a social constructionist perspective, where language is seen as productive, they are aware that this is a choice they have made — it is *their* construction. The rich child produces other riches. They argue that 'if you have a rich child in front of you, you become a rich pedagogue and you have rich parents', but if instead you have a poor child, 'you become a poor pedagogue and have poor parents'.

In this construction of the 'rich' child, learning is not an individual cognitive act undertaken almost in isolation within the head of the child. Learning is a cooperative and communicative activity, in which children construct knowledge, make meaning of the world, together with adults and, equally important, other children: that is why we emphasize that the young child as learner is an active *co*-constructor. Learning is not the transmission of knowledge taking the child to preordained outcomes, nor is the child a passive receiver and reproducer, a 'poor' child hopefully awaiting receipt of adult knowledge and enrichment. What children learn, all their knowledge, 'emerges in the process of self and social construction (since) children do not passively endure their experience but become active agents in their socialisation, co-constructed with their peers' (Rinaldi, 1993: 105).

Rather than an empty vessel awaiting enrichment, from the start of life the young child is a 'rich' child engaging actively with the world; he or she is born equipped to learn and does not ask or need adult permission to start learning. In fact, the young child risks impoverishment at the hands of adults and, rather than 'development', the loss of capabilities over time. In the words of Loris Malaguzzi, 'a child has got a hundred languages and is born with a lot of possibilities and a lot of expressions and potentialities which stimulate each other — but which they are easily deprived of through the education system' (quoted in Wallin, Maechel and Barsotti, 1981). As such, the young child should be taken seriously. Active and competent, he or she has ideas and theories that are not only worth listening to, but also merit scrutiny and, where appropriate, questioning and challenge.

Last, but not least, the young child is understood and recognized as being part of, a member of, society. He or she exists not only in the family home, but also in the wider world outside. This means being a citizen, with citizen's rights and, as he or she is capable of assuming them, citizen's responsibilities. It also means that the young child is not only included, but in active relationship with that society and that world. He or she is not an innocent, apart from the world, to be sheltered in some nostalgic representation of the past reproduced by adults. Rather, the young child is in the world as it is today, embodies that world, is acted upon by that world — but also acts on it and makes meaning of it.

This active engagement of young children with the world, and the need for adults to take this engagement seriously, is illustrated from an account by a Swedish pedagogue of a visit to an early childhood institution in Reggio Emilia.

I would here like to share with you an experience I once had in Reggio Emilia. One day when I visited the Diana preschool [an early childhood institution] in Reggio Emilia and entered a fairly large room of the preschool I got very astonished. The whole room was emptied and on the floor a lot of commercialized playthings were lying around; such as He-Man figures, My Little Ponies and other similar figures. As a Swedish pedagogue and also a mother of two children I got really confused. What was going on here? How could they allow such tools? For my eyes in this moment saw the typical, pedagogically developed wooden playtools used in Swedish preschools.

I asked the Italian pedagogues what they were working with and they answered that it was a project work on modern fairy tale figures. Once again I was surprised. These plastic and luridly coloured figures, were they modern fairy tale figures? The pedagogues continued to tell me how often they observed children talking about figures and stories they saw on TV and how little they as pedagogues knew about these figures and stories. They also found out how little they listened to the children when they talked about such figures. Often they said to the children, 'we don't talk about that here', or 'we'll talk about that another time'. They thought it would be interesting for the children to work with a project on modern fairy tale figures, and as is common in Reggio, the pedagogues began the project by getting more knowledge themselves through watching the programmes the children also were watching. They interviewed the children too about their knowledge and ideas. To their surprise they found one boy could mention more than 25 characters from these programmes, not only their names, but also what kind of role many of them had. As a start for the project the children were asked to bring all kinds of modern fairy tale figures to the preschool and the project moved out from the children's experiences, stories and ideas.

Returning home from Reggio, I reflected on this experience and how we in the early childhood institutions in Sweden had always forbidden toys like this. I also remembered how I had quarrelled with my son in the mornings when he wanted to bring his He-Man figures to his centre. He had often hidden them in his pockets, and I had to feel ashamed in front of the staff. In the early 80s we also had a discussion in educational journals, where the message was that children should be allowed to bring their most precious things with them to the preschool, as they were seen, from a psycho-analytical perspective, as transitional objects. As a result children in many preschools were allowed to bring these figures with them — if they left them in the entrance hall.

I also remembered how often when out shopping with my son, I tried to avoid passing the windows of the toy shop. One day we were anyway in front of the toy shop window and he said to me in a serious tone: 'Mum, now I really have to have a He-Man figure.' I answered very seriously. 'Haven't I told you, you won't get another one?' Then he looked at me even more seriously and said, 'Mum, you haven't understood anything.' Then I asked, 'What haven't I understood?' 'You haven't even understood that He-Man is good.'

Later I thought, what an opportunity as an adult to take children's theories, hypotheses, dreams and fantasies seriously, instead of seeming not to have heard anything or telling children that they should not talk about these things. Children do embody the world, corrupt or not, like us as adults, and as adults we need to take responsibility to listen to them at the same time as we also have to give them counter-images, but not in any simple way. (Dahlberg, 1997)

This construction of the young child has profound implications for the construction of motherhood. Mothers, together with fathers, continue to have the main responsibility for their children, and the home and family provide an environment and relationships of vital and unique importance to the young child. But the young child does not require exclusive maternal (or parental) care in the family home. Indeed, exclusive parental care constrains the young child's opportunities for inclusion in society, the exercise of citizenship, and of fulfilment from interaction with other children and other adults, interaction which has a vital role to play in the active child's co-construction of knowledge, identity and culture.

Understanding the young child as a co-constructor and active participant, wanting and responding to a wide range of relationships, in the home and outside, with other children and adults, we can move away from the restrictive, dualistic thinking to which the belief in exclusive maternal care has given rise: *either* maternal care, which is good, *or* non-maternal care, which is bad or, at least, an inferior substitute. Instead, we can open up the possibility of a childhood of many relationships and opportunities, in which *both* the home *and* the early childhood institution have important, complementary but different parts to play. This possibility has been recognized by the children in Reggio Emilia,

who understood sooner than expected that their adventures in life could flow between two places. [Through early childhood institutions] they could express their previously overlooked desire to be with their peers and find in them points of reference, understanding, surprises, affective ties and merriment that could dispel shadows and uneasiness. For the children and their families there now opened up the possibility of a very long and continuous period of [children] living together [with each other], 5 or 6 years of reciprocal trust and work. (Malaguzzi, 1993b: 55)

Childhood and Pedagogy in Conditions of Modernity

We have argued that constructions of childhood and children are *productive* of practice; in other words, pedagogical work is the product of who we think the young child is. The construction of the young child as an empty vessel and reproducer gives rise to an idea of pedagogy or education as a means of transmitting to, or depositing within, the child a predetermined and unquestionable body of knowledge, with a prefabricated meaning. Pedagogy is the administration of knowledge, a banking concept in which 'knowledge is a gift bestowed by those who consider themselves knowledgeable on those they consider know nothing' (Freire, 1985: 46).

We view this concept of pedagogy as located within, and produced by, conditions of modernity because it is part of an Enlightenment narrative which tells of education as a site for transmission of scientific knowledge to produce autonomous subjects who are supposedly made free by the information they receive. This narrative has not only understood education in a particular way, as the transmission of preconstituted knowledge to empty vessels, but freedom also, as the individual transformed by knowledge into an autonomous subject, self-sufficient and independent of obligation — Man at the centre. This narrative further speaks of education as a linear process that 'transforms children who are, by definition, dependent upon adults, into independent beings, free citizens' (Readings, 1996: 158). This narrative, therefore, values children primarily for what they will become, for the task of education is to transform the 'poor' and dependent child into the 'rich', autonomous and mature adult subject. Early education is understood in foundational terms, equipping young children for what will follow, to be judged in terms of long-term outcomes. In this outcome-driven approach, 'events and experiences hold significance only if our narratives of education and child development name them as stepping stones on the paths towards positive or negative developmental outcomes . . . [and we] value activities that we believe will have a long-term payoff at the expense of activities that seem frivolous or pointless because they are not correlated with success later in life' (Tobin, 1997: 13–14).

In this pedagogy, the pedagogue has a privileged voice of authority, and commitment to the ideals of autonomy and truth puts an end to real questioning. Instead, a typical pedagogical practice is the pattern of *question–answer*, in which the pedagogue poses questions to the children — but questions which actually are not real questions as the pedagogue already knows the 'true' answers and only listens for these answers. This method of work is often associated with the tradition in schools, but not in early childhood institutions. However, studies show that it does appear in the practice of these institutions, especially during more pedagogically-oriented moments such as 'morning sessions' or 'circle times' (Haug, 1992; Hedenqvist, 1987; Rubenstein Reich, 1993). The following episode, from a morning session at a Swedish early childhood institution, vividly illustrates the power of the question–answer pattern (Hedenqvist, 1987). Siv, who is the pedagogue, sits with the children, including Bosse and Alvar, in a circle on the floor.

Siv:	There is something that does not exist in the air in the wintertime. They are in the air now. Some birds are eating them . . . something that flies in the air . . . that we talked about last week and that has come back now . . .
Bosse:	What?
Siv:	Yes, what is flying around in the air now . . . a lot of them . . .
Bosse:	Birds! Bees! Bumble-bees!
Siv:	Yes, I'm thinking of a very small insect. You said a . . .
Bosse:	A bumble-bee,
Siv:	Yes, (hesitating) and what other kinds of small insects are there?
Bosse:	Bees!

Siv:	Hm, there are some more insects . . . those which come and bite you. Do you know which they are, Alvar? The ones which bite us in the summer and then it itches?
Alvar:	A bee . . . ?
Siv:	Yes, but . . . (imitating a buzzing sound),
Bosse:	A wasp!
Siv:	I'm thinking of mosquitos.
Bosse:	What . . .
Siv:	Mosquitos

This small excerpt shows children busy trying to grasp the code of what is expected of them from the teacher in a game of what one could call 'Guess what I am thinking of?' It shows how the question–answer pattern is embodied in the pedagogue and the children. It shows how, in this type of exchange, very poor and helpless a child appears, a child seen as an object without his or her own resources and potentials, a child to be filled with knowledge but not challenged.

Childhood and Pedagogy in Postmodern Conditions

> The potential of the child is stunted when the endpoint of their learning is formulated in advance. (Rinaldi, 1993: 104)

> The transgressive force of teaching does not lie so much in matters of content as in the way pedagogy can hold open the temporality of questioning so as to resist being characterized as a transaction that can be concluded, either with the giving of grades or the granting of degrees. (Readings, 1996: 19)

We have argued that we are living through a period of great change, in which what might be called postmodern conditions are emerging. If we view childhood as a social phenomenon located in a particular context, then it seems to us that the child as *co-constructor*, rather than reproducer, *of knowledge, identity and culture* can be understood to be living a postmodern childhood. What does this mean? What characterizes a postmodern childhood? What are the implications for the function and construction of early childhood pedagogy?

To live in a society that is characterized by postmodern conditions means that individual children have to adjust to a high degree of complexity and diversity, as well as to continuous changes. In a more stable society the children's biography and knowledge were almost predetermined (Asplund, 1983), much the same as their parents. In such conditions, the function of early childhood pedagogy can be understood as enabling children to assume their true identity, their essential identity, and the reproduction of knowledge and cultural values, predetermined earlier by religion and later by a supposedly value-free, objective science and reason.

But in a society of rapid change, the demands and requirements that the future will hold for children can be difficult to anticipate. If the past no longer provides guarantees for the future, if traditional reference points, such as the church, political party and class, weaken, then life increasingly becomes a project that you have to construct yourself. As Melucci (1989) and others have observed, a postindustrial society is characterized by a high degree of reflexivity.

But even more fundamental, living in postmodern conditions calls for a new way of understanding knowledge, requiring us, first and foremost,

> to abandon the 'grand narrative' of a theoretical unity of knowledge, and to be content with more local and practical aims. This means abandoning one of the deepest assumptions (and hopes) of Enlightenment thought: that what is 'really' available for perception 'out there' is an orderly and systematic world, (potentially) the same for all of us — such that, if we really persist in our investigations and arguments, we will ultimately secure universal agreement about its nature. (Shotter, 1992: 69)

The postmodern perspective, therefore, questions the Enlightenment idea and hope that there is objective, or innocent, knowledge, through the accumulation of which we can get nearer the truth that will tell us how the world is, who we are and how to act in the world in ways that are universal and just. Instead it offers a quite different understanding: knowledge as perspectival and ambiguous, contextualized and localized, incomplete and paradoxical, and produced in diverse ways: 'there is a change in emphasis from confrontation with nature to a conversation between persons, from correspondence with an objective reality to negotiation of meaning' (Kvale, 1992: 51).

There is much discussion about 'constructivist' and 'social constructivist' teaching, and the different approaches and concepts covered by these terms (cf. Richardson, 1997). From our perspective, it is different understandings of knowledge that distinguish our postmodern *social constructionist* perspective from the *constructivist* movement which has had a revival in educational reforms in recent years. Both view the child as active and flexible and expect the pedagogue to start from the child's everyday understanding and construction of the surrounding world. But from a constructivist perspective knowledge seems to be seen as something absolute and unchangeable, as facts to be transmitted to the child, and thus as separate from the child, independent of experience and existing in a cultural, institutional and historical vacuum. Constructivism eschews the socially constructed nature of knowledge, and its rules of reason inscribe a fixed world of school subjects that children internalize through flexible strategies of problem solving (Popkewitz, 1993).

By contrast, a pedagogue working with a social constructionist perspective would give the child the possibility to produce alternative constructions before encountering scientifically accepted constructions. The child can then place constructions in relation to scientific constructions, and make choices and meanings (Lenz Taguchi, 1997). This is understood to be a learning process not only for the child but also for the pedagogue, if he or she is able to encounter the child's ideas, theories and hypotheses with respect, curiosity and wonder.

So, both perspectives see an active and problem-solving child. But unlike the social constructionist perspective, the constructivist perspective sees that child existing within a context of standardized, stable and objective concepts. Popkewitz

(1993), for example, has argued that educational reforms which have been influenced by the constructivist revival have focused on how learning occurs in classroom interaction so that children acquire subject matter. The consequence is a valuing of children's thoughts and values as right or wrong according to whether they agree with a predetermined definition of knowledge and a pedagogy which never gives children the chance to explore their own theories.

Taking a postmodern perspective means that we can no longer fall back on knowledge as universal, unchanging and absolute, but must take responsibility for our own learning and meaning making. The same goes for making moral choices. We must take responsibility for making moral choices, no longer being able to abandon this responsibility in favour of conformity to universal rules and absolute truths, reproduced in children through processes of cultural transmission. Postmodern ethics means each of us, from childhood, must take responsibility for making difficult decisions. We are our own moral agents, bearing responsibility for making — constructing — moral choices: there is no truth 'whose name might be invoked to save us from the responsibility for our actions' (Readings, 1996: 168).

This places increasing requirements on children to form and shape their own understanding of the world, knowledge, as well as identity and lifestyle. This process of individualization means having a high degree of self-control or self-government of your own choices and actions, individually and collectively. This calls for a trust in your own ability to make choices and argue for your standpoints. It also means that children gain an increased responsibility for themselves and for realizing their own possibilities.

These changes are often analysed negatively, as a threat to security and a source of alienation. But they can be understood as opening up tremendous possibilities — which are not always desirable — but can be. Realization of these possibilities requires highly developed capacities for learning, self-reflection and communication, and open and questioning relationships. It presupposes what Ziehe has called 'extraordinary learning processes' (1989), processes which are neither linear nor isolated, and which give children opportunities to use their curiosity and creativity, to experiment and take responsibility, to make choices concerning their life and future.

Living in postmodern conditions therefore puts considerable demands on the process of pedagogy. The challenge is to provide a space where new possibilities can be explored and realized through enlarging the reflexive and critical ways of knowing, through construction rather than reproduction of knowledge, through enabling children to work creatively to realize the possibilities and handle anxiety. It can contribute to the emergence of a pluralistic patchwork quilt of co-existing world views and life experiments.

But it is not just a matter of children constructing knowledge in changing times. They also construct identity. The project of modernity, believing in a knowable world of universal truths and universal properties, has sought a universal human nature and an identity of the subject that is coherent and unified, stable and knowable, to be assumed or realized. By so doing, it has threatened to reduce difference in identity, replacing complexity and contradiction with unity and coherence.

As we have discussed in the previous chapter, postmodern thinkers like Derrida and Foucault and many feminists have questioned the idea of a unified and stable subject, a fixed entity or essence of the individual, an inner self that the individual can discover and know truly through introspection, transparency and consciousness. Identity, both across groups and within individuals, is understood as complex and multiple, fragmented and ambiguous, contradictory and contextualized:

> we are seen to live in webs of multiple representations of class, race, gender, language and social relations; meanings vary even within one individual. Self-identity is constituted and reconstituted relationally, its boundaries repeatedly remapped and renegotiated . . . Identities are continually displaced/replaced. The subject is neither unified nor fixed. (Lather, 1992: 101)

In this context, the issue of taking difference seriously, treating it as an opportunity rather than a threat and finding ways to relate to others, without making them the same, assumes great importance.

If Man was at the centre of the Age of Enlightenment, in a postmodern age man and woman are *de*centred, and the individual subject 'is dissolved into linguistic structures and ensembles of relations' (Gergen, 1992: 40). Inherent to the modernist concept of the free and self-determining individual is a static and essentialized self. But postmodernity's focus on the fundamentally relational nature of identity results in the historically constituted and shifting self (Lather, 1992).

Identity therefore is no longer understood, from a postmodern perspective, as taking on predetermined, rigid and universal forms through processes of socialization and reproduction. Rather, as a relational and relative concept, identities are constructed and reconstructed within specific contexts — contexts which are always open for change and where the meaning of what children are, could be and should be cannot be established once and for all. Postmodern children are inscribed in multiple and overlapping identities, in whose construction they are active participants. We can see how children and young people co-construct these multiple and overlapping identities in a dynamic and fluid fashion through the example of the increasing numbers of children and young people who have one parent who is 'white' and one parent who is 'black'. There is a long history of the construction of so-called 'mixed parentage' as necessarily problematic, partly as a result of an acceptance that there are clearly differentiated 'races' which are, in essence, necessarily polarized. People with one black and one white parent have usually been classified as black, but they have also been identified as separate from black and white people and classified using terms which tend to pathologize them for not fitting into a racialized binary opposition, for example 'half-caste', 'mixed race', 'biracial', 'maroon' and 'mulatto'. In this way, an arbitrary division is constructed between those of mixed parentage and others, even though the populations of the world are, in reality, intermixed (Phoenix and Owen, 1996).

But in the diversity of today's societies, there is movement away from the idea that racial identity is given or reproduced, towards the idea that 'people of mixed-parentage must be allowed to assert their racialized identities in whichever ways

they feel are most appropriate . . . [and] conceptualising identities as "both/and"'
(Phoenix and Owen, 1996: 129–30). A British study of social identities shows how
this happens in practice, with young people of mixed parentage proving active in
resisting external pressures and in constructing their own shifting, multiple and
contextualized identities.

> It was not uncommon for the young people to explain how they described them-
> selves in different ways at different times and in different contexts. In this they
> appeared to have a range of ways in which they could individually express their
> racialized identities which could be said to be congruent with notions of postmodern
> plurality and flexibility. In expressing these identities, some seemed to accept, and
> others to reject, the dualism inherent in the treatment of 'black' and 'white' as
> oppositional categories . . . Most of the young people were clear that they made
> their own decisions about whether to accept or reject the constructions their par-
> ents, teachers and friends attempted to persuade them to use. (Phoenix and Owen,
> 1996: 131–2)

There is a similar movement away from understanding culture as a given, an
heirloom to be handed down and taken up from generation to generation. Instead,
culture is also increasingly understood as complex, fluid and contextualized, co-
constructed by individuals in relations with others.

> The appropriation of cultural tradition becomes more dependent upon the creative
> hermeneutic of contemporary interpreters. Tradition in the modern world loses its
> legitimacy of simply being valid because it is the way of the past. The legitimacy
> of tradition rests now with resourceful and creative appropriations of it in view of
> the problems of meaning in the present . . . [T]he reflective effort and contribution
> of individuals becomes crucial. (Benhabib, 1992: 104)

Postmodern conditions bring processes of individualization. But they also foreground relationships. Knowledge, identity and culture are constituted and reconstituted in relation to others — they are *co*-constructed. Relational concepts abound:
dialogue, conversation, negotiation, encounter, confrontation, conflict. If knowledge
is no longer viewed as an accumulation and reproduction of facts, but as perspectival
and open-ended, then knowledge can be viewed as an open-ended conversation,
privileging no party and seeking neither consensus nor a final truth. Constructing
identity not in essentialistic but pluralistic terms implies that a child is connected to
many different groups of shifting ethnic, religious, cultural and social character. For
this reason, as well as the importance attached to the ethics of an encounter, pedagogy for postmodern conditions is based on relationships, encounters and dialogue,
with other co-constructors, both adults and children.

This 'pedagogy of relationships', in which children are understood to be
actively engaged in co-constructing their own and others' knowledge and identities,
has been described by Loris Malaguzzi in writing about Reggio Emilia:

> Children learn by interacting with their environment and actively transforming
> their relationships with the world of adults, things, events and, in original ways,

their peers. In a sense children participate in constructing their identity and the identity of others. Interaction among children is a fundamental experience during the first years of life. Interaction is a need, a desire, a vital necessity that each child carries within . . . Children's self-learning and co-learning (construction of know-ledge by self and co-construction of knowledge with others), supported by inter-active experiences constructed with the help of adults, determine the selection and organization of processes and strategies that are part of and coherent with the overall goals of early childhood education . . . Constructive conflicts [resulting from the exchange of different actions, expectations and ideas] transform the indi-vidual's cognitive experience and promote learning and development. Placing children in small groups facilitates this process because among children there are not strong relationships of authority or dependence; therefore, such conflicts are more attractive and advantageous . . . If we accept that every problem produces cognitive conflicts, then we believe that cognitive conflicts initiate a process of co-construction and cooperation. (Malaguzzi, 1993a: 11–12)

So important are relationships to the thinking and work in Reggio that they do not talk of being 'child-centred', with its implication of the child as an autonomous, isolated and decontextualized being. Rather they would say that relationships — between children, parents, pedagogues and society — are at the centre of every-thing they do, viewing the early childhood institution as 'an integral living organ-ism, a place of shared lives and relationships among many adults and very many children' (Malaguzzi, 1993b: 56). For nothing and no-one exists outside of context and relationships.

Nor is the idea of a pedagogy of relationships confined to early childhood. In his discussion of the university — how it has been, is and might be — Readings argues passionately for this understanding of pedagogy: 'I want to insist pedagogy is a relation, a network of obligation . . . (in which) the condition of pedagogical practice is an infinite attention to the other' (1996: 158).

When the human encounter — relationships — is the basis for pedagogy, communication is seen as the key to children's learning. In Reggio, they view the child as a communicative individual from the start, from the very first moment of life. They want to have a child who is an active interacter, not a passive receiver. Pedagogy and the pedagogical milieu have to stimulate children's own activity and their possibilities for communicating their own experiences; they want to find many ways for children to communicate, to use 'the hundred languages of childhood'. Through communication, children can establish belongingness and participation, laying the ground for taking different perspectives; view their own experiences in the light of others'; discuss, make choices, argue for one's choices — stand up for them, and handle new situations. To cite Loris Malaguzzi again:

When children are born they are washed by an ocean of words, by signs, and they learn the art of speech itself, the art of listening, the art of reading, and to give signs meaning. I mean that upbringing implies the finding of a solution to an increasing competence as far as communication is concerned. Actually, in commun-ication the child's whole life is contained, man's whole life: the logical tools of thought, communication as a base for socialization, and the feelings and emotions which pass through communication. To learn how one can speak and listen are some of the big questions of life. (Malaguzzi, 1993b: 57)

Foregrounding relationships and communication, also produces a 'pedagogy of listening', an 'approach based on listening rather than speaking' (Rinaldi, 1993: 104). This means listening to the ideas, questions and answers of children, and struggling to make meaning from what is said, without preconceived ideas of what is correct or valid. 'Good' listening distinguishes dialogue between human beings, which expresses and constitutes a relationship to a concrete Other, from monologue, which seeks to transmit a body of knowledge and through so doing make the Other into the same. Again taking up the same theme, but in relation to universities, Readings (1996) also argues for the importance of 'listening to thought' in pedagogical work, which he distinguishes from the production of an autonomous subject or an autonomous body of knowledge:

Rather it is to think besides each other and ourselves to explore an open network of obligation that keeps the question of meaning open as a locus for debate . . . Doing justice to thought means trying to hear that which cannot be said but which tries to make itself heard — and this is a process incompatible with the production of even relatively stable and exchangeable knowledge. (1996: 165)

One other feature of the pedagogical work of Reggio should be mentioned here: a refusal to be time governed. Most children attend early childhood institutions for at least a full school day, and for at least three years, often longer. Time is not organized by the clock, but according to children's own sense of time, their personal rhythms and what they need for the projects on which they are working. All this gives children time to get engaged, time not to have to hurry, time to do things with satisfaction. This questions, for example, the tight time governance of British 'nursery education', where attendance is normally confined to a short morning or afternoon session on the grounds either that this is all the time young children can manage or that no better outcomes can be secured by longer attendance. More generally, it questions a reduction of education to what Readings calls 'a logic of accounting', which is concerned increasingly with ever faster progress up the ladder, acquiring a predetermined body of knowledge ever more rapidly and cost-effectively.

From our understanding, and a theme we take up again in Chapter 6, the pedagogical work in Reggio Emilia can be said to anticipate various themes of postmodernity. It has turned away from the modernist idea of unity, and recognized the enormous power of forces which insist on system, structure, centralization, hierarchy, coherence and normalization. It has turned towards the postmodern idea of complexity and contradiction, and has recognized the great opportunities that arise from recognizing difference, plurality, otherness and unpredictability. Over the years, Reggio has struggled to find a pedagogical practice of multiple languages and co-construction, of relationships and dialogue, rich in paradox and irony, valuing both cooperation and confrontation, welcoming doubt and amazement as much as scientific enquiry. Working through pedagogical tools such as documentation, it has sought a learning culture characterized by participation, reflection, solidarity, pleasure and wonderment. What has made this possible is not only the establishment and support of a network of early childhood institutions, but a construction of them as forums in civil society, where children and adults can engage together in projects of social, cultural, economic and political significance. We consider this construction of the early childhood institution further in the next chapter.

Note

1   'Childhood' is a stage in the life course, and a permanent phenomenon in society. Children live through childhood.

Chapter 4

Constructing the Early Childhood Institution: What Do We Think They Are For?

Introduction

> From a social constructionist perspective [early childhood institutions], as well as our images of what a child is, can be and should be, must be seen as the social construction of a community of human agents, originating through our active interaction with other people and with society . . . [Early childhood] institutions and pedagogical practises for children are constituted by dominant discourses in our society and embody thoughts, conceptions and ethics which prevail at a given moment in a given society. (Dahlberg, 1997)

Early childhood institutions are socially constructed. They have no inherent features, no essential qualities, no necessary purposes. What they are for, the question of their role and purpose, is not self-evident. They are what we, 'as a community of human agents', make them. This chapter is an exploration of a few of the many different constructions of the early childhood institution; it is by no means exhaustive. These constructions are constituted by and in turn constitute constructions of the young child, linking to our discussion of early childhood in the previous chapter. They are also productive of pedagogical practice. What we think these institutions are determines what they do, what goes on within them.

The chapter falls into two main parts. The first examines some constructions of the early childhood institution that are dominant in many parts of the Minority World today — the early childhood institution as producer of child outcomes or as a substitute home or as a business. In the second part we examine an alternative and less common construction of the early childhood institution — as a forum in civil society where children and adults engage in projects of social, cultural, political and economic significance.

Dominant Constructions of the Early Childhood Institution

Producer and Business

> It seems to me that early childhood programmes are increasingly in danger of being modeled on the corporate/industrial or factory model so pervasive in

elementary and secondary levels of education . . . factories are designed to transform raw material into prespecified products by treating it to a sequence of prespecified standard processes. (Katz, 1993: 33–4)

Three major, often conflicting purposes for child care create the child care dilemma we [the United States] as a society suffer today. First, child care supports maternal employment . . . Second, child care serves children's development, which can be enhanced by high quality early childhood programs, whether or not their mothers are employed. Third, child care has been used throughout this century to intervene with economically disadvantaged and ethnic minority children and socialize them to the cultural mainstream. (Scarr, 1998: 98)

The Key Note Market Report on Childcare [in the UK] has observed that wealthy companies are becoming increasingly attracted to the childcare market . . . [Nord-Anglia Education, the second largest company] was floated on the stock market last year. It has opened four purpose-built nurseries, runs nursery units in each of its 20 independent schools and bought the Princess Charlotte nanny college earlier this year. (Report headed 'Big business sees profit in childcare' in *Nursery World*, 27 August 1998)

The dominant construction of the early childhood institution is as a producer of care and of standardized and predetermined child outcomes. Linked to the modernist constructions of the young child discussed in Chapter 3, in particular as reproducer of knowledge, identity and culture, the broad and increasingly important task of these institutions as producers is to fill the empty vessel that the young child has often been understood to be. This task is mainly to be achieved through education, now recognized as a central concern not only in nursery education but also in child care and day care: 'due to this emphasis [in American policy on the relationship between early childhood and later educational achievement] more and more Americans are realizing that *all* programs for young children are about education' (Kagan et al., 1996: 13).

Some of the more specific outcomes that the early childhood institution is expected to produce are now widely recognized in early childhood policy and literature, in particular enhancing children's development and preparation for compulsory schooling which includes starting school 'ready to learn'. Other outcomes are more implicit, although nonetheless real, in particular the reproduction of culture, including values. For example, early childhood institutions help to reproduce cultural values concerning gender; the highly gendered nature of the workforce in early childhood institutions and the lack of gender awareness in most pedagogical work produces a powerful discourse, for children and indeed adults, about appropriate gender roles and relationships (Jensen, 1996).

As parental employment grows, so increasing importance is attached to early childhood institutions producing child care for parents and employers. In an attempt to resolve the contradiction between a still dominant construction of motherhood, which asserts that exclusive maternal care is the best way to bring up very young children (discussed in more detail in the previous chapter), and an economic reality in which an increasing number of mothers are unable or unwilling to provide such exclusive care, the objective is often a very particular concept of care: to provide a *substitute* home reproducing, as closely as possible, the model of maternal care. This is sought either through individualized forms of care (for example, family day carers or nannies); or through the organization of early childhood institutions and the structuring of relationships between children and staff in these institutions, with importance attached to high ratios of staff to children and the need for close and intimate relationships between staff and children. This idea — that mother care is needed for secure development and that, in its absence, non-maternal care requires to be modelled on a dyadic mother–child relationship — has been termed 'attachment pedagogy' by Singer (1993), who argues that it has had a powerful influence on ideas about children's upbringing, both in the home and in institutions.

The individualistic approach taken to working with children in many early childhood institutions in Britain and the United States can be explained, in part at least, by this construction of these institutions as substitute homes. A comparison between nurseries in Britain, Spain and Italy illustrates how the staffing structure in the British nurseries encouraged staff to see themselves as individuals rather than, as in Spain and Italy, also as part of a group, sharing and working towards common objectives (Penn, 1997b). This was reflected in how the staff perceived and worked with the children.

> There was little sense of the children as a group able to influence or to help each other, and in general the organizational format of the nurseries would make it difficult to achieve, even if it were considered a worthwhile objective. The overall objective was instead the surveillance and monitoring of individual children to make sure they did not come to harm . . . [I]n so far as any theoretical assumptions underpinned the approach to children in the UK nurseries, it was that of Bowlby . . . [which] holds that emotional security, and therefore learning, only takes place in a one to one adult–child relationship, and all other situations are irrelevant. The contribution of the peer group is completely disregarded. (1997b: 52, 53)

This construction of the early childhood institution as producer of a particular form of home-like care has perhaps been most marked in Britain and the United States, with their strong ideological commitment to maternal care, their high valuation of individuality and their ambivalence to more collective relationships and ways of working (New, 1993). But it has also been productive in other countries. The development of a comprehensive system of early childhood institutions in Sweden, starting from the 1930s, was strongly influenced by a discourse of the home; centres for children up to the age of 7 years have been represented as 'professional homes', have been called *daghem* ('day home'), and have organized children into *syskongrupper* ('sibling groups'). This discourse of the early childhood institution as home can in turn be related to a construction of Swedish society as a large community, represented by the metaphor of *Folkhemmet* (the 'People's Home'). But it was also a means of shaping the encounter between the private and the public, the individual and the state: 'it can be seen as an active incorporation and blending of discourses connecting the family and the private into discourses concerning the social and the public . . . [B]inding symbols and representations of the people, the interests of the nation and the home together was a technique that made the world on the one hand intelligible and on the other hand manageable as an object of intervention' (Dahlberg, 1998: 5).

More recently, Sweden has entered a period of uncertainty about the role of the state and public intervention. The metaphor of the *Folkhemmet*, to describe the relationship between the state and the individual, has been problematized and faded. However, the construction of early childhood institutions as producers of substitute home care has gained further legitimation. Concerns have developed about the impersonal and bureaucratic character of both schools and early childhood institutions, and about the need to protect early childhood institutions from becoming more school-like. One response to these concerns has been a new emphasis on early childhood institutions as substitute homes, through privatizing public institutions and encouraging greater closeness between children and adults in a quasi-parental relationship.

The recent history of early childhood institutions in Sweden is also a reminder that the outputs that these institutions are understood to produce are not confined to individual development or conditions for economic success; they can be framed in terms of social progress, with outputs of benefit to society as a whole. Throughout this century, the expansion of early childhood institutions in Sweden has been motivated by a succession of social outcomes, connected by 'modernist visions and revisions of building a progressively better society, an improved human race and freer individuals' (Dahlberg, 1998: 1). Thus, the kindergarten movement of the early twentieth century envisaged early childhood institutions as a means both to liberate children from the constraints of tradition and to re-establish moral order (transforming the poor family into the moral family) and the spirit of community, badly disrupted by industrialization and urbanization (Hultqvist, 1990). The discourse of a comprehensive early childhood pedagogy, which opened up in the 1930s in the context of developing a broad welfare state, took forward the idea of early childhood institutions contributing to the production of a spirit of community, and added other social outcomes — freedom, emancipation, gender equality and solidarity between different social groups.

The production of social outputs, but of a more targeted variety, also constitutes one of the purposes of early childhood institutions in Britain and the United States: social control through processes of normalization. Within the American context, Sandra Scarr refers to one output, social cohesion through 'socializing' economically disadvantaged and minority ethnic children into mainstream culture. In both countries, a strong motive for increasing public investment in early childhood institutions is their role in 'welfare to work' programmes, intended to reduce welfare payments and to reverse the perceived social and moral damage caused by prolonged dependency on these payments, by establishing labour market participation as a normative expectation of all adults. A third output is the prevention or reduction of later problems or disorders in schooling, employment and adult life, and the high costs they impose on society. The most quoted example is the High/Scope Perry Pre-school Project, an intervention with 123 poor black children in a town in Michigan in the United States, which concluded that for every $1 of public funds invested $7 was later saved, mainly through reduced criminality (Schweinhart, Barnes and Weikart, 1993).

In all these instances, the early childhood institution is understood as a means of social intervention, capable of protecting society against the effects of poverty, inequality, insecurity and marginalization. It offers a quasi-medical treatment, a form of social immunization or medication which will reduce current social ills or protect against future infection. In all cases, the early childhood institution is embedded in a construction of the young child as weak, dependent and 'in need', 'the poor child — the deficit [child] or the child at risk, with limited capacities and in need of protection' (Dahlberg, 1995: 14), yet also potentially threatening and antisocial.

Whatever the outcome and whoever the beneficiaries envisaged for early childhood institutions, this construction of these institutions as producers has a common theme. Like most other institutions for children, early childhood institutions are provided primarily to serve adult interests (Mayall, 1996), or to protect children from adults. They constitute places where children are acted upon to produce predetermined, desirable outcomes, places where children are developed, educated, cared for, socialized, and are compensated. If these institutions are proposed in the interests of children and childhood, as places *for* children and childhood, rather than places where children are acted upon, adults (or at least those with the power to make decisions) remain, as Sharon Kagan and her colleagues observe, 'largely uninterested'.

This construction of the early childhood institution as producer of outputs brings to mind, as Lilian Katz observes in the quotation at the beginning of this section, the metaphor of the factory, a place where young children ('the raw material') are processed, to reproduce a body of knowledge and dominant cultural values ('prespecified products') that will equip them to become adults adapted to the economic and social needs of society, and/or to protect society from the consequences of social, familial and individual dysfunction. Just as the factory seeks to adopt standardized methods for efficient production anywhere, so the search is on in early childhood institutions for effective methods of processing that can be exported and reproduced anywhere, irrespective of context, and expressed in the language of 'models' or 'programmes', and the question 'what works?'

There is one other construction of the early childhood institution which is increasingly prominent: as a business. Early childhood institutions are still understood to be producers, but they are additionally understood as businesses competing in a market to sell their product(s) — for example, developmental outcomes, school readiness, care in a substitute home, prevention of later delinquency — to customers or consumers, invariably adults, never children (who lack the means to be consumers), most often parents, but also employers or public agencies.

This development is again most apparent in Britain and the United States. In recent years, these countries have witnessed a huge expansion of private markets in 'child care services' (day nurseries, family day care, nannies and so on) competing for the business of a growing number of parents who want care and education for their children and a growing number of employers who want to offer 'child care' support as part of their package of employee benefits. But the concept has also taken hold in public services, for example, in early childhood institutions in Sweden where, in the context of a shift towards a more market-oriented social welfare system, 'the work being carried out in child care centres is often compared with the work carried out in private business' (Dahlberg and Åsén, 1994: 161).

These constructions of the early childhood institution produce matching constructions of the early childhood worker. First, she is a *technician*, whose task is to ensure the efficient production of the institution's outcomes, however framed, for example, transmitting a predetermined body of knowledge to the child or supporting the child's development to ensure that each milestone is reached at the correct age. The technology she administers incorporates a range of norms or standards: where the child should be at his or her current stage of development and the achievable goal; what activities are appropriate to the child's stage of development; what the answers are to the questions she puts to the child, and so on. The outcomes are known and prescribed, even though the child may be allowed some choice and freedom in how he or she achieves them. From a Foucauldian perspective, she is the effect of disciplinary power, but also exercises power in her work with children and parents, embodying the discourse of developmental psychology which produces understandings of the child and shapes practice with him or her.

Second, she is a *substitute parent* providing a close, intimate relationship with the children in her charge. 'She' is significant. Because of the gendered nature of parenting, with mothers still viewed as primarily responsible for actual caring, the substitute parent is expected to be a substitute mother. This in turn contributes to the production of a highly gendered workforce.

Finally, she is an *entrepreneur*. She must successfully market and sell her product. She must manage the institution to ensure high productivity and conformity to standards, in short ensuring an efficient production process.

The Early Childhood Institution, the Nation State and Capitalism

Viewed from the perspective of the project of modernity, early childhood institutions have been increasingly considered a necessary technology for progress. Many constructions of the early childhood institution, as indeed of other institutions for children such as schools, embody an idea of social redemption through the application of science to children, an ideal which has strongly influenced modern life (Popkewitz, 1998b). Such institutions have come to be seen not only as places for the transmission of knowledge, but also as places where social and psychological problems can be solved with the careful application of behavioural and social sciences.

> This emerging reliance on science and technology, coupled with a romantic view of the purity and perfectability of the child, led to the perception that children are appropriate vehicles for solving problems in society. The notion was that if we can

somehow intervene in the lives of children, then poverty, racism, crime, drug abuse and any number of social ills can be erased. Children became instruments of society's need to improve itself, and childhood became a time during which social problems were either solved or determined to be unsolvable. (Hatch, 1995: 118–9)

This redemptive theme runs through the history of early childhood institutions, up to the present day. But we can also see changes in the influences shaping early childhood institutions and their purposes. Readings (1996) argues that, faced by the related changes in capitalism and the power of the nation state discussed in Chapter 1, universities are transforming themselves from being the ideological arm of the nation state, striving together to recognize the idea of a national culture and identity, to bureaucratically organized and relatively consumer-oriented corporations at the service of transnational capitalism.

> Global fusion and national fission go hand in hand and work together to efface the linking of the nation state and symbolic life that has constituted the idea of 'national culture' since the eighteenth century. It is now pointless to seek the destiny of the university in its capacity to realize the essence of a nation state and its people . . . Contemporary students are consumers rather than national subjects . . . Consumerism is a sign the individual is no longer a political entity, not subject to the nation state. (1996: 51, 53)

Although it is not as clear as for the university, we can still see how these economic and political changes have also affected early childhood institutions. We have already noted how the development of early childhood institutions in Sweden has been closely related to the development of a vision of Swedish society and the formation of a modern, industrialized nation state. Similarly in France, the *écoles maternelles*, or nursery schools, have been closely connected to the nation state, being viewed as a means of introducing the young French child into citizenship and civic values. As another example, the British government expanded nursery provision rapidly during the Second World War in the interests of the nation state, to ensure a supply of female labour for war industries (then ran down this provision when war ended and it was decided that the national priority was employment for men demobilized from the armed forces).

But the more recent growth of early childhood institutions, over the last three decades or so, can be seen as related to the weakening of the nation state and the growth of deregulated global capitalism discussed in Chapter 1. In a world in which the economic is no longer subjugated to the political and capitalism 'swallows up' the notion of the nation state, increasingly powerless nation states become increasingly managerial (Readings, 1996), seeking to entice transnational corporations by providing conditions for profitable investment. Amongst the conditions is the assurance of a ready supply of competitive labour, which means sufficient numbers of women and men in their 'prime working years' (i.e. between 25 and 50 years old), with the skills required in the modern workplace and prepared to work 'flexibly' and intensively.

In this scenario, early childhood institutions are a necessary means for ensuring labour supply, providing care for the children of today's labour force and, it is argued, enhancing the performance of tomorrow's labour force. While the dominance of the economic over the political, of transnational capitalism over the nation state, is further reflected in the language of business, management and consumerism which more and more permeates early childhood institutions, their purposes and practice. In this context, as already noted, early childhood institutions are increasingly seen as businesses, whether operating as autonomous for-profit 'service providers' within a private market, as in much of the English-speaking world, or within a publicly financed and managed system, as in Sweden.

However, things are not quite as simple as this outline may suggest. Many different discourses are interacting, as we can see if we take the case of Sweden. Recently, early childhood institutions in Sweden have been integrated into the *national* educational system (previously being within the social welfare system), and have got their first *national* curriculum, which might suggest even closer association with the nation state. At the same time, however, we can observe how local authorities, who are actually in charge of these institutions, are abandoning the justification of these institutions as vehicles for national culture and goals. In effect, a process of redefinition has begun where early childhood institutions, even if still financed by the state, are changing from a very close ideological relation to the state to being bureaucratically organized, relatively autonomous and consumer-oriented; the same transformation is occurring among local authorities themselves, which behave increasingly as autonomous consumer-oriented organizations, rather than political and cultural centres related to the nation state. From being closely connected to the common good, both institutions and authorities are more and more turned into business enterprises (Dahlberg, 1998; Dahlberg and Åsén, 1994).

In this process parents and children will be constructed and think of themselves less and less as members of a community and more and more as consumers of services, something which is also obvious in the rhetoric. Even if profit is not yet on the agenda, the language of economic management and free choice is introduced and words such as *parents* are exchanged for words such as *consumers*. This change in language symbolizes a shift in which early childhood institutions are no longer seen as essentially ideological and tied to the self-reproduction of the nation state. They become a human resource for the market place instead of a means for the development of a national culture. In this process, where the early childhood system turns from being an institution connected to the nation state into a business organization serving the needs of business, knowledge has itself become commodified as information and as a good that can be sold on a market (Bernstein, 1990; Dahlberg, 1998).

In a situation like this it is easy to become nostalgic or enter into cynical despair when the lost mission of liberal education becomes visible. This is also how we can understand the struggle that we can see today for going back to the Enlightenment project, and the relationship it posits between educational institutions and the nation state, national culture and national identity. But given the complexity of the space in which early childhood institutions are presently located, we no longer think that it is fruitful to do this.

Looking back, we do not want to give up the hope that these institutions can still be connected to the broader social, political and cultural tasks of the nation state. However, through working more closely into the postmodern critique of the modernist project we are now more aware of the difficulties attached to realizing this hope. We cannot any longer position early childhood institutions by appealing to values of reason as the predetermined goal to strive for, nor values such as autonomy and culture. For these values have been constituted through the meta-narratives of modernity, and as such have functioned as a means of unification, normalization and totalization. How then to take a stand against consumerism before early childhood care and education embarks irrevocably upon the path of becoming bureaucratic businesses dedicated to the service of global capitalism?

The Construction of the Early Childhood Institution as a Forum in Civil Society

Civil Society

The words 'civil society' name the space of uncoerced human association and also the set of relational networks — formed for the sake of family, faith, interest and ideology — that fill up that space. (Walzer, 1992: 92)

Participation is not seen as an activity that is only and most truly possible in a narrowly defined political realm, but as an activity that can be realized in the social and cultural spheres as well . . . This conception of participation, which emphasizes the determination of norms of action through the practical debate of all affected by them, has the distinctive advantage that it articulates a vision of the political true to the realities of complex, modern societies. (Benhabib, 1992: 104–5)

The increasing numbers of early childhood institutions in most Minority World countries are part of a recent shift of 'reproduction', including the care and education of young children, away from the private domain of the household and the extended family (although these remain very important). But when this happens, to where is 'reproduction' shifted? In the case of early childhood institutions, there are choices. Where these institutions are located has implications for the social construction of the early childhood institution: what we think they are, how we understand their purposes. In many cases, early childhood institutions have been situated either within the domain of the state (i.e. provided by central or local government) or within the economic domain (i.e. provided by the workplace or as businesses operating within a private market). But early childhood institutions can be situated in a different domain — civil society.

Civil society has several contradictory meanings. For example, liberal theory of democracy, whose origins lie in Locke's development of Hobbes' theory, has seen society as constituted of two spheres: the state and civil society, the latter viewed as a society of individuals integrated only through their economic relations. The state is differentiated from social life and should restrict its intervention in the civil society to protecting individual rights, in particular the right to property. In contrast republican theory, going back to ancient Greek society, distinguishes the state from the household, and regards the state as the only form of public sphere and the only possibility for social life; there is no distinction between political and civil society. As in liberal theory, the state does not deal with economic matters, but unlike liberal theory should be engaged with the realization of the good life.

Our understanding of civil society is somewhat different again. It has much in common with the definition of civil society 'as a sphere of social interaction between economy and state, composed above all of the intimate sphere (especially the family), the sphere of associations (especially voluntary associations), social movements and forms of public communication' (Cohen and Arato, 1992: ix). We would however view the 'intimate sphere' as a distinct and fourth area, apart from but in relationship with the state, the economy and civil society. Civil society can therefore be seen as being between and in relationship with these other three areas and their institutions (for example, government at different levels; the market, work organizations and trade unions; households and families). Civil society is 'the space of uncoerced human association' where individuals can come together to engage in activities of common interest, which may be of many kinds — cultural, social, economic and political.

Among the defining features of civil society, Cohen and Arato refer to *social movements* and *associations*. Since the 1960s, there has been a strong emergence of what Melucci (1989) calls new social movements. These have been analysed in relation to economic change and the continuing evolution of capitalism, gaining ground against older political movements such as mass political parties and trade unions, which were built around homogeneous and stable class identities produced during the period of 'organized capitalism' and industrialism. New social movements reflect weakening and fragmentation of these identities in increasingly complex post-industrial societies and a new phase of what has been called 'disorganized capitalism'. They have also been analysed from a postmodern perspective, embodying the 'death of metanarratives' and a new 'politics of difference' which draws attention to the particularities of group, place, community and history (Kumar, 1995).

New social movements can be seen therefore as one expression of what has been called a radical and plural democracy, responsive to the complexity, fluidity and ambiguity of identity and in which '*différance* is construed as the condition of possibility of being' (Mouffe, 1996b: 246). Rather than an essentialist notion of groups with given, stable and coherent interests and identities, new social movements can be seen to open up possibilities for shifting forms of alliances which recognize multiple interests and identities. From this perspective, consensus is a dangerous utopia, threatening to absorb otherness into a smothering and oppressive oneness and harmony, while 'recognition of undecidability is the condition of existence of democratic politics' (Mouffe, 1996b: 254). Conflict and confrontation, far from being signs of imperfection, indicate a democracy that is alive and inhabited by pluralism: 'that is why, in Derrida's words, democracy will always be "to come", traversed by undecidability and for ever keeping open its element of promise' (Mouffe, 1996a: 11).

Of particular importance to our subject, Melucci sees social movements as social constructions, in which a collective identity is constructed through an interactional process. They are systems of action, complex networks connecting many different elements, which through communication, negotiation and confrontation between the actors involved produce meaning, decisions and collective action. Without the challenges these new movements pose, Melucci argues, complex societies would not be capable of posing questions about meaning, and could not challenge the accepted wisdom or dominant discourse.

Some social scientists today, including many feminists, consider that rejecting a universal and essentialist perspective jeopardizes the democratic ideal of the Enlightenment. It seems to us, however, that it opens up the possibility for a new understanding of democracy in postmodern times, which seeks to avoid the oppression of reducing our identity to one single and constant position — be it class, race, gender or whatever. This new understanding of democracy calls for new forms of collective action and the proliferation of public spaces or forums in which collective action can take place. Melucci finds in new social movements a potential for new societal forms of collective action and thus an enlargement of democracy in complex societies. Collective action need no longer be channelled only through the established state and economic institutions (parliament, trade unions, etc.) but can also be expressed through democratic institutions situated in the framework of civil society; it is not a matter of 'either/or' but of 'and/also'.

Cohen and Arato also emphasize the democratic potential of civil society through

> a notion of self-limiting democratizing movements seeking to expand and protect spaces for both negative liberty and positive freedom . . . [T]he rights to communication, assembly and association, among others, constitute the public and associational spheres of civil society as spheres of *positive freedom* within which agents can collectively debate issues of common concern, act in concert, assert new rights, and exercise influence on political (and potentially economic) society. (1992: 17, 23, original emphasis)

Association is an important feature of civil society. In his study of Italian regional government, the American political scientist Robert Putnam (1993) describes civic associations as networks of civic engagement, which 'represent intense horizontal interaction', citing as examples 'neighbourhood associations, choral societies, cooperatives, sports clubs, mass-based parties and the like'. He argues that civic associations make a major contribution to the effectiveness of both economic life and democratic government, demonstrating that Italian regions with successful economies and regional governments (in particular, the region of Emilia Romagna, in which Reggio Emilia is located) also have the greatest number of civic associations. The key to understanding this relationship is what Putnam calls

'social capital' — trust, reciprocity, respect and other features of social organization which are an important condition for the economic and political success of
a society. Networks of civic associations constitute 'an essential form of social
capital', instilling in their members habits of cooperation, solidarity and public-
spiritedness; 'the denser such networks in a community, the more likely that its
citizens will be able to cooperate for mutual benefit' (1993: 173).

Forums in Civil Society

Early childhood institutions can be understood as *public forums situated in civil
society in which children and adults participate together in projects of social,
cultural, political and economic significance*. Before considering these projects in
more detail, we need to examine the concept of a 'forum'.

Forums are an important feature of civil society. If civil society is where
individuals — children, young people and adults — can come together to participate and engage in activities or projects of common interest and collective action,
then forums are places where this coming together, this meeting, occurs. They have
much in common with Putnam's concept of 'civil association', and also with the
concept of 'public space', described below by Henri Giroux in relation to the
school:

> The school is best understood as a polity, as a locus for citizenship . . . To bring
> schools closer to the concept of polity, it is necessary to define them as public
> spaces that seek to recapture the idea of critical democracy and community . . . By
> 'public space' I mean, as Hannah Arendt did, a concrete set of learning conditions
> where people come together to speak, to engage in dialogue, to share their stories
> and to struggle together within social relations that strengthen rather than weaken
> possibilities for active citizenship. (1989: 201)

Forums provide a locus for active citizenship through participation in collective action and the practice of democracy. A strong and vibrant civil society
requires this type of engagement by active citizens in forums — and out of such
activity may come new social movements. Forums can therefore be understood as
democratic institutions, operating beyond 'a narrowly defined political realm' in
'social and cultural spheres'. But this does not mean they are substitutes for political institutions. They are complementary, representing a new autonomous political
arena alongside more institutionalized arenas (such as the state and the market) and
offering an enlarged sphere for the operation of politics. Political institutions can
support the idea and promote the availability of forums; while forums provide
opportunities within civil society for politicians (as representatives from the state's
political institutions) and others to meet together to engage in matters of common
interest. To do this effectively — for forums to engage politicians and others in
dialogue — requires *decentralization* of political authority to the most local level
possible for the subjects of engagement, such as pedagogy for younger and older
(school age) children and personal social services.

The operation of the forum as a locus of participation and dialogue, enabling politicians and others to engage actively and productively, to deepen their understanding, also requires procedures and conditions that support this function. Some procedures have been developed specifically in early childhood institutions, and might have wider applicability. These include *documentation*, which in Reggio has been seen as 'a democratic process to inform the public about the contents of the [early childhood institutions]' (Rinaldi, 1993: 122); and the participation of 'wise helpers', such as *pedagogista* or pedagogical advisers and philosophers, another feature of Reggio. Both are discussed in more detail in Chapters 6 and 7.

They also require 'the conditions of *universal moral respect* and *egalitarian reciprocity*' (Benhabib, 1992: 105). The principle of universal moral respect concerns 'the right of all beings capable of speech and action to participate in the moral conversation', which implies the participation of children. While the principle of egalitarian reciprocity requires each participant having the same rights 'to various speech acts, to initiate new topics, to ask for reflection about the presuppositions of the conversation'. The cultivation of moral and cognitive abilities is also important, for example, the capacity 'to reverse perspectives, that is, the willingness to reason from the Others' point of view, and the sensitivity to hear their voice'; and the ability to see the Other as equal but different. These procedures and conditions not only contribute to democratic participation and practice in forums, but also to the ethics of an encounter.

However, it is important to recognize that the comprehensive and perfect application of such procedures and conditions is unlikely. They are extremely demanding and may not even be universally agreed. Consensus may be neither required nor desired, and conflict or confrontation may be considered a healthy element of dialogue, but disagreement can become destructive. There are issues of power which can reduce possibilities for participation and dialogue. In many ways we are offering an ideal construction, how we would like things to be, but in practice things are unpredictable, we cannot be certain which way they will go. The forum in civil society is a possibility worthy of struggle, not a certainty guaranteed of success if only instructions are followed.

The Early Childhood Institution as a Forum in Civil Society

It seems to us that early childhood institutions have the possibility of being forums in civil society. But this is a choice to be made and an aspiration to be worked for; they are not inherently so. To be forums, early childhood institutions must choose to understand themselves as such and actively assume the task. They must locate themselves within civil society, rather than within the state or the economy, being in relationship with both of these spheres but remaining separate.

Early childhood institutions which wish to be forums in civil society need to be open to *all* families with young children — both children and adults — and to the world. Access should not be constrained either by cost or by admission criteria, for example, the employment status of parents. Early childhood institutions which operate purely as businesses within the private market or for the employees of particular employers are situated in the economic sphere; they cannot also be forums within civil society. To be so, early childhood institutions should be largely or wholly publicly resourced (but not necessarily publicly managed) and available as of right to all local children, as such being not only forums, but also community institutions. To this end, employers can make an important contribution, by paying an equitable share of taxation from which early childhood institutions open to all children can be adequately resourced. They can also contribute by engaging in the forums constituted by the early childhood institution, alongside other adults and children.

For some years now there has been a widespread decline in the vitality of public life, marked by falling participation rates in various activities and a widely-remarked turn to private life and pursuits (Kumar, 1995; Putnam, 1995). Many types of civic association or forum which flourished in industrial society are in long-term decline, for example, colliery brass bands or working men's clubs in certain British communities where their significance has reduced with the contraction of mining and heavy industry. Early childhood institutions are increasing everywhere. They offer the possibility of forming part of a new generation of forums and civic associations, embedded in and attuned to the world we live in today, which could revitalize the public sphere through a rich variety of projects.

Nor is this wishful thinking. The early childhood institutions of Reggio Emilia can be seen as vivid examples of early childhood institutions as forums in civil society. Influenced by systems theory, they see themselves as systems of relationships and communication located within and inextricably part of the larger system of society, closely linked to their local community, including families and local government. Nor is Reggio alone: there are many examples, from many countries, of early childhood institutions beginning to assume this role and explore the opportunities it affords.

The Projects of the Early Childhood Institution

If early childhood institutions can constitute forums in civil society where children and adults may participate together in projects of social, cultural, political and economic significance, *what are these projects*? There can be no final, definitive agenda. Determining these projects — answering the basic question 'what are early childhood institutions for?' — is one of the political projects of the institution as forum, as well as for the wider society; it is an issue for continuous dialogue between children and adults, including local and national politicians. The only generalization that can be made is that the early childhood institution viewed as forum in civil society is a place *for* children to live their childhoods. It is a permanent feature of the community offering many opportunities and possibilities, not always knowable from the start, not an intervention of fixed duration, known purposes and predetermined outcomes.

Despite not knowing for sure what the projects of the early childhood institution should or will be, we can suggest four possibilities by way of illustration. First and foremost is *the project of pedagogical work or learning*. We have argued in Chapter 3, from a postmodern perspective, that knowledge and identity are constructed and that construction occurs not from young children being taught but from what children do themselves, as a consequence of their activities, relationships and the resources available to them — by being in relation and dialogue with the world. When the human encounter is the basis for pedagogy, as well as for ethical relationships, then to facilitate and accomplish these encounters becomes the 'true' role of early childhood institutions. Viewed in this way, the early childhood institution provides a space for activities and relationships, enabling the co-construction of knowledge and identity. A similar idea of creating public spaces for dialogic learning inspired Paulo Freire's work in Brazil, in this case in adult education projects:

> [Cultural centers] were large spaces that housed cultural circles, rotating libraries, theatrical presentations, recreational activities and sports events. The cultural circles were spaces where teaching and learning took place in a dialogic fashion. They were spaces for knowledge, for knowing, not for knowledge transference; places where knowledge was produced, not simply presented to or imposed on the learner. They were spaces where new hypotheses for reading the world were created. (Freire, 1996: 121)

More specifically, early childhood institutions provide children with tools and resources for exploring and problem solving, negotiation and meaning making. These include: thematic project work based on everyday experience, giving children the possibility to express themselves in many languages; the support and inspiration of reflective practitioners; and opportunities for small groups of children to work together in exploring and interpreting the surrounding world, and, by doing so, to take responsibility for their own learning or knowledge construction. The early childhood institution offers a pedagogy based on relationships and dialogue and the ethics of an encounter. This pedagogy recognizes that the child is co-constructing knowledge, not being taught an existing corpus of knowledge; and that producing knowledge, making meaning, is done in relationship with other co-constructors, both adults and children, who must not only take the young child's ideas and theories seriously, but be ready to confront and challenge them.

This pedagogical project of early childhood institutions, in which children are understood to be actively engaged in co-constructing their own and others' knowledge, has been described by Loris Malaguzzi, referring to the pedagogical work in Reggio Emilia:

> The wider the range of possibilities we offer children, the more intense will be their motivations and the richer their experiences . . . All people end by discovering the surprising and extraordinary strengths and capabilities of children linked with an inexhaustible need for expression . . . Children are autonomously capable of making meaning from experiences — the adults' role is to activate the meaning-making competencies of children . . . Between learning and teaching, we [in Reggio

Emilia] honour the first; the aim of teaching is to provide conditions for learning. (Malaguzzi, 1993b: 72–3, 77)

As we have already discussed in the previous chapter, this ideal of pedagogical work presupposes early childhood institutions which are permeated with active participation and a reflective culture, and which are open to, and engaged in dialogue with, the surrounding world. It assumes an active interest in the times we live in, such as questions concerning our environment, peace, justice and human coexistence, and new debates and achievements within science and philosophy. Kirsti Hakkola, a Finnish pedagogue, has expressed this idea in a very evocative way in relation to her own early childhood institution in Helsinki: 'I want our pre-school to be a preschool without walls, and which is placed on a public square.'

The second important project, already introduced in the preceding discussion of forums, is to *promote an informed, participatory and critical local democracy*. Early childhood institutions have the potential to be places where parents, politicians and others (including employers, trade unions and the general citizenry) can come together with pedagogues and children to engage in dialogue on a range of subjects. There is no closed and definitive agenda of subjects, but several subjects might be suggested.

First and foremost, early childhood institutions as forums in civil society provide an opportunity for *constructing a new public discourse about early childhood* itself, an important part of what might be called a 'politics of childhood'. For early childhood institutions are one obvious place for the public discussion of issues such as pedagogical work and of questions such as: How do we understand early childhood? What is our construction of the young child? What is the relationship between young children and society? As we shall discuss further in Chapter 7, which is about pedagogical documentation, this first requires problematizing the dominant discursive regimes in pedagogical practice as well as in social and behavioural sciences, including the constructions of the child, early childhood institutions and the work of these institutions that they produce. Doing this, the way is opened up to reconstruct alternative images of the child, early childhood institutions and early childhood pedagogy.

Understood in this way, working with parents does not mean pedagogues giving to parents uncontextualized and unproblematized information about what they (the pedagogues) are doing, nor 'educating' parents in 'good' practice by transmitting a simplified version of a technology of child development and child rearing. Rather it means both parents and pedagogues (and others) entering into a reflective and analytic relationship involving deepening understanding and the possibility of making judgments about the pedagogical work (within the 'discourse of meaning making' discussed in Chapter 5), and in which pedagogical documentation (discussed in Chapter 7) plays an important part. 'Parental participation' in this context is a description of democratic practice rather than a means of social control or technological transfer.

Another subject for a politics of childhood may be called *issues of the 'good life'*. In the case of early childhood institutions, 'good life' questions might include

'What do we want for our children?' and 'What is a good childhood?'. By using the term *good life* we do not assume that there is one true good life to be discovered and lived, one conception of the good life that will prove equally acceptable to all. There may well be many conceptions in a plural democracy. The point is, however, that the early childhood institution as forum provides opportunities to enter into dialogue with others about good life issues, and the possibility of searching for some measure of agreement without any guarantee of or need for finding agreement.

> It may very well be that discourses will not yield conceptions of the good life equally acceptable to all . . . [But] it is crucial that we view our conceptions of the good life as matters about which intersubjective debate is possible, even if intersubjective consensus, let alone legislation, in these areas remains undesirable. However, only through such argumentative processes can we . . . render our conception of the good life accessible to moral reflection and moral transformation. (Benhabib, 1990: 349–50)

A third possible subject area concerns *the relationship between employment and caring for children*. At the same time that they provide care and enable parents to participate in the labour market, early childhood institutions can also provide opportunities for the relationship between employment and caring for children to be problematized and debated, through children and adults — including parents, politicians, employers and trade unionists — engaging in critical dialogue based on actual practice and experience. In this way, the early childhood institution can avoid uncritical collusion with the demands of the labour market, however unsympathetic to parenting these demands may be, and resist the mechanistic role of simply ensuring an adequate supply of labour (thus being reduced to serving the same function as a company car park or works canteen). Instead, it can become a space for democratic debate and deepening understanding about the important subject of the relationship between production and reproduction and, more generally, between capitalism and society, leading in turn to the possibility of challenge and action.

The democratic project of the early childhood institution can also be embodied in the pedagogical work itself, as it has been in Scandinavia where ideas of common good and democracy have always been influential. For example, the Danish system of early childhood institutions pays great attention to democratic values, in government guidelines that emphasize that children must be listened to, in the training of pedagogues and in the everyday life of the institutions themselves. Democracy is understood to involve 'the child's right to play an active and creative part in his/her own life — from the very early years onwards'; experiencing democracy in early childhood institutions 'will lead to [the child gaining] an understanding of and insight into modern democracy' (Lauridsen, 1995: 3).

This vision of a democratic project for the early childhood institution can be related to our earlier discussion of new societal forms of democracy situated in civil society. Early childhood institutions operating as forums in which there is active democratic practice addressing important subjects — and we understand early child-hood and pedagogical work to be very important subjects — have the potential to contribute to the enlargement of democracy in complex postindustrial societies. More specifically, they can form part of a reconstruction of democracy at local level based on new relationships between elected representatives from established political institutions (local authorities, municipalities, communes, regional govern-ments) and new democratic forums. We can also see in the pedagogical work in Reggio Emilia, and in the way it has inspired pedagogical work in many other places (the subject of Chapter 6), that early childhood institutions have the potential to generate new social movements.

The preceding projects — pedagogical work as co-construction of knowledge and identity and opening up new possibilities for democracy — can be viewed as contributing to *the exercise of freedom*, understood in a Foucauldian sense as being able to think critically — to think opposition, to promote 'reflective indocility' — and by so doing to take more control of our lives, through questioning the way we view the world and increasing our ability to shape our own subjectivity. Thinking critically makes it possible to unmask and free ourselves from existing discourses, concepts and constructions, and to move on by producing different ones. It is

> a matter of flushing out . . . thought and trying to change it: to show that things are not as self-evident as one believed, to see that that which is accepted as self-evident will no longer be accepted as such. Practising criticism is a matter of making facile gestures difficult . . . As soon as one no longer thinks things as one formerly thought them, transformation becomes very urgent, very difficult and quite possible. (Foucault, 1988: 155)

Understood in this way, exercising freedom is not some revolutionary activity. Rather it is the 'art of not being governed so much' by power (Foucault, 1990). It is a 'practice to dislodge the ordering principles' and make 'the forms of reasoning and rules for "telling the truth" potentially contingent, historical and susceptible to critique' and by doing so creating a greater range of possibilities for the subject to act (Popkewitz, 1998b).

Exercising freedom does not mean or require absence of doubt, through estab-lishing some unchallengeable body of facts on the basis of which we can say that we now know the world. In his book *Fear of Freedom*, the psychoanalyst Erich Fromm (1942) contrasts this 'compulsive quest for certainty', with what he terms 'positive freedom', the freedom to act spontaneously and to think for ourselves, a freedom which does not, however, eliminate what he calls 'rational doubt'. For the person, adult or child, who experiences positive freedom is not only free to ques-tion, but also welcomes uncertainty. Freedom may therefore mean feeling free to 'not know' and resisting pressures to foreclose by reaching definitive positions.

The third project of the early childhood institution arises from its potential for the *establishment and strengthening of social networks of relationships*, between children, between adults (both parents and other adults engaged in the institution) and between children and adults. The early childhood institution as 'a place of shared lives and relationships, among many adults and very many children' (Malaguzzi, 1993b: 56) can help to counter the 'loneliness, the indifference and the violence that more and more characterize modern life' (Malaguzzi, 1993a: 10), and provide sources of social support. They can contribute to the cohesion of local communities and, more generally, civil society. They can provide opportunities for what Putnam (1993) refers to as 'intense horizontal interaction', and the increase of 'social capital' by fostering reciprocity and trust, cooperation and solidarity.

A fourth possible project of early childhood institutions, and the last we discuss in detail here, concerns *the care they provide for children which enables parents to participate in the labour market*. This child-care task supports gender equality in the labour market and employed parents in their struggle to manage the relationship between employment and family life. It is also of economic significance, making an important contribution to an efficient use of labour and to the successful performance of both private and public sectors in the economy. It is self-evident that in societies where most parents are employed, provision must be made to ensure the care of children while parents are at work. In our view, however, child care should never be the only or dominating purpose of early childhood institutions as forums in civil society; indeed such a focus is incompatible with this construction of the early childhood institution. As we have already argued, early childhood institutions as forums should be open to all children whether or not their parents have employment, and they should house a variety of projects, including pedagogical work that is important to all children, irrespective of their parents' employment status. Child care becomes a major, often dominating, concern in societies which have neglected to make adequate provision for this requirement (such as in Britain, where faced by growing parental employment and past political indifference, the Labour Government elected in 1996 gave high priority to what it termed a 'national child-care strategy'). Where adequate provision is made, as in the early childhood institutions of Reggio Emilia or Stockholm, 'child care' need no longer be a dominating concern and attention can focus on a range of other projects such as pedagogical work.

The early childhood institution, operating as a forum in civil society and undertaking the sort of projects outlined above, has an important contribution to make not only to the reconstruction of local democracy, but also to a reconstruction of the welfare state. As we have already suggested, the early childhood institution is one of a range of new or transformed *community institutions of social solidarity* that have the potential to foster and support new relationships of cooperation and solidarity in changing societies distinguished by increasing diversity, complexity and individualism. As such, they can help to give meaning to 'community'. These institutions of a reconstructed welfare state are open to all — children and adults, whether within or without the labour market, irrespective of income or class. They are committed to equality — but an equality that recognizes the Other as different — and to a democratic practice that replaces earlier welfare state institutions located within large, top-down bureaucratic systems with a commitment to equality as sameness. Reflecting the broad aims of a reconstructed welfare state, early childhood institutions as forums can serve multiple purposes: as a means of *inclusion*, for children and adults, in civil society; creating opportunities for *the exercise of democracy and freedom*, through learning, dialogue and critical thinking; offering wide-ranging and flexible forms of *social support* for parents, both in and out of the labour market; and providing a mechanism of *redistribution* of resources towards children as a social group.

For us the question has been how to re-vision early childhood institutions and pedagogy, transgressing ideas of them primarily as ideological apparatus of the nation state or as bureaucratic organizations committed to consumerism and transnational capitalism. This is not to say that they can be divorced entirely from either; it would be misleading to pretend that early childhood institutions are not participants in both the nation state and the capitalist system. What is at stake is how they participate in and contribute to both, and whether and how they may find other purposes in other spheres.

We have tried to explore one possibility, of early childhood institutions as forums in civil society. We have seen them as contributing to pedagogy, welfare and community, conceptualizing them as community institutions for promoting learning, democracy, social solidarity and economic well-being, but also with many other possibilities. Rather than being places for finding truth through transmitting an autonomous body of knowledge, for prioritizing the establishment of consensus and unity, for forming a unified identity or for applying techniques of normalization, we see forums as places that are always open for discussion and questioning. Our ideal of early childhood institutions as forums is that they are places which encourage 'indocility' and confrontation, keep questions of meaning open, value listening to thought: in short that they serve as 'loci of debate and dissensus', and as 'sites of obligation, loci of ethical practices' (Readings, 1996: 154). Instead of viewing early childhood institutions as ideal communities, with ideal children and ideal parents and pedagogues, we see them more as places where *the question of being together is posed*, in which it is recognized that communication is neither transparent, nor grounded upon and reinforced by a common cultural identity.

Forums, not Substitute Homes

It will be apparent from our construction of the early childhood institution as a forum in civil society that we do not envision it as part of the state or the economy. But neither indeed do we see it as part of the private domain of the household. It is *not* to be understood as a substitute home. Young children — both under and over 3 years of age — are seen as able to manage, and indeed to desire and thrive on, relationships with small groups of other children and adults, without risking either their own well-being or their relationship with their parents. Not only is there no need to try in some way to provide a substitute home, but the benefit from attending an early childhood institution comes from it *not* being a home. It offers something quite different, but quite complementary, so the child gets, so to speak, the best of two environments.

If we approach early childhood institutions as forums in civil society, the concept of closeness and intimacy becomes problematic. It can turn public situations and institutions private. As such, it not only creates a 'false closeness' and risks trying to duplicate, necessarily unsuccessfully, the important learning processes that occur outside the institution. But it also hinders the ability of the institution to realize its own social life and relationships and devalues or trivializes the idea of a public space.

To abandon ideas of intimacy, closeness and cosiness does not leave indifference, callousness and coldness. It does not mean being uncaring. Instead, Ziehe (1989) offers a contrasting concept to closeness, the concept of *intensity of relationships* implying a complex and dense web or network connecting people, environments and activities which opens up many opportunities for the young child within a vision of the rich child and a co-constructing pedagogy. This is in line with the pedagogical work in Reggio Emilia, which constantly challenges the child's thinking and 'has encouraged multiple languages, confrontation, ambivalence and ambiguity . . . the whole milieu speaks of a collective adventure . . . one could almost say that Reggio has created a new university' (Dahlberg, 1995: 17).

If the early childhood institution is not understood as a substitute home, then the early childhood worker is also not to be understood as in any way a substitute parent. What then is the role of the pedagogue, the early childhood worker, in this postmodern construction of the early childhood institution? First and foremost, she (or he) is a co-constructor of knowledge and culture, both the children's and her own, in a pedagogy that 'denies the teacher as neutral transmitter, the student as passive and knowledge as immutable material to impart' (Lather, 1991: 15). The early childhood worker mobilizes children's meaning-making competencies, offering themselves as a resource to whom children can and want to turn, organizing space, materials and situations to provide new opportunities and choices for learning, assisting children to explore the many different languages available to them, listening and watching children, taking their ideas and theories seriously but also prepared to challenge, both in the form of new questions, information and discussions, and in the form of new materials and techniques.

The role also requires that the pedagogue is seen as a researcher and thinker, a reflective practitioner who seeks to deepen her understanding of what is going on and how children learn, through documentation, dialogue, critical reflection and deconstruction (Malaguzzi, 1993b; Rinaldi, 1993).

What Place for the Future and for Interventions?

Our discussion of the early childhood institution as a forum in civil society has taken us far from the beginning of this chapter when we presented an alternative construction, whose concern seems often to be less with the childhood that young children are living and more with the school children and adults they will become, and views these institutions as factories producing specified outcomes or intervention technologies preventing or treating social ills. Are these different constructions totally incompatible?

Our construction of what the early childhood institution can be foregrounds early childhood as an important life stage in its own right and the early childhood institution as a place for the young child and for the life she lives, *here and now*. But can it also be for the future, for the older child, the young person and the adult that the young child will become? An initial hesitancy in answering arises from wishing to avoid any implication that consideration of the future must be at the expense of the present, that we must choose between being and becoming. But if we can be confident in our constructions of the child and early childhood institution, then it seems to us that the answer should be yes, that early childhood institutions can be concerned both with the present and also the future, in that they enable children to relate to and participate in the wider society, in which they live today and will live tomorrow — at school, at college, in work, in families. The questions are, however, what type of society and what type of relationship?

We have discussed in Chapter 3 how the pedagogy of the early childhood institution can be made relevant to living in postmodern conditions. The early childhood institution we have talked about also presumes an information and life-long learning society, as well as a democratic and welfare society. By understanding young children as active co-constructors of their own knowledge, as critical and imaginative thinkers and as the possessors of many languages, the early childhood institution enables young children to acquire a range of complex abilities that active participation in such societies calls for and which will equip them for further learning, future employment and continued citizenship: to adapt to new situations; to take a critical stand; to make choices; to integrate different experiences into a common understanding; to take on board the perspective of others; to articulate their own position and to communicate effectively; and to take initiatives and to be self-assertive (Denzik, 1997).

The language here is particularly difficult. The concept of early childhood education as a *foundation* for lifelong learning or the view that the early childhood institution contributes to children being *ready to learn* by the time they start school, produces a 'poor' child in need of preparation before they can be expected to learn, rather than a 'rich' child capable of learning from birth, whose learning during early childhood is one part of a continuous process of lifelong learning, no more nor less valid and important than other parts. The language of *school readiness* is also problematic from our perspective. Rather than making the child ready for school, it seems to us that the issue is whether the school is prepared for the child who has been in the questioning and co-constructive milieu of the early childhood institution constructed and operating in the way we have outlined above.

Indeed, our discussion of early childhood and early childhood institutions inevitably raises important and challenging questions about schooling and employment. What is the purpose of education? Are schools simply reproducers of knowledge, institutions where the individual is supposed to acquire a specific body of knowledge sanctioned by society, or are they institutions where children co-construct knowledge and their understanding of the world? Are schools also to be constructed as forums in civil society, and if so, what are their projects — economic, social, cultural and political? Do they 'seek to capture the idea of critical democracy and community'? Are schools best understood, as Giroux argues that they should, 'as a locus for citizenship . . . in which students and teachers can engage in a process of deliberation and discussion aimed at advancing the public welfare in accordance with fundamental moral judgements and principles' (1989: 201)? Are schools, in the words of Paulo Freire 'an instrument which is used to facilitate the integration of the younger generation into the logic of the present system and bring about conformity to it or (as) the practice of freedom, the means by which men and women deal critically and creatively with reality and discover how to participate in the transformation of the world?' (1985: 14).

We repeat that we would consider our constructions of the young child and the early childhood institution to be compatible with and supportive of school children and workers who are well attuned to learning and working and living in a postmodern world and in a society of lifelong learning, democracy and welfare. But it seems to us that this long-term perspective is neither the main project of the early childhood institution; nor should we expect the early childhood institution to provide a smooth ride for the schools and the labour market that follow. Indeed, by encouraging critical thinking among young children, and providing a forum for discourse about issues such as the relationship between employment and caring for children, early childhood institutions should challenge conformist practices and oppressive relationships.

Can our construction of early childhood institutions as forums in civil society accommodate the narrow and more instrumental understandings of these institutions as producers of outcomes? This is difficult because such different perspectives are involved. What we have called the dominant construction of the early childhood institution, at least in the United States and Britain, assumes that the young child is located in the private domain of the family. Early childhood institutions come into play when the family is understood as being unable to manage the ideal, as some sort of default arrangement: when parents work and substitute care is needed; when teachers can better educate children over 3; when children are deemed to be at risk or families in need of intervention. Not only does this approach construct the 'poor' child, it introduces dividing practices which classify children according to certain criteria and even allocate children in many cases to different types of institution according to these criteria (in Britain, for example, children classified as needing child care are directed towards private nurseries, many children identified by social workers as in need will be referred to so-called family centres, while children needing education mostly go to classes in primary schools).

We, however, see the child as located in civil society as well as the home, a citizen as well as a family member, requiring relationships with other children and adults to make full use of their tremendous capabilities for learning and to live a good childhood. We see the early childhood institution as a right of citizenship, a means of inclusion in civil society, a pedagogical opportunity, but also as part of the infrastructure that is needed for a strong civil society, democracy and welfare state. The early childhood institution as a forum opens up many opportunities and possibilities, and many things can and do happen in this space.

In this context, the children are not attending an early childhood institution because they are classified as in some way disabled or otherwise in need, or because their families are classified as unable to meet their needs, but because the early childhood institution is a place *for* all children, a recognized part of early childhood. Moreover, as we discuss later, following the pedagogical work in Reggio, our idea of the early childhood institution is a place of close relationships between children, parents and pedagogues, where the work is always the subject of rigorous and public pedagogical documentation and one of the critical questions is 'do we see the child?' In these circumstances, children (or parents) who may need additional resources or other support will be apparent and the necessary resources or support assured. In these circumstances, ensuring children's rights to learn and to relationships and recognizing the potential and capabilities of all children are foregrounded, rather than targeted intervention and meeting needs. Pedagogues work together with parents to mutually deepen their understanding of the child and the pedagogical work, rather than applying technologies of normalization to children and parents.

Given our understanding of the early childhood institution as a complex and multi-faceted organism embedded in civil society, located in a particular context, engaged in co-constructive pedagogical work, fostering solidarity and cooperation and a site for democratic and emancipatory practice, the question, 'Does it work?' seems simplistic and normalizing. Instead, we need to find ways of deepening our understanding of what is going on in the institution, which may suggest new or modified forms of organization or ways of working. What this might entail and how it might be done are major themes of the next three chapters.

The early childhood institution as a forum in civil society opens up many possibilities for the inclusion of the young child in civil society and placing early childhood and early childhood pedagogy high on the agenda of that society. It engages young children with adults, beyond the private domain of the home, and makes young children audible and visible to the wider community. As such, it contributes to giving meaning to the idea of the child as citizen.

In many parts of the Minority World, there has been much debate about the relationship between *care* and *education* in early childhood *services*. Should these services be limited to one function or the other? Should they, in some way, attempt to combine these functions? It seems to us, however, that these are not very productive questions. Today, most children need some non-parental care, for one reason or another, most often because they have parents in the labour market; early childhood institutions, as we have already made clear, need to be geared to provide such child care. Far more productive are questions arising from the subject of this chapter, how we construct early childhood institutions. Who do we think these institutions are for? What do we think they are for? What are their projects? Where do we situate them — in the state, the economic domain or civil society? How do we understand their relationship to democracy and the welfare state?

There are profound choices to be made here, and these choices are never neutral; they are permeated with values. They always carry social implications and consequences. They say a lot about the role and position we give to young children and about how we envisage our democracies, welfare states and societies overall. For early childhood institutions carry great symbolic importance. They are statements about how we, as adults, understand childhood and its relationship to the state, the economy, civil society and the private domain.

Chapter 5

Beyond the Discourse of Quality to the Discourse of Meaning Making

Introduction

> Taxonomy, classification, inventory, catalogue and statistics are the paramount strategies of modern practice. Modern mastery is the power to divide, classify and allocate — in thought, in practice, in the practice of thought and in the thought of practice . . . It is for this reason that ambivalence is the main affliction of modernity and the most worrying of its concerns. (Bauman, 1991: 15)

The age of quality is upon us. But 'quality' itself is not a neutral word. It is a socially constructed concept, with very particular meanings, produced through what we refer to as 'the discourse of quality'. In this chapter, we deconstruct this discourse, look for its origins and analyse its application to the early childhood field where it has become a dominant discursive regime.

It seems to us that the discourse of quality can be understood as a product of Enlightenment thinking, and modernity's zest for order and mastery. As such, it views the world through a modernist lens, and complements modernist constructions of the young child and early childhood institution. The language of quality is also the language of the early childhood institution as producer of pre-specified outcomes and the child as empty vessel, to be prepared to learn and for school, and to be helped on his or her journey of development.

But looking through the lens of postmodernity brings new ways of understanding the world, including young children and their institutions. As we become accustomed to looking through this lens, a new discourse comes into focus. What we call the 'discourse of meaning making' foregrounds deepening understanding of the pedagogical work and other projects of the institution, leading to the possibility of making a judgment of value about these projects. If the 'discourse of quality' can be seen as part of a wider movement of quantification and objectivity intended to reduce or exclude the role of personal judgment, with its attendant problems of partiality and prejudice, self-interest and inconsistency, the 'discourse of meaning making' can be seen as reclaiming the idea of judgment — but understood now to be a discursive act, always made in relationship with others.

The Discourse of Quality

Enlightenment Thinking and Trust in Numbers

Since 1945, and especially since the early 1980s, quality has moved to the top of the agenda in private business and public services. But to fully understand the emergence of a dominant 'discourse of quality', it is necessary to adopt a longer time frame. In the pre-industrial world, where most communication was local in nature, every region, sometimes even different towns, had their own measures: 'this was at least an inconvenience, if not an obstacle, to the growth of large-scale trading networks, and the expansion of capitalism was one important source of the impetus to unify and simplify measures' (Porter, 1995: 25). By contrast, quantification, based on standardization of measurement, is a technology of distance. As such, it has been a necessary condition for increasing globalization — of trade and science — in which communication increasingly went beyond the boundaries of locality and community: 'reliance on numbers and quantitative manipulation minimizes the need for knowledge and personal trust'.

The pre-industrial world privileged personal judgment over objectivity. By contrast, the modern world privileges objectivity, the withdrawal of human agency and its replacement by impartial uniformity, what Porter calls 'trust in numbers'. Quantification has become the great aid to achieving objectivity, acquiring an increasing role not only in economic relationships and in various fields of science, but also in democratic government. Science and democracy have been closely linked in this project, and in both cases the United States has taken a leading role. Following the overwhelming success of quantification in the social, behavioural and medical sciences in the postwar period, there was a major effort to introduce quantitative criteria into public decision making in the 1960s and 1970s:

> It is no accident that the move towards the almost universal quantification of social and applied disciplines was led by the United States and succeeded most fully there. The push for rigor in the disciplines derived in part from the same distrust of unarticulated expert knowledge and the same suspicion of arbitrariness and discretion that shaped political culture so profoundly in the same period. (Porter, 1995: 199)

It has provided a means to replace personal judgments, which have increasingly come to be regarded as undemocratic: 'objectivity means the rule of law, not of men; it implies the subordination of personal interests and prejudices to public standards' (1995: 74).

This growing 'trust in numbers' and the developing technology of quantification that held out the possibility of reducing the world in its complexity and diversity to standardized, comparable, objective, measurable categories can be understood not only as a response to economic change and political imperatives. It is an integral part of the project of modernity and Enlightenment thinking. It is a necessary technology for practices of dividing, classifying and allocating and, as such, a means to impose order and for the exercise of disciplinary power. It represents the application of uniquely rational procedures to the search for certainty, unity and foundations, shedding the shackles of time and place and the limitations of judgment. Yet, as Adorno and Horkheimer (1944, 1997 edition) argue in their analysis of the destructive potential of Enlightenment thinking, 'trust in numbers' carries great risks: 'It makes the dissimilar comparable by reducing it to abstract quantities . . . that which does not reduce to numbers, and ultimately to the one, becomes illusion . . . what cannot be made to agree, indissolubility and irrationality, is converted by means of mathematical theorems . . . it confounds thought and mathematics' (7, 24–5). In laying down the foundations of certainty, meaning may be buried and lost.

The Emergence of the Discourse of Quality

The growing importance of quality in the field of early childhood institutions can be understood in relation to the modernist search for order and certainty grounded in objectivity and quantification. It can be located as part of a wider movement in which the 'discourse of quality' has become increasingly central to economic and political life, a movement which began in the business world and the production of private goods and services. The world of business is therefore a good starting point for seeking to understand the 'discourse of quality', and the meaning of the concept of quality within that discourse.

The concepts of quality control and quality assurance were created in the 1920s (Mäntysaari, 1997). But the 'discourse of quality' gained new momentum in the immediate post-war years, not at first in North America or Europe, but in a Japan that was rebuilding its economy devastated by war and seeking to re-establish its position in the world trading order. An important influence was the American quality expert W. Edwards Deming, who first presented his methods to a Japanese audience in 1950. Faced by increasingly successful competition from Japan, based on a reputation for high-quality goods, American and European companies began to take a heightened interest in quality: 'the Total Quality Management bandwagon started to roll in the early 1980s (and) by the end of the decade, quality was widely recognised as one of the most important factors of success in global markets' (Dickson, 1995: 196).

Bank (1992) gives definitions of quality offered by some of the gurus in the field. Edwards Deming emphasized that quality was about reliability, dependability, predictability and consistency — 'if I had to reduce my message to managers to just a few words, I'd say it all had to do with reducing variation'; Joseph Juran talks about quality as 'fitness for use or purpose'; Philip Crosby refers to quality as conformance to requirements; while William Conway defines quality in terms of consistent, low-cost products and services that customers want and need. The American Society for Quality Control, which 'is considered the leading authority on quality in the world' recognizes that quality is 'a subjective term for which each person has his or her own definition'; but goes on to state that 'in technical usage, quality can have two meanings: (1) the characteristics of a good service that bear on its ability to satisfy stated or implied needs; and (2) a good or service free of deficiencies' (quoted in Bedeian, 1993: 656–7). More recently, however, definitions of quality have begun to emphasize the satisfaction of the customer:

> Traditionally quality has been defined as 'conformance to requirements'. However in the 1980s, quality came to be symbolized by customer satisfaction — the quality movement in the 1980s assumed a customer focus . . . The ultimate aim of improved quality is total customer satisfaction. (1993: 56, 656)

The discourse of quality has spread not only globally, but from industry to industry (Bank, 1992). It has also spread from the private to the public sector:

> The concept of quality has been wholeheartedly embraced [in the 1980s] by those seeking to rationalise and shake up the public sector in the UK . . . because it includes notions of efficiency, competition, value for money and empowering the customer. More traditional supporters of a strong public sector have adopted quality to show that equal opportunities and other people-centred issues are inextricably linked to good outcomes; that welfare services can justify their cost in terms of tangible benefits and measurable efficiency; and that the empowerment of service users and staff is the best way to remove the dead hand of old-fashioned bureaucratic public control. Quality has thus become part of the mainstream of UK public life in many sectors. (Williams, 1994: 5)

Quality management and assurance in 'human services' have spread from the United States to Europe, especially in the current decade and in the context of a particular economic and political climate:

> under the influence of massive privatisation programmes and the search for cuts in social welfare budgets, a particular *discourse on quality* has become increasingly prominent, one which relies very much on a business-based approach . . . [T]he concepts coming from the market sector clearly prevail . . . in line with the fact that the global ideological trends have shifted towards an increasing impact from market liberalism. (Evers, 1997: 1, 10, emphasis added)

This process involves, once again, a shift from more individual and 'professional' judgments, to more quantifiable, objective and open methods of assessment, 'a move away from purely connoisseurial evaluation and towards much clearer and more specific definitions of quality' (Pollitt, 1997: 35).

The spread of the 'discourse of quality' from business to public services has had another effect. It has involved a new emphasis: 'business approaches are concerned with consumer quality (or 'user quality'), that is services which are tailored to satisfy consumer requirements and expectations' (1997: 34). But as we shall see, the expansion of the discourse of quality into the public sector has raised issues that contribute to the problematization of the concept of quality.

Gaining Control and Coping with Uncertainty

We have already alluded to several of the influences which have driven the 'discourse of quality' to its present dominant position: modernity and Enlightenment thinking; the need for 'technologies of distance' in market economies operating on an expanding scale; growing global economic competition; the increasing dominance in human services of business culture and market economics, with concepts like 'quality' permitting the 'integration of all activities into a generalized market' (Readings, 1996: 32); and a democratic desire for impartial and transparent methods of assessment to replace personal judgments. But still other influences can be seen at work.

As well as growing global competition and the resurgence of market forces, the 1980s saw the start of a strong movement, among companies and governments, to decentralize. But as companies and governments decentralized, some sought to retain control through the application and evaluation of quality criteria.

> In the context of the economic and fiscal crisis and efforts to change the public welfare system in Sweden (and in many other western countries) decentralization, goal-setting and evaluation have become new 'prestige' words . . . Goal governing has become a new way to direct and control services. The main idea of goal governing is that rules and relatively detailed plans are replaced by clear goals — 'management by objectives' — and strategies for evaluation of goal attainment. With increased decentralization and deregulation, evaluation of the quality of early childhood education and care programmes will grow in importance as an instrument for governing. (Dahlberg & Åsén, 1994: 159)

Quality and its evaluation can thus become an integral part of a new control system, assuming a policing function (Lundgren, 1990; Popkewitz, 1990), so that 'the power that decentralization gives away with one hand, evaluation may take back with the other' (Weiler, 1990: 61).

But the increasing prominence of quality can also be understood at a more personal level. As the world becomes more complex and demanding, each of us becomes involved with and dependent on ever more services, organizations and technologies. We are subjected to increasing quantities of information, much of it intended to enable us to be good consumers and much of which is meaningless without further investment of time and effort. Time pressures mount, particularly for women and men in their 'prime working years' (between 25 and 50), as child rearing increasingly coincides with peak participation in the labour market. At the same time, the rapid pace of change means that former sources of authority — for example, kin or religious codes of behaviour — may no longer be able to reassure or offer relevant guidance in making decisions.

Overwhelmed by information and choices, pressed for time and lacking a presumed expertise, unable to rely on traditional sources of authority or to trust the self-interested claims of producers, it is unsurprising if, to help us make sense of the world and to make decisions, we come to rely increasingly on 'expert systems

... of technical accomplishment or professional expertise that organise large areas of material and social environments ... [and which] remove social relations from the immediacies of context and provide "guarantees" of expectations across distanciated time-space' (Giddens, 1991: 27). Methods of quantification, including measures of quality, are one feature of these expert systems, minimizing, as we have already seen, the need for knowledge and personal trust.

So in the field of early childhood, we can see a growing body of experts — researchers, consultants, inspectors, evaluators and so on — whose job it is to define and measure quality. Increasingly, we rely on this expert system to make judgments for us about the services we want or need for ourselves and our children. We look to these experts to tell us that what we are getting is good 'quality'. Increasingly overloaded, we seek reassurance rather than understanding, we want the guarantee of expert assessment instead of the uncertainty of making our own judgments.

This search for reassurance goes beyond simply needing guidance for decision making. It is also about coping with the uncertainty, complexity and increased risk that characterize living in the world today, which Giddens (1991) has likened to riding a 'juggernaut' — a powerful and disturbing image which evokes an explosive mix of unpredictability and uncontrollability, dangers and opportunities. One response to these conditions is to seek shelter in the reduction of complexity to simple certainties.

What all these developments and movements have in common is a search for certainty and trust in authority, based on rigour, objectivity and impartiality. People look to experts to provide these. But, paradoxically, experts themselves increasingly lack security and public trust, either because they represent newer disciplines or because public confidence in previously trusted disciplines has diminished (for example, as the gains from various physical sciences and technologies come to be overshadowed by the risks they are found to produce (Beck, 1992)). Where expert judgment is no longer sufficient, if it ever was, experts have to build, or rebuild, trust through the development of quantifiable methods. In this context, quantification can be understood as a response to conditions of mistrust and exposure to outsiders (Porter, 1995).

The 'discourse of quality' has an obvious appeal as part of a search for clear, simple and certain answers underwritten by academic, professional or other authority. Part of us may know we need to learn to live with uncertainty — but another part of us may still desire objectivity and a 'quest for stable criteria of rationality'. Secure in modernity's belief that facts can be split from values, we hope to treat definitions and choices as technical issues and leave them to expert technicians, without the need to question how and why they are arrived at. The 'discourse of quality' offers us confidence and reassurance by holding out the prospect that a certain score or just the very use of the word quality means that something is to be trusted, that it really is good. Indeed, one of the wonders of a cynical age is the trust and credibility accorded to numbers or other forms of rating, as if numbers or stars or whatever symbol is used must, by their very existence, represent reality (just as we may end up believing the map is the same as what is mapped, the name the same as the named) — rather than being a symbol whose meaning can only be arrived at by critical reflection and judgement.

Constructing the Concept of Quality

[Logical positivism is based on a] firm conviction that the social-political world [is] simply 'out there' waiting to be discovered and described . . . that it [is] only by means of applying logical (and empirical) criteria that we are able to distinguish genuine, objective knowledge from mere belief . . . Research, according to a positivist account, is a systematic and methodical process for acquiring genuine, positive scientific knowledge. . . .

Given the influence of positivist epistemology, we have come to equate being rational in social science with being procedural and criteriological: To be a rational social enquirer is to observe and apply rules and criteria for knowing . . . to be rational is not to engage in moral and political speculation, critique, interpretation, dialogue, or judgement. (Schwandt, 1996a: 58, 59, 60, 61)

[In the quantitative paradigm in evaluation literature] the research enterprise resembles a search for a single and objective truth. As far as the social researcher is concerned there is a social reality which is amenable to quantitative measurement . . . The quantitative paradigm assumes that it is possible to separate the researcher from the researched. The investigator is seen to be able to adopt an objective, value-neutral position with regards to the subject matter under investigation. This scientific detachment is made possible by the use of research tools and methodologies . . . which serve to limit the personal contact between researcher and researched and provide a safe guard against bias. (Clarke, 1995: 7–8)

The discourse of quality is firmly embedded in the tradition and epistemology of logical positivism, whose main features are described above by Thomas Schwandt and Alan Clarke, which itself is deeply embedded in the project of modernity. The concept of quality is primarily about defining, through the specification of criteria, a generalizable standard against which a product can be judged with certainty. The process of specification of criteria, and their systematic and methodical application, is intended to enable us to know whether or not something — be it a manufactured or service product — achieves the standard. Central to the construction of quality is the assumption that there is an entity or essence of *quality*, which is a knowable, objective and certain truth waiting 'out there' to be discovered and described.

The discourse of quality values and seeks certainty through the application of scientific method that is systematic, rational and objective. At the heart of this discourse is a striving for universality and stability, normalization and standardization, through what has been termed 'criteriology', 'the quest for permanent or stable criteria of rationality founded in the desire for objectivism and the belief that we must somehow transcend the limitations to knowing that are the inevitable consequence of our sociotemporal perspective as knowers' (Schwandt, 1996a: 58).

How is the essential quality of a product to be defined? How is 'the quest for permanent and stable criteria of rationality' to be conducted? The specification of criteria of quality is undertaken by a particular group whose authority to specify comes from various sources, including expert status or political, bureaucratic or managerial position. Production of criteria is a process of construction, permeated by social, cultural, political and moral influences. Typically, though, the definition of criteria is treated as a technical process based on the application of disciplinary knowledge and practical experience (or alternatively political, managerial or other types of authority), free of values. In line with the positivist distrust of philosophy (Schwandt, 1996a), the question 'on what philosophical basis has quality been defined?' is almost entirely absent. The discourse of quality eschews the first person proposition 'we mean' or 'it seems to us', for the third person assertion 'it is'.

Because definition of quality is regarded as a process of identifying and applying 'objective' and indisputable knowledge, the process itself receives relatively little attention, analysis or further justification (except perhaps some rationale which explains the linkage between the knowledge base and the specified standard). Defining 'quality' therefore is an inherently exclusive, didactic process, undertaken by a particular group whose power and claims to legitimacy enable them to determine what is to be understood as true or false; it is not a dialogic and negotiated process between all interested parties. Once defined, criteria are then offered *to* others and applied *to* the process or product under consideration. Quality is presented as a universal truth that is value and culture free and applicable equally anywhere in the field under consideration: in short, quality is a decontextualized concept.

As the definition of quality is taken for granted and treated as a given, the main focus of the 'discourse of quality' is the achievement and evaluation of this expert-defined specification, rather than the construction (or deconstruction) of the specification. The discourse places more emphasis on the question 'how do we identify quality?' than on the preceding questions 'what do we mean by quality and why?' and 'how and by whom has quality been defined?' This in turn *prioritizes methods*, especially methods of measurement: within the positivist perspective 'many social scientists believe that method offers a kind of clarity on the path to truth that philosophy does not . . . method has become a sacred prescription' (Schwandt, 1996a: 60). Because the essence of quality is its absolute and universal nature, it is particularly important to remove any element of personal speculation, interpretation or judgement, any whiff of subjectivity. These suspect behaviours must be replaced by methods of measurement that are reliable and open to scrutiny and undertaken by disinterested measurers who are clearly separated from the subject of their measurement: objectivity rules. Not only does the discourse assume a reality, a thing called *quality*; it assumes that this reality can be perfectly captured, given adequate and carefully controlled means.

The overriding aim is to reduce the complexity and diversity of the products measured and the contexts within which they exist and operate to a limited number of basic measurable criteria which can then be encapsulated in a series of numerical ratings — the dream of modernity. Typically, this encapsulation involves processes of representation and normalization. Rather than engaging with what is actually going on, with all its complexity and contradictions, the discourse of quality seeks to depict or map in relation to certain criteria held to represent the essence of quality for the product under consideration. The purpose is to assess the conformity of the product — for example, an early childhood institution — to the criteria, and the norms that underlie these criteria, rather than seek understanding of the subject.

The contrast between the complexity of the everyday life of the early childhood institution and the simplification involved in the process of representation is discussed below by a Danish pedagogue, who struggles with the apparent contradiction that two very different approaches can both be called 'quality' (the contradiction disappears when we see that he is describing different ways of understanding the world, within the projects of modernity and postmodernity):

> In the past, 'quality' was generally used to provide a brief reference point in describing an experience and as a way of expressing in shorthand a complexity which was hard to define otherwise without using thousands of words — and if thousands of words were used, the feeling remaining would often be that the description had only scratched the surface of what had actually been experienced. The concept of quality is used differently today, especially in Danish business life . . . Quality charts, certificates, points and grades are being produced at a furious rate by business, a sort of 'quality inflation'. And after all many things can be weighed and measured or recorded in a table, formula or graph . . . My fear is that if this approach to quality, with its emphasis on weighing and measurement, comes to dominate the discussion in services for children then it will spoil more than it improves. A society with clearly defined ideas of how to measure art will be regarded as authoritarian and narrow-minded: true quality, like true art, cannot be reduced to simple statements. (Jensen, 1994: 156)

Quality, Customer Satisfaction and Public Services

Our argument has been that the discourse of quality is essentially about the quest for an absolute standard for products, objective and generalizable, defined in terms of criteria. But how does this relate to the other definition of quality, emanating from the business world — customer satisfaction? In some ways, it is quite compatible. Customer satisfaction, expressed through surveys or some other means, can be treated as one of the relevant criteria for determining quality, one indicator of product performance. Alternatively, and more complex, the customer, or the customer's requirements, can determine the criteria that define standards, what has been called a 'constructivist' approach to quality definition, 'where services' users play a major role in defining and valuing the dimensions along which quality will be sought, measured and assessed' (Priestley, 1995: 15). In other words, the particular group specifying criteria in this case are the customers, and it is being customers that gives them authority.

The idea of customer satisfaction is, however, problematic, in particular when it proves necessary to move beyond the simple notion of the individual customer seeking personal satisfaction from a product purchased within a private market, to a wider recognition of the social and political significance of many institutions and services, especially those that are provided in the public sector. Matters then become complex and multi-dimensional, and business approaches to quality 'do not and sometimes cannot grasp some of the peculiarities of the area of personal social services' (Evers, 1997: 11). There may be problems in some cases with the customer expressing themselves about the services they receive or are entitled to receive. In the context of personal social services, many users are frightened, alienated and/or disabled, members of weak and vulnerable groups (Evers, 1997; Pollitt, 1997). If young children are regarded as the customers for early childhood institutions, they too are unlikely to be able to act as customers according to the theory of market relations. At the very least, to make the idea of customer and customer satisfaction meaningful requires considerable further thought and ingenuity.

To assume a simple customer–provider relationship begs many questions, for 'the question of the customer is a complicated one' (Mäntysaari, 1997: 59). The growing enthusiasm for consumerism in public services 'bypasses some important prior questions about the whole character of [that] consumerism' — in particular, who is the consumer? (Pollitt, 1988). There is the person currently using the service (although whether in the case of services for children the user is the child, the parents or both is not discussed). But, there are also *potential* users and *future* users, and other members of the community who may also be affected by the provision of public services and the taxpayer. Moreover, consumers of public services are also citizens.

Hambleton and Hoggart (1990) similarly question the appropriateness of the model of the individual consumer, emphasized in the private market, applied to quality of public services because it fails to address important issues including the wider collective responsibility and accountability of the public sector. Gaster suggests that 'a further dimension to the question "What is quality?" must be the democratic element both through representative democracy and participatory democracy . . . If a quality service is one that meets as nearly as possible the needs of consumers and the wider community, it follows that the definition of quality needs to emerge from a dialogue with that community' (1991: 260, 261). Pollitt (1988) similarly makes the case for developing inclusive and dialogic approaches to quality in public services, 'guided by a normative model of a (potentially) active, participative citizen-consumer, concerned with a range of values of which efficiency is only one' and a recognition that 'every set of performance indicators, however "hard" the measures, is thoroughly suffused with values and judgemental uncertainties' (1988: 86).

This work in the personal social services demonstrates the impossibility of limiting discussions of quality to a discreet and decontextualized consumer and his or her satisfaction. Because many of these services are public goods, other people — beyond the 'customer-provider' dyad — have to be brought into account, as well as other considerations that go beyond whether or not the customer is satisfied: 'providers have to design their services according to specific social-policy criteria of distributional justice, which are non-existent or far less relevant than in private business'; and public services have to adopt standards of professionalism which 'are not only agreed with direct recipients of the service, but with a broader public as represented by administrators and legislators' (Evers, 1997: 20). Last but not least, when democracy comes into play, matters become messy if diversity is to be taken into account:

> In many countries, PSS [personal social services] units or parts of them are inter-
> twined with local communities, subcultures and networks; they are finely tuned
> with demands arising from there, as well as by their respective values and
> aspirations . . . Preserving a dimension of localism in PSS can be a very controver-
> sial issue. Taking a position which does not want to abolish it but prefers to
> develop it further as part of a rich and diversified landscape of care and PSS
> providers, will have consequences when assessing QA [quality assurance] con-
> cepts. Because for this specific local and moral economy, the takeover of models
> of standard-setting and control coming from the big hierarchical systems will be
> problematic. The challenge would be to develop methods for quality improvement
> which respect the peculiarities of this local economy. (Evers, 1997: 19)

The preceding discussion draws largely on work in the personal social services field. By questioning the private market concept of the isolated and decontextualized consumer or customer and by introducing a political and social context which takes account of societal relationships and democratic goals, it seems to us that many writers about quality in the personal social services are problematizing the concept of quality as constructed within the discourse of quality. Much of this work raises many of the issues concerning quality that have been raised in relation to early childhood institutions (quite independently, since there seems to be little commun-ication between personal social services and early childhood when it comes to discussion of quality), and which led us in Chapter 1 to conclude that there was a problem with quality. Can the discourse of quality recognize context and the pecu-liarities of different contexts? Can it recognize and live with the values and judg-mental uncertainties that suffuse any set of indicators or criteria? Who defines quality and how can this process cope with the multiple perspectives of a genuinely democratic process?

The Discourse of Quality in Early Childhood

Since its emergence on the scene in the early 1980s, the discourse of quality has been applied to the field of early childhood institutions in a number of ways, including research, measures, standards and guidelines on good practice. These have all involved, in various forms, the development and application of criteria, to enable evaluation of the standards or performance of early childhood institutions. These criteria mainly fall into three groupings: structure, process and outcome.

Structural criteria (sometime referred to as 'input' criteria) refer to resource and organizational dimensions of institutions, such as group size, levels of staff training, adult to child ratios and the presence and content of a curriculum. *Process* criteria refer to what happens in the institution, in particular the activities of chil-dren, the behaviour of staff and interactions between children and adults. This category can be extended to cover relationships between the institution and parents. *Outcome* criteria have mainly been defined in terms of certain aspects of child development, assumed to be desirable, but also to young children's later school, social and economic performance sometimes stretching as far as adulthood. Another outcome is also receiving some attention (although less than in many other fields): customer satisfaction with parents the assumed consumers of early childhood services. This emerging emphasis on parental satisfaction, it has been argued, reflects 'a broadened conception of child care quality that takes the interests and concerns of parents into account' (Larner and Phillips, 1994: 47).

A reviewer of the different approaches to quality in early childhood services concludes that every approach 'can be analysed in terms of its Input, Process and Outcome' although he adds that 'some methodologies are stronger on one aspect than another' (Williams, 1994: 17). In particular, outcome criteria are less often evaluated, mainly because there are difficulties, financial and methodological, in collecting and interpreting data about children's development and performance in a way that enables it to be neatly related to the performance of early childhood institutions. For example, in the messy real world children may attend a number of different institutions during their early childhood making it difficult to tease out the outcomes from attending any one particular institution; and a child's development needs to be tested both before starting to attend an institution and after leaving to get a clear idea of the impact of that particular institution. Consequently, structural and process criteria have been used as a proxy for outcomes, so that researchers and others often 'identify "quality" with characteristics of care facilities that correlate with favourable scores on developmental tests' (Singer, 1993: 438).

The discourse of quality has influenced the early childhood research field over the last 20 years or so. It has generated many studies, mainly American, although an increasing number are coming from other countries, indicating the spread of the discourse of quality in the early childhood field. One of the main consequences of this research has been to establish relationships between some structural and process criteria on the one hand, and some outcome criteria: 'research in child development and early childhood education has identified several clear indicators of quality care, defined in terms of their predictive significance for children's development' (Phillips, 1996: 43).

Another product of this research work within the discourse of quality has been the development of measures which have come to be used by many researchers as a tried and tested means of assessing quality. The best known and most widely used example is the Early Childhood Environmental Rating Scale (ECERS). The ECERS was developed by two American early childhood specialists, Thelma Harms and Richard Clifford, in the early 1980s, and has been described by its authors as 'a relatively short and efficient means of looking seriously at the quality of the [early years] environment . . . [covering] the basic aspects of all early childhood facilities' (Harms and Clifford, 1980: iv). Designed for use in a variety of forms of early childhood institution in the United States, a country with a very particular economic, social, cultural and political context, it has nevertheless been used increasingly in other countries across the world by both researchers and practitioners and seems set to become a global standard and the basis for an increasing body of cross-national comparisons of early childhood institutions.

The ECERS is an observation schedule comprising 37 individual items, with the scores from subsets of these items aggregated to provide 7 scale scores, intended to provide an overall picture of the surroundings that have been created for the children and adults who share the setting that is being rated. The development of the measure involved an initial formulation by the authors, which was validated against the views of American experts in the early childhood field. Seven 'nationally recognized experts' were asked to rate each item on the scale in terms of its importance to early childhood programmes. Subsequently, the scale was tested by comparing its ability to distinguish between classrooms of 'varying quality' as judged by early childhood trainers in the US. The ECERS is not explicit about its values (Brophy and Statham, 1994), although the authors refer to 'the lack of universally acceptable norms for early childhood environments' (Harms and Clifford, 1980: 38).

The discourse of quality has generated another field of activity, the development of standards and good practice guidelines for various forms of early childhood provision, which although not framed as measures or evaluation methods in effect provide definitions of quality. In the UK, for example, 'many agencies with particular interests . . . have produced explicit standards and recommendations for practice. These specifications of quality standards have been fundamental to the development and assessment of services aimed at providing a good experience for the child' (Williams, 1994: 3). One of the best known examples from the United States is *Developmentally Appropriate Practice in Early Childhood Programs*, the first edition of which was published in 1987 by the American National Association for the Education of Young Children (Bredekamp, 1987). Founded on 'child development knowledge', it produces guidelines that 'define a "universal" child rearing practice to foster this development by distinguishing between appropriate and inappropriate practises, a dualism that makes it difficult to consider other options' (Lubeck, 1996: 151). This decontextualized approach, 'premised on modernist assumptions', 'serves to foster the development of an isolated being . . . with the end goal being the autonomous individual' (1996: 156).[1]

As in other fields, the discourse of quality in early childhood has been constituted by a search for objective, rational and universal standards, defined by experts on a basis of indisputable knowledge and measured in ways that reduce the complexities of early childhood institutions to 'stable criteria of rationality'. Method has been emphasized at the expense of philosophy, the 'how' rather than the 'why' prioritized. Consequently, the discussion of quality in early childhood institutions rarely starts by seeking important and productive questions   about children, childhood or early childhood institutions — and offering some answers, however partial and uncertain.

Developmental Psychology and the Discourse of Quality

The 1930s opened up a discourse (in Sweden) of a comprehensive early childhood pedagogy — a discourse that became an important part of the choreography of a

> political rationality holding modernist visions and revisions of a better society . . .
> Developmental psychology was an important instrument in this strategy, in which
> the child is supposed to bring her(him)self into agreement with social normativity,
> universality and the principle of reason. To use a concept from Foucault, one could
> say that from now on developmental psychology and child-centered pedagogy
> became a form of 'discursive regime of truth' which governed what was seen as
> important to do in practice, but also what could be thought and said and not
> thought and said about children. (Dahlberg, 1995: 3, 4)

> Developmental psychology based on positivist and universalist goals with a bio-
> logical basis has dominated theorizing about children and profoundly influenced
> policies towards them. (Mayall, 1996: 19)

As we have already discussed in Chapter 2, developmental psychology is 'a paradigmatically modern discipline' (Burman, 1994: 18), and has been a very important, indeed dominant, discursive regime in the field of early childhood institutions,
at least in the Anglo-American world: 'child development knowledge has been so
foundational to the field of early childhood education that erasing it would seem to
leave us in a mindless limbo' (Lubeck, 1996: 158). One reason why the discourse
of quality has been taken up so readily, and unquestioningly, in the early childhood
field is because it shares so many of the perspectives and methods of this dominant
discipline. Both are products of the project of modernity — 'development' and
'quality' are quintessentially modernist concepts.

The discipline of developmental psychology and the discourse of quality in
early childhood have fitted like hand in glove. Child development has offered, as
certain and objective truth, the individual's progress through universal developmental stages, a 'grand narrative' that has done much to produce the constructions
of young children and early childhood institutions discussed in earlier chapters, as
well as criteria for definitions of quality in these institutions. Both the discourses of
child development and of quality adopt a decontextualized approach or, at best,
attempt to bring 'context' in as an explanatory variable, divorcing the child and the
institution from concrete experience, everyday life, the complexities of culture, the
importance of situation. Both are 'driven by the demand to produce technologies of
measurement' (Burman, 1994: 3), including systems of classification which attempt
to reduce complexity so that processes which are very complex and interrelated in
everyday life are isolated from one another and placed into abstract systems and
ideas; assessments of children's development and of quality both end up producing
abstract maps which simplify and normalize, saying how children or institutions
should be, while distracting our attention from finding out how they really are. Both
discourses assume and seek to discover objective, universal and generalizable innate
truths, treating both children and institutions as 'independent pregiven objects about
which [they] make "discoveries"' (Henriques et al., 1984: 101–2). Both are highly
individualistic in orientation, the discourse of quality focusing on individual outcomes and relationships, while the discourse of child development believes 'in the
individual and self-contained child . . . the idea that the child is a social construction
and a continuing social construction seems uncongenial to the spirit of American
culture and child psychology' (Kessen, 1983: 32).

In sum, both discourses — quality and child development — are strongly modernist, positivistic in approach and committed to the importance of generating objective forms of knowledge. Both have adopted the assumptions of the natural sciences — with their emphasis on the universal and rational — rather than the assumptions of the cultural/historical sciences — with their emphasis on the constructed and local nature of both problems and answers (Cole, 1996).

In these circumstances, it is not surprising that developmental psychologists have played a leading role in work on quality in early childhood institutions — as expert authorities for defining quality criteria, as producers of methods of measurement and as researchers into quality and its determinants. It would be unfair, however, to imply that this dominance is simply the result of imperialistic tendencies; developmental psychology has been given a clear run because other disciplines have not been interested (Mayall, 1996). In particular, until recently sociology has tended to ignore children and childhood, regarding them as the province of psychology and accepting psychology's definition of children as cognitively incompetent and therefore essentially passive: 'psychologists' designation of children as developing non-people and as socialization projects has allowed sociologists to write children out of their scripts' (Mayall, 1996: 19). But whatever the reason, the field of early childhood has been the poorer for its dependency on one discipline and its neglect by others. These 'absent' disciplines might have felt more ill at ease with the positivist assumptions underlying the 'discourse of quality'. Had they been actively engaged, it is possible that the 'discourse of quality' in the field of early childhood would have been problematized sooner.

History provides one example of the potential benefits of alternative disciplinary perspectives. Even a cursory examination of the history of early childhood institutions shows how ideas about these institutions — their purposes, the nature of pedagogical work, their understanding of the young child — are the subject of recurring construction and reconstruction (cf. the discussion of the recent history of early childhood institutions in Sweden in Chapter 4; of nursery education in Britain from Robert Owen to the present day in Moss and Penn, 1996; and of the North American infant school movement of the 1820s and its relationship to contemporary early childhood dynamics in the United States and Canada in Pence, 1989). More broadly, many historians have a fundamentally different understanding of children and childhood than developmental psychologists.

> Historians take for granted and indeed know in their bones: that human behaviour is invariably contingent and that social action is crucially conditioned by context . . . [But] can the developmentalists abandon the positivist presumption of homogeneity and give up the positivist goal of universality? Can they authentically accept radical contingency and indeterminancy and come to terms with situation-specific particularity? Are they about to quit the quest for unchanging childhood on which their field was founded? Can they surrender the conviction that the child is . . . a natural kind rather than a social and historical kind? . . .
>
> Operating on notions of the child as a natural kind and notions of themselves as natural scientists, studying predictable processes of that natural kind, developmentalists have been disinclined to struggle with portents of the relativity they are

nonetheless feted to face . . . [While historians'] extended experience with [relativity] doubtless conditions our receptivity — to the proliferation of perspectives that attended the emergence of the new social history. . . . We recognise that we cannot pronounce reliable regularities on which to base predictions because we cannot countermand the inexorable contingency of the human condition. (Zuckerman, 1993: 231, 235, 239–40)

Developmental Psychology and Quality in Crisis

The project of developmental psychology as the presentation of a general model which depicts development as unitary, irrespective of culture, class, gender or history means that difference can be recognised only in terms of aberrations, deviations and relative progress on a linear scale . . . The notion of 'progress', whether of societies or through the 'life span', implies linear movement across history and between cultures. Comparison within these terms is now being recognised as increasingly untenable. In particular, the implication that there is a detached, disinterested set of devices and techniques for this purpose, such as developmental psychology illustrates the extent to which we have come to believe in the abstract, disembodied psychological subject and dismiss all it fails to address as merely supplementary or inappropriate . . . The issue is to bring to light and acknowledge the investment and hidden subjectivity that lie beneath the claims to disinterested and true knowledge. (Burman, 1994: 185, 188)

Though developmentalism and functional models of socialization theory have suffered a beating in the last 20 years, they remain remarkably powerful . . . Whilst the critiques of established child development theories have come from many quarters, over a considerable time, not only do these theories have very considerable resilience in policy and practice fields concerned with child health, welfare and education, but the construction of a more wide-ranging child psychology paradigm has also proved difficult. (Mayall, 1996: 52, 55)

In Chapter 1, we described how the concept of quality in early childhood has been problematized during the 1990s. Developmental psychology, the discipline that has been so closely associated with the application of the discourse of quality in the early childhood field, has been going through a similar, but more exhaustive and extended, process of problematization and deconstruction, both from without the discipline but also from within and including some of the most well-known names in the discipline (cf. Bronfenbrenner et al., 1986; Burman, 1994; Cole, 1996; Elder et al., 1993; Henriques et al., 1984; Kessen, 1979, 1983; Lubeck, 1996; Mayall, 1996; Morss, 1996; Prout and James, 1990). The features of developmental psychology which are being problematized are similar to those being problematized in the discourse of quality in early childhood (not surprising since both are so deeply embedded in the project of modernity): the positivist approach and its methods, including the reduction of complexity to simplified and quantifiable representations, and its suspicion, even rejection, of subjectivity and philosophy; a belief in general laws and universal truths, personified by the decontextualized view of development as a biologically-determined sequence of stages; a focus on the individual as the centrepiece of enquiry; the strong normalizing tendency; its implication in processes of regulation and control; the very concept of 'development' itself.

Both developmental psychology and the discourse of quality can be said to be in crisis, based as they both are on a positivistic programme of 'establishing permanent criteria and uncovering an indisputable foundation for knowledge [that has] proved to be unattainable' (Schwandt, 1996a: 59). It is difficult to find today philosophers who subscribe to this programme (Shadish, 1995). Positivism has been displaced and 'the programme of making everything knowable through the supposedly impersonal norms and procedures of "science" has been radically questioned' (Apple, 1991).

In some respects, none of this should cause concern. We have already argued that crisis can be viewed optimistically, opening up new possibilities and horizons, alternative enquiries and solutions, and opportunities for new understandings: 'the critique that has amassed over the last 20 years or so regarding the inadequacies of positivist assumptions in the face of human complexity has opened up a sense of possibilities in the human sciences' (Lather, 1991: 2). Moreover, there is no need to be prescriptive, to insist on either/or; those who choose to understand the world through the modernist perspective are free to do so.

In practice, however, there are causes for concern. For despite the intellectual breakdown of positivism, it still remains influential in publication, funding, promotion and tenure in many academic fields (Fishman, 1995), while the Cartesian dream of certainty lingers on and motivates a continuing search for definitive and universal criteria (Schwandt, 1996a) as in the discourse of quality. Developmental psychology and quality are still dominant discursive regimes, which continue to govern people's understanding of early childhood and early childhood institutions. Many policy-makers and practitioners in the field of early childhood are unaware that developmental psychology has 'suffered a beating': they continue to rely on it to provide them with a 'true' account of childhood and a foundation for policy and practice. Not only do alternative approaches and perspectives go unexplored, but early childhood programmes, measurements of quality and constructions of 'normal' child development are exported from the United States, the heartland of the positivistic discourses of quality and child development, to be applied unquestioningly in other countries throughout the world. The project of modernity may be increasingly questioned; but its belief in progress and universal truth continues to exert a powerful and problematic global influence, which we shall consider in more detail in Chapter 8.

Beyond Quality to Meaning Making

What can be done about the 'problem with quality'? Can quality be reconceptualized to accommodate diversity, subjectivity, multiple perspectives and temporal and spatial context? For example, can an item 'context' be added as a variable to the study of quality, leading to statistical calculations of the effect of this item on the variance of scores produced from measurements of quality? Can we qualify definitions of quality to indicate to which society or culture they specifically refer and apply, ending up with, for example, Swedish or British or Canadian variants of some basic standard of quality? If more stakeholders were to be consulted, and if they were to be better informed, could a more inclusive and consensual definition of quality be constructed based on a shared understanding? Should quality be left to every individual centre or community to define, in isolation and according to its own interests, values and understandings, assuming all definitions to be equally valid?

It seems to us that none of these questions leads very far. The idea that context can be separated out and its effect independently measured requires a conceptualization of context as 'that which surrounds'. But this conceptualization has been problematized as a reductionist simplification. An alternative conceptualization, 'context as that which weaves together', precludes the possibility of separating context out as an independent variable (Cole, 1996). For some psychologists this has meant, for example, a move from looking at culture as an independent variable affecting cognition, to regarding cognitive processes as inherently cultural (Rogoff and Chavajay, 1995). Applied to the study of early childhood institutions, this perspective would mean recognizing that these institutions are similarly inherently cultural — inextricably interwoven with culture as well as the other strands that make up context.

The view that early childhood institutions are inherently cultural might suggest that the notion of, for example, 'Swedish quality' or 'British quality' or 'Canadian quality', could prove productive. Yet the very words, this qualification of quality, seem rather strange, almost absurd, not least because we never see them in other settings, for example, in adverts for cars or other products where 'quality' is never qualified in this way but always assumed to be a universal yardstick, a 'technology of distance'. The problem is a basic contradiction: the notion that understandings of quality in early childhood institutions might be societally or culturally specific is incompatible with the concept of quality being a universal and objective norm. Once you allow for some diversity and recognize the possibility of multiple perspectives, where do you draw the line? Are you not forced to accept that you are looking at different understandings of what is going on or what people would like to be going on? As the possibility of standardization fades in the face of diversity and complexity, why not seek an understanding of how the institution really is rather than evaluating its conformity to an increasingly problematic norm?

Stakeholders, even if consulted and better informed, might still disagree and arrive at different understandings on quality. Unless, of course, we assume that there is a single right answer, probably based on expert knowledge, which will enable conflicts of definition to be eventually reconciled — an assumption which takes us back to the idea of quality as a universal, knowable truth. Even members of one particular stakeholder, cultural or other group, while sharing much in common, may still differ amongst themselves on many important issues or form subgroups and sub-sub-groups. Indeed it would be surprising, and perhaps worrying, if members of such broadly defined groups were in complete agreement, since stakeholder (or other groups) do not consist of uniform clones, but individuals with many differences: 'as but one example, upon close inspection, "women" become fragmented, multiple and contradictory both across groups and within individuals' (Lather, 1991: xvi). In any case this discussion begs the question of whether consensus is viewed as desirable or problematic (Karlsson, 1995).

Finally, few people are comfortable with the idea of unqualified 'anything goes' relativism, especially when its consequences affect a relatively powerless group such as young children. We address the issue of relativism in more detail later in this chapter (pages 116–19), locating our discussion within a wider ethical context.

It seems to us that the underlying problem is with the concept of quality itself. Is it an empty vessel which we can fill and refill with different meanings? Or is it a filled vessel, with a very particular and immutable content of meaning? It seems to us that the concept of quality does have a very particular meaning, that of a universal, knowable and objective standard, and that it is situated within a particular modernist understanding of the world. Quality is a 'technology of distance', a means of excluding individual judgment and for crossing group and community borders. Quality cannot be reconceptualized to accommodate complexity, values, diversity, subjectivity, multiple perspectives, and other features of a world understood to be both uncertain and diverse.

The 'problem with quality' cannot be addressed by struggling to reconstruct the concept in ways it was never intended to go. If we try to make an accommodation with, for example, subjectivity or multiple perspectives, then an increasingly desperate search for quality will prove to be a wild goose chase. For the concept of quality in relation to early childhood institutions is irretrievably modernist, it is part of the Cartesian dream of certainty and the Enlightenment's ambition for Progress and Truth. It is about a search for definitive and universal criteria, certainty and order — or it is about nothing. Working with complexity, values, diversity, subjectivity, multiple perspectives and temporal and spatial context means taking another position which understands the world in a different postmodern way and which will be productive of new discourses, concepts and questions — not struggling to reconstruct quality. The problem with quality is not really a problem once we recognize that it is not a neutral concept, but that it is a concept which we can choose to take or leave.

The Discourse of Meaning Making

In place of talk about programs and projects, we prefer to talk about conjectures and images and contradictions and ambiguities that accompany ideas that we value when we choose our way of life and society. We believe that we will never fully understand and nail down these ideas because their meanings will continue to shift and drift. These are not reasons for despair. It is just the way things are, as we understand them, when we cope with education, society and living. (Cherryholmes, 1994: 205)

Even at the core of 20th-century physics, idiosyncrasies of persons and cultures cannot be eliminated . . . Within a humanized Modernity, the decontextualization of problems so typical of High Modernity is no longer a serious option ... 'To every human problem' [said the commentator Walter Lippmann], 'there is a solution that is simple, neat, and wrong'; and that is as true of intellectual as it is of practical problems. (Toulmin, 1990: 201)

We have argued that the modernist discourse of quality in early childhood institutions (or any other settings) involves the decontextualized quest for certainty through the detached and objective application of universal and timeless criteria. The intention is to assess how far the institution conforms to some preordained ideal of performance. Because it is situated within the project of modernity, the discourse of quality 'is inadequate for understanding a world of multiple cause and effects, interacting in complex and non-linear ways all of which are rooted in a limitless array of historical and cultural specificities' (Lather, 1991: 21). It seems to us that such understanding requires a different discourse situated within the project of postmodernity, which is at home with diversity, complexity, subjectivity and multiple perspectives, and which, as part of an emancipatory practice, enables us to act as agents, to 'produce rather than reflect meaning' (1991: 37).

We term the postmodern discourse, *the discourse of meaning making*. It shares much in common with the sceptical approach adopted by sixteenth-century humanists (overtaken in the seventeenth century by the Cartesian dream of certainty), which in recent decades has made its reappearance in philosophy (Toulmin, 1990). This discourse is also situated within the ethical position we have outlined previously, the ethics of an encounter, foregrounding the importance of meaning making in dialogue with others. These requirements distinguish this approach both from the concept of personal or expert judgment, dependent on the individual seeking to discover truth in isolation from others; or from the concept of quality, involving the application or reproduction of standardized and quantified criteria which replaces reliance on individual judgment, however expert, with trust in numbers and objective scientific methods.

In the field of early childhood, the discourse of meaning making speaks first and foremost about constructing and deepening *understanding* of the early childhood institution and its projects, in particular the pedagogical work — to make meaning of what is going on. From constructing these understandings, people may choose to continue by attempting to make *judgments* about the work, a process involving the application of values to understanding to make a judgment of value. Finally, people may further choose to seek *some agreement with others* about these judgments — to struggle to agree, to some extent, about what is going on and its value. However, the discourse does not assume that all three stages must be followed. Indeed, it may be considered sufficient to confine making sense to deepening understanding, without going on to judge or to seek some agreement.

There are continuities between the discourse of quality and the discourse of meaning making. In particular, a desire to make sense of what is going on can be said to motivate both the modernist discourse of quality and its postmodern counterpart. We could even say that the different discourses both seek answers to the questions of what is *good work* in our early childhood institutions, how can it be defined and how can it be carried out. However, the two discourses have very particular and different understandings of what it means to make sense and to enquire into good work, using very particular and different methods. For instance, within postmodernity *good* is not understood as an inherent, substantial and universal category, an idea in which the Enlightenment believed and which it tried to legitimate. Rather good is understood as the product of discursive practice, and is always contextualized (specific to time and place), often subject to disagreement and inevitably subject to negotiation. While recognizing the possibility of *some* agreement, the 'discourse of meaning making' does not require or even seek consensus and unanimity, for 'it is in the graveyard of universal consensus that responsibility and freedom and the individual exhale their last sigh' (Bauman, 1997: 202). Nor can answers to what good work in early childhood institutions is, can be and should be stand in isolation from understandings of early childhood, early childhood institutions and early childhood pedagogy, the sorts of issues we have discussed in the preceding chapters.

Each discourse involves the making of choices, or judgments. But whereas the discourse of quality speaks of value-free technical choices, the discourse of meaning making calls for explicitly ethical and philosophical choices, judgments of value, made in relation to the wider questions of what we want for our children here and now and in the future — questions which must be posed over and over again and which need to be related to even larger questions about 'what is the good life?' and 'what does it mean to be a human being?' The answers we give tell a lot about how we understand the position of the young child in society, as well as our forms of democracy.

'Making sense of what is going on' within postmodernity is about the construction or making of meaning. We do this, each of us, acting as agents — but always in relation to others, understanding *us* to be situated in a particular spatial and temporal context and to be 'finite, embodied and fragile creatures, and not disembodied cogito or abstract unities' (Benhabib, 1992: 5). 'Making sense' involves processes of dialogue and critical reflection, drawing on 'concrete human experience', rather than exercises in abstracting, categorizing and mapping.

The discourse of meaning making therefore not only adopts a social constructionist perspective, but relates to an understanding of learning (discussed in Chapter 3) as a process of co-construction, by which in relationship with others we make meaning of the world. It assumes that each person co-constructs his or her own understanding of what is going on. In contrast, the discourse of quality relates to an understanding of learning as reproducing a predetermined body of knowledge, with the expert technician acting as the transmitter of this knowledge. In short, the two discourses can be seen as about different ways of learning about what is going on in early childhood institutions.

The ability to make meaning and deepen understanding — what we would call *wisdom* — is neither equally spread nor unsusceptible to change; some are wiser than others and wisdom can be cultivated. Nor does rejecting the search for certainty that figures so highly on the modernist agenda mean rejecting rigour and openness, trust and fairness. The discourse of meaning making must seek to avoid 'the danger of rampant subjectivity where one finds only what one is predisposed to look for, an outcome that parallels the "pointless precision" of objectivism' (Lather, 1991: 52). The discourse of meaning making foregrounds the need for democratic and public accountability, for example, of the work of early childhood institutions, but at the same time 'refuses to equate accountability with accounting' (Readings, 1996: 131).

Meaning making requires very precise, demanding and public conditions that create an interactive and dialogic process in which prejudices, self-interest and unacknowledged assumptions, with the distortions and limited vision that they produce, will be confronted and challenged. In the context of the early childhood institution, these conditions include:

- situating meaning making of pedagogical work and other projects of early childhood institutions within a wider, continuous and critical enquiry into 'good life' issues (such as, What do we want for our children? What is a good childhood?), constructions of early childhood and early childhood institutions, and pedagogical philosophy;
- the application of critical and reflexive thinking, including problematization and deconstruction;
- pedagogical documentation as a tool to assist critical and reflexive thinking and understanding of pedagogical work, by enabling us 'to submit practice to strict, methodological and rigorous questioning' (Freire, 1996: 108). Because of its importance, we devote Chapter 7 to exploring what we mean by pedagogical documentation and what it involves;
- the importance of encounters and dialogue, applying to them the principles of universal moral respect and egalitarian reciprocity, and cultivating moral and cognitive abilities such as the sensitivity to hear others' voices, the ability to see the Other as equal but different and the capacity to reverse perspectives (Benhabib, 1992). This capacity to reverse perspectives presents particular challenges in the early childhood institution, since it involves not only other adults, but also young children. As we shall see, the process of documentation provides one means to enable adults not only to see the young child but also to gain understanding of the perspective of the young child;
- the participation of facilitators, or wise people, drawn from a range of backgrounds and experience, including pedagogical work and philosophy; in the next chapter we present the example from Italy of the *pedagogista*.[2] Such facilitation can also be a role for evaluators, where enabling people to deepen their understanding and to cultivate the ability to make judgments — what Schwandt below calls 'practical wisdom' — is acknowledged as the ethical aim of evaluation (other ethical aims for evaluation include enlightenment and emancipation, and each assumes a different role for the evaluator):

> Evaluation practices that aim to cultivate an ethic of practical wisdom decenter the place of social enquiry in social life. At best, social scientific

enquiry serves as but one source of insight or self-awareness that supple-
ments or complements our ordinary struggles to understand ourselves and
to do good. In a phrase, social scientific inquiry is secondary or ancillary
to praxis . . . The task of evaluation here is to help clients cultivate this
capacity [to make judgments of the qualitative worth of different ends in
practice] . . . The evaluators use their special knowledge about what it
means to evaluate and how to come to warranted conclusions of the worth
of evaluands to add to the conversation about practice that clients and
stakeholders routinely conduct. But such knowledge is used in a complementary or supplementary manner. It is not knowledge in the form of
a pronouncement from an allegedly detached, objective and disinterested
observer who enlightens practitioners . . . [T]here is no knowledge that
the evaluator 'transmits' to parties in the evaluation. (Schwandt, 1996b:
17, 18)

One reason why the discourse of meaning making is so rigorous is that it is not
abstract. On the contrary, it is very concrete; it is about what is going on in the
pedagogical work and other projects of the early childhood institution, in particular
making visible and public what children are actually doing, through various forms
of documentation, and about different people entering into dialogue about that
work. In this discourse people address the institution, the children and the work
directly, not through attempts at representation such as measures which purport to
show how 'good' or 'bad' the institution is or how 'normal' the children are in
relation to some theory of child development. The intention is to study and make
meaning from actual practice, recognizing that in fact there may be many meanings
or understandings, not attempt to reduce what is going on to fit preconceived
categorical criteria.

Contextualization — locating the work of the early childhood institution within
a particular place and time — is therefore critical to the discourse of meaning
making. Schwandt emphasizes this point in his discussion of the implications of
taking 'practical wisdom' as the ethical aim of evaluation:

[In theories of evaluation practice aiming at cultivating practical wisdom] human
practices are essentially characterized by their mutability, indeterminacy and par-
ticularity that makes judging their goodness inaccessible to systems of general
rules and principles. Good judgment thus requires cultivating perceptual awareness
of concrete particulars. At the same time, human practices are constructed around
standing commitments to what is good and right; they are oriented towards agreed-
upon social aims. Right action — in this case, the activity of judging the worth of
a practice — is not however dictated by these general principles. We cannot
engage in some (relatively simple) process of weighing alternative goals, values,
criteria and the like that reduces judgment of what constitutes good practice to
calculation. Rather, we must engage in strong evaluation judging the qualitative
worth of different ends or aims of our practices. (1996b: 18)

We have so far been at pains to emphasize the rigour of the discourse of meaning
making, and to specify procedures to promote this rigour. But we do not expect, nor

indeed want, simple answers, certain conclusions, in short to establish mastery and control. Pedagogical work is embedded in life and the world we live in. It is not some decontextualized abstraction that can be readily measured and categorized. Simple and neat solutions are also likely to be wrong solutions. Instead, making meaning, deepening understanding, or attempting then to make judgments, will be a struggle, full of 'contradictions and ambiguities' (Cherryholmes, 1994: 205), of 'the unavoidable complexities of concrete human experience' (Toulmin, 1990: 201). It can offer no certainties and no guarantees, only judgments to be made, always in relationship with the Other, for which each one of us must take responsibility. It will also be a continuous struggle. There are no endings, only beginnings, for 'we will never fully understand and nail down these ideas because their meanings continue to shift and drift' (Cherryholmes, 1994: 205). The endeavour is inherently messy, and like Cherryholmes, we accept that these are 'not reasons for despair [because] it is just the way things are' (ibid).

Meaning making is messy in another way. The discourse of meaning making is, first and foremost, about producing meaning, deepening understanding. But in a world of diversity and multiple perspectives, in an activity that is unavoidably subjective, the result will be multiple and diverse understandings. Again, this is no cause for despair: 'tolerating the resulting plurality, ambiguity, or the lack of certainty is no error', being in Stephen Toulmin's memorable phrase 'the price that we inevitably pay for being human beings and not gods' (1990: 30).

But there is also no reason for not seeking some agreement about what is going on, in the sense of some degree of shared understanding and judgment about the work of the early childhood institution. This undertaking does not require complete agreement. Indeed, consensus may be undesirable. The process of dialogue and seeking agreement may be as important as the outcome in terms of agreement or consensus:

> When we shift the burden of the moral test in communicative ethics from consensus to the idea of an ongoing moral conversation, we begin to ask not what all would or could agree to as a result of practical discourses to be morally permissible or impermissible, but what would be allowed and perhaps even necessary from the standpoint of continuing and sustaining the practice of the moral conversation among us. The emphasis now is less on *rational agreement*, but more on sustaining those normative practices and moral relationships within which reasoned agreement *as a way of life* can flourish and continue ... [I]t is the process of [moral] dialogue, conversation, and mutual understanding, and not consensus, which is our gaol. (Benhabib, 1990: 346, 358)

Seyla Benhabib is here talking about moral conversations and moral judgments. Is this relevant though to making sense of what is going on in the early childhood institution? It seems to us that it is entirely relevant. Seeking to understand what is going on in these institutions, and making judgments, involves moral issues that each of us have to confront and struggle with. It is not just about the application of supposedly value-free and morally neutral technical expertise. Making sense requires each of us making value-based, and therefore moral and political, choices about how we understand young children, the nature of early childhood, the position of young children and early childhood institutions in society and democratic process and the projects of early childhood institutions.

Evaluation and the Discourse of Meaning Making

Evaluation will be associated in many people's minds with the discourse of quality and with the aspiration of the modernist project to discover the truth about the world — or at least that part of the world that is to be evaluated. Yet, evaluation, or at least one part of the field, is engaged in a process of reflection, debate and reconstruction that is specifically located in the context of the shift from the project of modernity to the project of postmodernity. We have found much in that process that resonates with, indeed illuminates, our own attempt to better understand the problem with quality.

In an extended review of Denzin and Lincoln's *Handbook of Qualitative Research*, Daniel Fishman (1995) describes the book as 'a major publishing event . . . [which serves] as a broad historical framework and conceptual umbrella for postmodernism as a large scale intellectual movement, both within program evaluation and across the social science field generally . . . and which should have an impact upon all program evaluators and other social science researchers in laying out alternatives to traditional, positivist, quantitative studies' (1995: 301, 307). He concludes:

> The *Handbook* makes clear that from the perspective of the postmodern critique of the positivist and post-positivist foundations of objective knowledge, there is no justification for 'pure' research whose goal is to discover truth about the world. Rather, postmodernism argues that in place of objective truth, there are simply alternative constructions and perspectives on particular, socioculturally and historically situated events and things . . . An implication of the postmodern idea that 'all meaningful research is applied' is that all research is 'political', that is, the human goals and purposes to which research is linked always take place within political contexts . . . Of course, to paraphrase Mark Twain, 'reports of the death of positivism and postpositivism's subsequent hegemony are greatly exaggerated' . . . However, the trend certainly seems very clear: [critical theory and constructivism] are gaining strength, and there is general support for them as the general culture moves from modernism to postmodernism . . . All this gives us as individual program evaluators much to think about. (1995: 307)

Thomas Schwandt, another American evaluator and critic of the modernist agenda in the field of evaluation, has similarly problematized situating evaluation within the modernist project, with its epistemology of logical positivism, belief in criteriology, its assumption of the disinterested social scientist and its distaste for philosophy and moral issues (Schwandt, 1996a).

> In the West and particularly in the United States, evaluation (as well as other professions involved in social policy, programming and administration) is heavily

influenced by the tradition of value-free social science. In this theory of science, the ethical register or domain is predefined as irrational, subjective, emotive and attitudinal . . . This is compounded by a second problem. As many commentators have noted, the modern self struggles with the grip of an epistemology of disengagement from and control of the social world. This way of knowing squeezes out the realm of the personal, the intuitive, the perceptual and the emotive, all characteristics of moral engagements. It is reflected in the modernist tendency in social science and management practice to convert what are essentially moral and ethical problems to technical and administrative ones. (1996b: 3)

The critique is leading to new ideas emerging about evaluation and social enquiry, with two central themes:

[First] the object of social science inquiry is both a social and linguistic construction, and hence, because this object is represented in social scientific discourse, it is partially constituted by this discourse . . . Second, as we abandon the modern attempts to model our practice on the natural sciences, we turn to social practice and practical philosophy . . . [which] means (a) that conceptions of the aim of social inquiry are now being shaped not by the demand for a 'neutral, objectifying science of human life and action' or for *episteme* but by the search for a better understanding of *praxis*; (b) that the kind of investigation required here must attend to both ethical and political concerns (ethical because praxis [action] is defined by habits, modes of thought, customs and mores and political because action is public and is concerned with our lives in the polis); and (c) that the rationality of everyday life (and the rationality of social scientific practice itself) is regarded as intrinsically dialogic and communicative. (Schwandt, 1996a: 62)

This analysis leads Schwandt (1996a) to argue that social inquiry, such as evaluation, should be reconceptualized as 'practical philosophy', inquiry *with* rather than *on* human actors, intended primarily to enable practitioners 'to refine the rationality of a particular practice for themselves'. Features of this approach include: inquirers seeking to establish a dialogic relationship of openness with participants in the inquiry; inquirers viewing the participants in an enquiry as themselves engaged in performing a practical art, in which decisions are both cognitive and emotional and always contextualized; the aim being a reflective examination of practice, in which the inquirers encourage practitioners to reflect critically on and reappraise their commonsense knowledge. Overall, Schwandt concludes that saying farewell to the 'bankrupt' project of criteriology 'means not that we have resolved this quest for criteria but that we have gotten over it or beyond it . . . What once was the critical problem of the correct criteria becomes the problem of how to cultivate practical reasoning' (1996a: 70).

Bill Readings has addressed the issue of evaluation in relation to universities, in the context of a critique of what he calls 'the discourse of excellence', 'excellence' having become the watchword for universities in the same way that 'quality' has for early childhood institutions. While critical of the discourse of 'excellence', he recognizes the importance of evaluation, but understood by him to involve an act of judgement and self-questioning 'embedded within a discursive or pragmatic context, a context that must be acknowledged' (1996: 133). Readings argues that evaluation produces a judgment of value; he is therefore critical of methods of evaluation which rely on the completion of standardized forms and the application of statistical calculation since they 'presume that evaluations can be directly deduced from descriptive statements, [which is to confuse] statements of fact with statements of value' (p. 131). Bringing issues of value into the reckoning means 'recognizing that there exists no homogeneous standard of value that might unite all poles of the pedagogical scene so as to produce a single scale of evaluation' (p. 165), and that 'evaluation can become a social question, not a device of measurement' (p. 124).

Judgments should be delivered not as a statement of fact but precisely as a judgment and be judged by others in turn. In other words, the judge must take responsibility for his or her judgment, 'rather than hide behind statistical pretension to objectivity' (p. 133), and taking responsibility for a judgment as a discursive act 'invokes an accountability that is radically at odds with the determinate logic of accounting . . . which only serves to prop up the logic of consumerism' (p. 134). Readings is at great pains to emphasize the provisionality of evaluation as judgment, the importance of keeping the issues open and subject to continuing discussion rather than seeking foreclosure, since the 'question of evaluation is finally both unanswerable and essential' (p. 133).

It seems to us that these discussions from the field of evaluation bear close relationship to what we have described as the discourse of meaning making, foregrounding the socially constructed nature of knowledge; the emphasis on constructing and deepening understanding of what is going on (i.e. practice or *praxis*); doing so by engaging with and being in dialogue with others, in particular practitioners, and through reflective analysis; recognizing that the process is value-based and therefore political and moral; and being comfortable with uncertainty and provisionality. Understood in these ways, evaluation can readily be part of the vocabulary of the discourse of meaning making.

Questioning the Discourse of Meaning Making

Conditions and Frameworks

We have put forward an alternative discourse for making sense of what goes on in early childhood institutions. Located within postmodernity, it is a discourse that speaks of personal agency and responsibility to produce or construct meaning and deepen understanding about pedagogical work and other projects, foregrounding practice and context, always in relationship with others and following rigorous procedures. It assumes multiple perspectives and voices and the possibility of finding some areas of agreement with others, while being wary of total agreement or consensus; uncertainty and indeterminacy are viewed as unavoidable.

This discourse of meaning making will be subject to many questions and objections. Some are the inevitable response to problematizing a dominant discursive regime which is assumed to be a permanent and unquestionable feature of the landscape and that governs us through having become embodied. To suggest that the very concept of quality is problematic, that it is located within a particular philosophical position, that it is the product of power and saturated with values may be so challenging that the suggestion is simply not heard or, if heard, ignored. Others arise from the need to make our so far abstract discussion more concrete, which we begin to do in the following chapters — although we also recognize that there is much work to be done.

Some may say that working within a discourse of meaning making, as well as enabling early childhood institutions to operate as forums in civil society as discussed in the previous chapter, is not possible without demanding conditions being in place: adequate numbers of trained and experienced staff; the availability of *atelierista* to support the hundred languages of children and the production of documentation in those different languages;[3] the availability of *pedagogistas* or other facilitators and of adequate time to enable staff and others to engage in meaning making; motivation of all concerned to undertake challenging and demanding work; organization that integrates care and learning into a single early childhood service; sufficient public resourcing to enable early childhood institutions to operate as forums in civil society; long-term political commitment and involvement and so on.

We agree. Structure and resources, together with political commitment, are necessary. There is no magic formula for a cheap and painless way to achieve a complex and demanding response to a complex and demanding issue. It is no coincidence that two of the main examples we give of work within the discourse of meaning making have emerged in parts of Europe — northern Italy and Sweden — where early childhood institutions have benefited from sustained public support, including sufficient tax-based resources, and an integrated approach to organization. (The third main example — from the First Nations in Canada — has arisen in a context of cultural suppression where communities have begun to question dominant regimes of truth.)

It seems to us that, as in the case of these Italian and Swedish examples, early childhood institutions should and need to operate within a publicly supported system (although the actual management of services may be by either public or private organizations), representing a political and community commitment to early childhood and early childhood institutions. But again, it is not inevitable that a publicly supported system will construct early childhood institutions in the way we have proposed (as forums in civil society) or adopt the discourse of meaning making that we have offered in place of the discourse of quality. Publicly supported systems may just as easily choose modernist constructions of young children and early childhood institutions, and go down the road of standards and quality criteria.

Adopting the discourse of meaning making, rather than quality, is not a recipe for neglect and indifference, for 'low cost' or 'cut price' solutions. Combined with our understanding of the importance of early childhood and early childhood institutions, it is a recipe for a system of well-organized and well-resourced early childhood institutions. It seems to us, however, that the way to achieve that system is not to establish a universal but static set of 'structural criteria', but to ask recurrently

'What do early childhood institutions require for their projects?', 'What do we need for the pedagogical work and the process of meaning making?'

We have attempted to delineate two alternative discourses and concepts — quality and meaning making — and we have argued that each is located within a very different philosophical position and premised therefore on very different assumptions and perspectives. It makes no sense to compare them in terms of which is better and which worse. Furthermore, *even if the discourse of meaning making were to be more widely adopted, it will co-exist alongside the discourse of quality for the foreseeable future*. For even though there may be a profound transformation underway, with a widespread feeling that we are moving either into postmodernity or, at the very least, a distinctive phase of late modernity, it is also still the case that we are living in the age of quality.

Individual institutions will almost always be working within regional or national frameworks which attempt to set certain common conditions or requirements — what might be called 'frameworks of normalization'. These frameworks may take various forms: legal rights for children; standards or regulations for the running of institutions; curriculum guidance; systems of inspection and quality assurance; and so on. Working within the discourse of meaning making does not preclude operating such frameworks of normalization, if required: it is not a case of having to choose between one and the other.

However, it is necessary to understand the limitations of these frameworks. Frameworks of normalization are themselves socially constructed, therefore value-laden, not revelations of inherent and value-free truth. For example, the concept of 'standards' begs many questions: 'What possibilities do we want to ensure or avert by setting standards?'; 'Why these possibilities and not others?'; 'Whose interests are being taken into account?'; 'What is the trade-off between these interests?' Once constructed, frameworks are still likely to be in constant need of interpretation. Unless we close our eyes very tight, we cannot avoid subjectivity and multiple perspectives. The more tightly frameworks are defined, to avoid local interpretation, the more likely they are to be accused of rigidity and irrelevance to local circumstances and so risk being ignored or side-stepped.

Frameworks are problematic in other ways. They can readily become normative, deadening innovation and aspiration. They focus our attention on the map, rather than the actual terrain. More generally, they can lead to a false sense of security, by seeming to offer certainties and guarantees. Ultimately, we must face the realization that there are no certain answers, no guarantees. We may decide to adopt a modernist perspective and the discourse of quality in the hope of reassurance and certainty of performance, hoping that 'there must be someone, somewhere, who knows how to set apart the right decision from the wrong one — a grandmaster . . . a supreme practitioner and/or a supreme theorist of the right choice' (Bauman, 1997: 202). But, it seems to us that all that this achieves is to get one perspective, one understanding of what is going on. And since everyone can learn what that perspective is, we risk a circular and self-defeating process in which institutions gear themselves to delivering the criteria that frameworks of normalization and their attendant inspectors determine, so that targets are met not because they are understood to be an important part of pedagogical work but because they are targets — resulting in the tail of evaluation wagging the dog of pedagogical practice. Moreover, by calling in the grandmasters, we opt out of taking responsibility for something for which we should be taking responsibility — young children and their lives.

If we can envisage situations where early childhood institutions operate both with the discourse of meaning making, but within frameworks of normalization, the balance becomes an issue. How many general rules, regulations and conditions? How much autonomy given to individual early childhood institutions to produce and make meaning of their own pedagogical work? It may prove illuminating to study what happens in countries that have chosen frameworks that quite deliberately leave much space for regional and local discretion and interpretation, for example, the national curricula for Early Childhood Education in Spain and Sweden.

The relationship between frameworks of normalization and local autonomy is emerging as an issue in other areas. In the field of development aid to Majority World countries (discussed further in Chapter 8), 'many professionals seem driven to simplify what is complex and to standardize what is diverse' (Chambers, 1997: 42), and there is a history of top-down attempts to manage complex relationships at local level. What emerges from this history is that

> not centralization and many complex rules, but decentralization and a few simple tendencies or rules, are the conditions for complex and harmonized local behaviour . . . The key is to minimize central controls, and to pick just those few rules which promote or permit complex, diverse and locally fitting behaviour. The practical conclusion is to decentralize, with minimum rules of control, to enable local people to appraise, analyse, plan and adapt for local fit in their necessarily different ways. (1997: 195, 200–1)

So, by all means let there be frameworks of normalization, if these are wanted. But equally let us not fool ourselves about what they are or what they can do. Let us recognize their limitations and dangers, their assumptions and values. Let them not be at the expense of ignoring other ways of thinking about and making sense of early childhood institutions and the work that they do.

The Great Bugbear of Relativism

One of the biggest concerns that many people have with problematizing quality and the construction of a discourse of meaning making is 'relativism'. There is a general anxiety here about chaos and anarchy, the breakdown of order and morality. How can we live in a world where there is no agreement about what is good or right or true? But there is also a more particular anxiety about what this might mean for young children and other vulnerable groups, since 'a slide into relativism (is seen as) dangerous for the dispossessed in its undercutting of the grounds for social justice struggle and its feeding of nihilism and quietude' (Lather, 1991: 115). There are two responses to these concerns, the first questioning the concept of 'relativism', the second about the capability of people to live in a world without foundational standards and the opportunities opened up by this world.

'Relativism' is used as a charge by people who adopt a modernist perspective against those who take a postmodern perspective. Indeed, 'relativism is a concept from another discourse [to postmodernism], a discourse of foundations that posits grounds for certainty outside of context' (Lather, 1991: 116). Relativism is an issue, therefore, if a foundational structure is held to exist and is then ignored (Cherryholmes, 1988), if there are universal and unshakeably founded laws and codes, if there is absolute knowledge. But from a postmodern perspective there are no foundations, no universal laws and codes, no external position of certainty, no universal understanding that is beyond history and society — and therefore no absolute truth against which other positions can be objectively judged: 'we just thought otherwise, believing in gods and kings and, more recently, the "objectivity" of scientists' (Lather, 1991: 117).

Postmodernism is 'modernity without illusions ... the illusions in question boiling down to the belief that the "messiness" of the human world is but a temporary and repairable state, sooner or later to be replaced by the orderly and systematic rule of reason' (Bauman, 1993: 32). Rather than 'relativism', we choose to speak of 'partial, locatable, critical knowledges' (Lather, 1991: 117) and of difference — of context and position, of perspectives and understandings. But recognition of difference is not just about taking account of the way the world is, its diversity and messiness: it also opens up possibilities and opportunities. For if there are foundations — principles, rules, codes, laws of universal validity — then all that is asked of us is to conform to them: to stick to the rules, to learn the codes, to ingest knowledge, to implement the standards. But if there are no foundations, then there is space for personal agency and responsibility, for making meaning and taking decisions — while at the same time recognizing the complexity and uncertainty that are an inevitable consequence of being human beings and not gods.

Zygmunt Bauman, in his study of postmodern ethics, discusses the heightened moral demands on the individual in postmodernity, but his comments could be applied more broadly to the situation of people struggling to make sense of the work of early childhood institutions:

> The probable truth is that moral choices are indeed choices and dilemmas are indeed dilemmas — not the temporary and rectifiable effects of human weakness, ignorance or blunders. Issues have no predetermined solutions nor have the crossroads intrinsically preferable directions. There are no hard and fast principles which one can learn, memorize and deploy in order to escape situations without a good outcome ... Human reality is messy and ambiguous — and so moral decisions, unlike abstract ethical principles, are ambivalent. It is in this sort of world that we must live; and yet, as if defying the worried philosophers who cannot conceive of an 'unprincipled' morality, a morality without foundations, we demonstrate day by day that we can live, or learn to live, or manage to live in such a world, though few of us would be ready to spell out, if asked, what the principles that guide us are, and fewer still would have heard about the 'foundations' which we allegedly cannot do without to be good and kind to each other. (1993: 32)

The American philosopher Richard Rorty likewise proposes that living and working without foundations places far greater responsibility on the individual to make choices (1980). He further argues that virtually no one actually adopts a relativist view: 'except for the occasional cooperative freshman, one cannot find anybody who says that two incompatible opinions on an important topic are equally good' (Rorty, 1982: 166). Like Bauman, he believes that many people get by without foundational beliefs and without giving up on making choices: 'the liberal societies of our century have produced more and more people who are able to recognise the contingency of the vocabulary in which they state their highest hopes — the contingency of their own consciences — and yet have remained faithful to those consciences' (Rorty, 1989: 46).

It seems to us that 'relativism' is a mystifying term, more used to stir up anxiety than further understanding. We prefer to talk about people finding ways to live in a world that is 'messy' and 'ambiguous', or complex and rich in diversity, which includes finding ways to understand and make judgments about complex issues such as early childhood pedagogy. There are ways, procedures, for supporting this task, and we believe, like Bauman and Rorty, that people have capacities and competencies that enable them to make decisions without universal codes. We have agency and responsibility, which carry with them the freedom or the burden of making choices — and from which there is no escaping uncertainty and ambivalence:

> [There is a] temptation to have one's cake and eat it, to taste in full the joy of choosing without fear of paying the penalty for a wrong choice, to seek and obtain a foolproof, patented and guaranteed recipe for the right choice — for freedom without anxiety . . . The snag is that foolproof recipes are to freedom, to responsibility and responsible freedom, what water is to fire . . . There is no such thing as freedom without anxiety . . . All in all, it is by no means certain what most of us would have chosen were they given the choice — the anxiety of freedom, or the comforts of such certainty as only unfreedom can offer. The point is, though, that the choice has not been and is unlikely to be given us. Freedom is our fate, a lot which cannot be wished away and will not go away however keenly we may avert our eyes. We do live in a diversified and polyphonic world where every attempt to insert consensus proves to be but a continuation of discord by other means. (Bauman, 1997: 202–3)

We do not lay claim to the only way of understanding the world and early childhood. Others will see them differently, through a modernist lens, and continue to be governed by the discourse of quality. We would not wish to prescribe how they think or what they do. The postmodern project values diversity and 'both/and', rather than the dualistic and 'either/or' approach. We can, for example, envisage a situation where many early childhood institutions adopted the discourse of meaning making, while at the same time having to conform to various standards and targets (what we have termed frameworks of normalization), democratically determined nationally or locally, which prescribed some of the work that they did. We can envisage different researchers operating within the different approaches, some, for example, comparing nurseries using ECERS or some other standardized measure, whereas others adopt other methods such as documentation to compare early childhood institutions from a different perspective and to reach different understandings. We recognize that the discourse of quality might be particularly useful for certain highly technical issues, perhaps, for example, food hygiene or building standards to ensure the physical safety of young children in early childhood institutions. Nor does adopting the discourse of meaning making imply rejection of quantification; a comprehensive and reliable system of information on such subjects as the supply and use of places, the costs of running institutions and the gender, ethnicity, training and other details of the workforce are necessary conditions for a system of well-organized and well-resourced early childhood institutions.

What we believe, however, to be important is for all those engaged with early childhood and early childhood institutions to recognize that there are different perspectives, that the work we do (whether as practitioners or parents or policy-makers or researchers) always takes a particular perspective — and that therefore choices — or judgments of value — are always being made from which flow enormous implications in terms of theory and practice. Our criticism of the modernist approach in early childhood — represented, par excellence, by the burgeoning work using standardized measures — is that it operates as if it was the only approach, the only true way, and in the process reduces complexity and diversity to methodological problems that can be controlled for and manipulated.

This modernist approach in the early childhood field, sustained by the power of United States research and developmental psychology and by the dominance of the discourse of quality across so many other fields, is an example of the hegemonic thinking that we raised in Chapter 1. For it is a feature of hegemonic practice, of a dominant discursive regime, that it takes itself for granted, assumes its premises to be neutral and unproblematic, denies and ignores or even remains unaware of the views and positions of others. The time has come, however, for researchers, practitioners and others who view the world from different perspectives to engage in dialogue with each other, not to *prove* who is right, but to seek mutual understanding and recognition and to understand how and why they have made their choices.

Notes

1   The NAEYC has recently produced a revised edition (Bredekamp and Copple, 1997), which takes more account of issues such as context and diversity. Although it still takes a modernist perspective, including a search for common principles and a dualistic division between 'appropriate' and 'inappropriate' practice, the shift represented by this new edition opens up new and welcome possibilities for dialogue with work choosing to adopt other perspectives.

2   The *pedagogista* is a pedagogical adviser who works with the pedagogues in a small number of early childhood institutions, to enable them to reflect on and better understand pedagogical practice and theory. This type of position is found in Reggio Emilia, but also in other parts of northern Italy.

3 *Atelierista* are pedagogues trained in the visual arts, working closely with other pedagogues and children in the early childhood institutions in Reggio. They both enable children to express themselves in a variety of non-verbal languages and assist adults to understand how children learn. Through their workshops *(ateliers)* and skills they help to produce a range of documentation, to contribute to processes of critical reflection on pedagogical work (Edwards, Gandini and Forman, 1993). It would be possible to have *atelierista* trained in other forms of artistic expression — music, dance, drama and so on.

Chapter 6

The Stockholm Project: Constructing a Pedagogy that Speaks in the Voice of the Child, the Pedagogue and the Parent

The Inspiration of Reggio

What is so terribly impressive and exceptional about the Reggio experience and the work of Loris Malaguzzi is the way they have challenged the dominating discourses of our time, specifically in the field of early childhood pedagogy — a most unique undertaking for a pedagogical practice! This was achieved by deconstructing the way in which the field has been socially constituted within a scientific, political and ethical context and then reconstructing and redefining children's and teachers' subjectivities. That is, they have tried to understand what kinds of thoughts, conceptions, ideas, social structures and behavioural patterns have dominated the field and how these discourses have shaped our conceptions and images of the child and childhood, the way we interact with children and the kind of environment we create for them . . . As I see it, all of this was possible because Malaguzzi was extremely familiar with the field and its traditions; but he also had the courage and originality to choreograph his own thinking. (Dahlberg, 1995: 9–10)

In Reggio they share a social constructionist view based on such concepts as construction, co-construction and reconstruction . . . Heinz von Foerster, to whom Malaguzzi often referred, argued that 'objectivity is a subject's false view that observing can take place without him'. For Malaguzzi, the notion that we cannot describe our world without taking notice and being aware that we are describing it was nurtured by the inspiration he drew from a variety of disciplines. In this connection he was known to cite scientists and philosophers representing, for example, the new quantum mechanics associated with Chaos Theory, the new cybernetics as well as the science of mathematics. Coupled with Malaguzzi's social constructionist perspective is his awareness of the power of the process of representation. As a result the pedagogues in Reggio have been very much against a textbook approach to their practice with prescribed rules, goals and methods. This explains why they do not have a 'programme or a curriculum' that can be readily transferred and applied to another cultural context. I recall Malaguzzi enquiring once, very seriously, in view of all the Swedish pedagogues visiting Reggio, whether many of them were working with the dove now — 'The Dove' being, by then, one of the most well-known thematic projects in Reggio. I couldn't help but answer yes! (Dahlberg, 1995: 11–12)

The pedagogical work in Reggio Emilia has become increasingly famous and a source of inspiration to more and more people over recent years. Many people from all over the world visit Reggio each year, staff from Reggio are frequently invited to lecture abroad, and the Reggio exhibition is in constant demand. In 1992, the American magazine *Newsweek* nominated Diana, one of the early childhood institutions in Reggio, 'the best in the world' (perhaps a rather problematic concept from the perspective of Reggio and this book, but nevertheless an indicator that Reggio is widely seen as very important for early childhood pedagogy).

But why is it so important? It is easy, especially from an Anglo-American perspective looking always for solutions without finding critical questions, to look for specific technical features, to try to locate a programme that can be described, classified and replicated irrespective of context. There are certainly important 'pedagogical tools': the procedure of pedagogical documentation, the role of specialist staff such as *atelierista* and *pedagogista*, the time built into the pedagogues' working week to analyse, debate and reflect on pedagogical practice. But these technical features are the surface manifestations of something much deeper, a pedagogical practice located in a profound understanding of young children in relation to the world and a philosophical perspective which in many respects seems to us postmodern.

The two quotations that start this section capture some of the elements of that practice, understanding and perspective: choosing to adopt a social constructionist approach; challenging and deconstructing dominant discourses; realizing the power of these discourses in shaping and governing our thoughts and actions, including the field of early childhood pedagogy; rejecting the prescription of rules, goals, methods and standards, and in so doing risking uncertainty and complexity; having the courage to think for themselves in constructing new discourses, and in so doing daring to make the choice of understanding the child as a rich child, a child of infinite capabilities, a child born with a hundred languages; building a new pedagogical project, foregrounding relationships and encounters, dialogue and negotiation, reflection and critical thinking; border crossing disciplines and perspectives, replacing either/or positions with an and/also openness; and understanding the contextualized and dynamic nature of pedagogical practice, which problematizes the idea of a transferable 'programme' or a universal 'dove' project.

This last point explains a hesitation in Reggio to 'text bind' their practice. For they are aware of how easy it is to construct universalized practice — a universal discourse with a universal dove, a seamless text which could be seen as the 'Reggio approach', a programme that can be exported and applied everywhere. Encountering the work in Reggio is more like encountering a series of projects or events, which range over a wide spectrum of contents. By respecting the *singularity* of these events, it becomes clear that there is not only one possible answer or way of working. It also becomes clear that this is dangerous, as it introduces uncertainty: 'its effect is to dethrone the Idea from its position of Truth' (Young, 1990: 82).

In these respects, we see many similarities between the work at Reggio and the work of Gayatri Chakravorty Spivak whose interests, broad and diverse like Reggio's, range over Marxism, deconstruction, feminism, psychoanalysis and critiques of colonialism and the institution and practices of pedagogy. Spivak recognizes how

> different disciplines interrelate and implicate each other . . . Instead of staking out a single recognizable position, gradually refined and developed over the years, she has produced a series of essays that move restlessly across the spectrum of con-temporary theoretical and political concerns, rejecting none of them according to the protocols of an oppositional mode, but rather questioning, reworking and reinflecting them in a particularly productive and disturbing way . . . Spivak's work offers no position as such that can be quickly summarized: in the most sustained deconstructive mode, she resists critical taxonomies, avoids assuming master dis-courses. To read her work is *not so much to confront a system as to encounter a series of events*. (Young, 1990: 157, emphasis added)

From our viewpoint, Reggio provides living witness to how the creation of *a crisis* in thinking and a struggle over meaning can produce opportunities, opening up the possibility of viewing children, early childhood institutions and early child-hood pedagogy in new ways — the child and the pedagogue as co-constructor of knowledge and identity, the early childhood institution as a forum in civil society and early childhood pedagogy as one of the main projects of that public space with the purpose of enabling children to have the courage to think and act for them-selves. Reggio proposes to us a practice permeated with active participation and a reflective culture, which values, but also problematizes, notions of democracy, dialogue and diversity, and which is open to the surrounding world and stands in communication with others. It is a practice further characterized by an active and enquiring relationship to many of the major issues of our times — childhood, gender, the environment, peace and human coexistence — as well as to develop-ments in science, philosophy and ethics. We can even suggest that by offering a new vision, with the prospect of new freedom and a new political culture, Reggio has become a new social movement and has created a new university.

The Swedish Connection

Reggio Emilia seems to have held a special attraction for Sweden. The Reggio exhibition, presenting the work of the early childhood institutions in the city, was first invited to Stockholm in 1981. That first exhibition was seen by around 90,000 Swedes and was followed by a new exhibition 5 years later. Since then interest, as well as wonder, in the work being carried out in the early childhood institutions in Reggio has continuously increased. During the last 10 years almost 3,000 Swedes have visited Reggio to study the pedagogical work, and many books and films about Reggio have been published in Sweden during the 1980s and 1990s (Barsotti, A., 1986, 1997; Barsotti, C., 1981, 1986, 1994; Wallin, 1986, 1996; Wallin et al., 1981).

Why are so many Swedes interested in the Reggio Emilia pedagogical philosophy and its practice? We think it is not just by chance. There are some striking similarities between Sweden and the Emilia Romagna region in northern Italy where Reggio is situated. Both have undergone somewhat similar processes of modernization. Both have high levels of parental employment and a relatively high standard of living. In the late 1960s and the 1970s, both developed an understanding of the structural changes taking place in society and attempted to respond to these changes with social planning and social welfare, including the building up of extensive systems of publicly funded early childhood institutions.

So, when Swedish pedagogues come to Reggio Emilia there is much with which to identify. But this goes beyond social, cultural and political conditions. There are connections also when it comes to concepts of early childhood institutions and pedagogical ideas. Since the 1960s, Sweden has tried to move away from a simple classification of 'children at risk' and 'children with special needs', related to a deficit concept and the role of institutions being to make good that deficit. Instead the emphasis has been on early childhood institutions for *all* children, where the idea of children with special needs has been changed into the idea of children who may need additional support. Reggio, with its image of the 'rich child', adopts a similar view of its early childhood institutions.

Although the expansion of the Swedish early childhood system was dominated by concerns about providing enough places to care for children with working parents, there was still space for an important and continuous discussion about pedagogical philosophy. As in Reggio Emilia, the concept of dialogue has, since the 1970s, been an important idea for early childhood pedagogy in Sweden. This concept was first introduced in reports from the Child Care Commission, published in 1972 (SOU, 1972). The Commission proposed that the early childhood system should, hence forward, be seen as a socio-pedagogical resource, helping to reduce inequalities in children's living conditions. In this context integration was a valued word, and was combined with an idea of dialogue pedagogy (*dialogpedagogik*).

The term 'dialogue' was chosen to symbolize a pedagogy that should transgress former early childhood traditions, traditions which had been based either in Gesellian theories of maturity or in theories of transmission where the child was seen as a passive and empty vessel that should be filled with knowledge (i.e. the child as reproducer as discussed in Chapter 3). The Commission was also challenging the unequal distribution of power between the child and the adult by constructing another relationship, more democratic and dialogic. In the Commission's 1972 report, the concept of 'dialogue pedagogy' was discussed in the following way:

> [Dialogue pedagogy] starts from the idea that there should be a continuous dialogue between the child and the adult, on both an inner and outer level, which implies a reciprocal giving and taking of emotions, experiences and knowledge . . . In the 'dialogue' between the child and the adult should exist respect for the child as an active individual, as well as the possibility for the child to experience meaningful human relations which in the long run can lead to the child developing such relations by her/himself. (SOU, 1972: 26, 46)

To provide theoretical and philosophical support for this concept, the Commission referred to the theories of Jean Piaget and Eric Homburger Erikson. Later, the thinking of Paolo Freire and George Herbert Mead became associated with, and legitimated, 'dialogue pedagogy' (Schyl-Bjurman and Strömberg-Lind, 1977; Selander, 1984).

In an appendix to the 1975 Commission report on a new training for pedagogues — *Utbildning i Samspel (Education for Relationships)* (von Euler, 1975) — it is argued that a dialogue pedagogy puts considerable demands on the staff. It requires an understanding of the child's development as a process and that knowledge is constructed in the relation between the child and the surrounding world. It is further argued that a positivistic perspective, which hitherto had been very common in curriculum studies

> becomes preposterous within the framework of a dialogue pedagogy. The child cannot be treated as a tool in a pedagogical situation characterized by a dialogue with an I and You relationship. If the child is seen as an object, a thing, the pedagogy (the methodology) will be seen as a tool for the pedagogue/teacher. The teaching risks becoming limited to a discussion concerning pedagogical tricks and techniques. In the same way as the aims for both children and staff must be the situation they are taking part in, the world they are a part of, in the same way the object for the teacher trainer and the student teacher above all must be the situation the student teacher will meet and how the human dialogue will be undertaken . . . Methods that result in measurements and quantifiable data (for example, ticking off schemas, estimations, assessment measures) will, because of their lack of explicit values, lead towards an objective view of the child, where the observer puts her/ himself outside what is happening. Such methods have a hidden effect, producing a technical view of pedagogical methods and excluding dialogue. (SOU, 1975: 338, 340)

For many reasons, the Commission's ideas faced difficulties in gaining ground in practice, and since the 1970s its ideas, and especially its concept of dialogue pedagogy, have been analysed and criticized from many perspectives (Callewaert and Kallos, 1976; Hultqvist, 1990; Selander, 1984). Nevertheless, the communicative perspective on pedagogy, which the Commission proposed, can be seen as epoch-making. Although there was no recognition of how developmental psychology is implicated with the growth of scientific classifications and normalizing discourses — power over life (as discussed in Chapter 2) — the Commission's work constituted a form of counter-discourse: it problematized, as Reggio has done, a traditional, instrumentalized idea of education, where the teacher is seen as a neutral transmitter of a body of predetermined and societally sanctioned knowledge and the child is constructed as a passive recipient. Instead the Commission's concept of pedagogy focused on the conditions and means through which knowledge is produced, by pedagogue and child together, and on the importance of pedagogues constructing a democratic relationship with children.

The Swedish connection with Reggio has become stronger over the years, culminating in the establishment in the early 1990s of a Reggio Project and a

Reggio Institute, both located in Stockholm. In the remainder of this chapter, one of us, Gunilla Dahlberg[1], tells the story of the Stockholm Project and the understandings it has provided both of the pedagogical work in Reggio and concerning the issues we have discussed in the previous chapters.

The Stockholm Project: Early Childhood Pedagogy in a Changing World

Starting Up

In 1988 a group of nine people, all engaged in one way or another in the field of early childhood pedagogy in Sweden, started a forum for discussing why so many Swedish pedagogues were attracted by the pedagogical philosophy in Reggio Emilia and what we could learn from the Italian experience. The group made visits to Reggio Emilia and had the opportunity to meet with the children and pedagogues there. We also arranged seminars at which pedagogues and local administrators from different municipalities in Sweden participated.

After a couple of years, all of us in the group felt we were becoming increasingly familiar with the Reggio Emilia philosophy, and more and more sophisticated in understanding and talking about the pedagogical practice and how it related to the underlying philosophical ideas. But we also came to realize, and this was very frustrating, that there was no pedagogical practice in Sweden that really took such a perspective seriously. A large gap existed between *the arena of formulation*, where pedagogical ideas are formulated into curricula and so on, and *the arena of realization*, where these ideas are actually practised (Lindensjö and Lundgren, 1986). It seemed to us that it was relatively easy to take on a view of the child as equipped with huge potential and many competencies or a view of the pedagogue as a reflective, co-constructive practitioner — at a surface level. But at a deeper level, what did the Reggio philosophy really mean, both theoretically and in relation to practice?

Fortunately for us, on one of the visits to Reggio Emilia, Loris Malaguzzi proposed that we should start a project together, Reggio and Stockholm. He also pointed out that, although there were a lot of differences between Sweden and Reggio Emilia, he thought we had a lot in common, and that generally speaking he believed that it was in the Scandinavian countries that children were treated with most respect. This faith was born out by what happened next. A project proposal was sent to the Ministry of Social Affairs. This led to the establishment in 1993 of the Stockholm Project which we called Early Childhood Pedagogy in a Changing World.

Before moving on to the project itself, one other preceding experience should be mentioned. The Project started out from postmodern conditions and their meaning for young children and for early childhood institutions. It was our conviction that, if we were to renew pedagogical practice and to restore the legitimacy of early childhood institutions, it was of paramount importance to understand the social phenomenon of childhood and relate that understanding to what kind of society children of today live in and what kind of society they will encounter in the future. For this understanding we have drawn a lot on a project undertaken in the late 1980s and funded by the Nordic Council, Modern Childhood in the Nordic Countries (the BASUN project).

In the BASUN project (Dencik, 1989) we started to analyse the relationship between early childhood institutions and work in industrial society and what consequences the change from an industrial society to a postindustrial information and knowledge society — *a learning society* — had for these institutions, both in relation to new risks, but also new possibilities for learning and meaning making, freedom and democracy. The Project began to open up discussion about what these societal changes might mean for the child's possibilities to handle life in a postmodern society and for the child's construction of his or her identity and biography, problematizing the idea of the child's identity as fixed (Dahlberg, 1992). This discussion in turn led the way to a deeper analysis and understanding of the universal ambitions of the project of modernity, discussed in earlier chapters, an understanding which has been very valuable for *our* understanding of Reggio Emilia.

The Design and Organization of the Project

From its inception, the Stockholm Project has been practice-oriented. It has been a very open project, not much planned in advance — something which has been hard for us to handle, but which has been a very dynamic force in the work. From the experience of Reggio, Malaguzzi gave us three important pieces of advice before we started: 'A project is difficult — when it ends it is as if it never existed'; 'Do not start a project only for the pedagogy, take in the whole organization'; 'Continue to change — do not stick with a method or organization'.

When we started the project, we had a number of ideas. The more we worked with the pedagogues in Reggio, the more we noticed a very conscious strategy of wrestling with and trying to unmask, to step outside and beyond, the dominant discourses and the homogeneous position ascribed to the child, the pedagogue and the parent through these discourses (Dahlberg, 1995). We wanted therefore to deconstruct the dominant discourses in the early childhood field, to be able to reconstruct other discourses. We also agreed to work in the following way:

- To work on thematic and project work: Swedish early childhood institutions have a long tradition of thematic work, but we wanted to take a critical view of the way this work has been carried out, in particular in relation to the practice of thematic work in Reggio.
- To work on observation and pedagogical documentation: in Sweden, these terms have been understood in relation to child developmental theories, i.e. using observations and documentation to assess and classify children against developmental norms. We wanted to look at the very different understanding of these terms produced by the pedagogical practice in Reggio.
- To create spaces for exchange of experiences, co-construction and reflection.

- To promote changes in the environment of early childhood institutions.
- To examine divisions of responsibility and use of time by pedagogues.
- To provide support for pedagogues, along the lines of the *pedagogistas* in northern Italy.
- To offer an *atelierista* consultant.
- To work closely with parents.
- To gain support and acknowledgement for the pedagogical work from the management of early childhood institutions.
- To work with a whole district (i.e. a local authority or municipality).

The design and organization of the Project were not laid down beforehand; they evolved throughout its four years. The Project chose to work with Åkervägen, an early childhood institution located in the district of Hammarby in Stockholm that had already been searching for inspiration from Reggio Emilia, but had found this to be difficult even though many of the pedagogues had visited Reggio. The Project offered to work with six other early childhood institutions from the same district,[2] connecting all seven institutions to the Project in a network. Each of these institutions selected one pedagogue from each group of children to participate in monthly network sessions held with the project group, and who in turn was to share her experience with her colleagues at her workplace. Their pedagogical work has been supported by an *atelierista* and a *pedagogista*, who have been able to act as tutors for the everyday practice in the network of institutions. Finally, the seven heads formed their own network together with the project leader.

An important consideration for us in choosing institutions for the network was that the whole staff group, and not just the head, was motivated to participate and willing to put in the extra work that was required. We offered no financial inducements. The institutions in the network had to work under the same financial conditions as the other 20 or so centres in the district. Another condition for participation, this time for the district management, was that they directed their in-service training to focus on themes prioritized by the project.

The selection of the seven institutions to form the network was a very hard process, raising difficult questions about democracy and change. In the Swedish democratic and bureaucratic tradition everyone in a district like Hammarby should get the same money and the same support at the same time. Typical responses to our insistence on being selective, of both institutions and pedagogues, were, 'In our district we have got 28 preschools — we have to have a project where everyone can take part and get new ideas' or 'Why can't every pedagogue from our preschools be part of the project?' However, in the project we have been troubled by this dominant view of democracy, which from the start we saw as potentially being a form of levelling down or dilution which would make change very difficult to achieve. We wanted to try out another idea that did not imply that everyone gets a little bit at the same time. From our perspective this meant that the lowest common denominator would prevail and very little change would take place.

The issue is how one understands how change takes place. How do you get change not only at the level of talk, but also in practice? What is democracy in this case? In our view, it was important to start with pedagogues who were motivated and engaged and who wanted to put some extra effort into making change happen. We were looking for good examples — 'good' not in the sense of being excellent, but 'good' in the sense of being documented examples of a process of change which can enthuse and inspire others.

At the same time, it was important to us not to create an elitist project, where institutions with the best conditions get support and the others get none. Those institutions that applied to participate in the network, but could not be accepted, were told that the work from the project would be regularly presented to them, and that they would be able to start up another network later with support from the first network and drawing on its experience. This has happened, so that today there are several networks in the district working with deconstruction and reconstruction of their practice.

We have made lectures which have been open to all pedagogues in the district, and which have offered another space for constructing new meanings and understandings of the child, ourselves as pedagogues and pedagogical practice. These lectures have been both theoretical and practice-oriented. Drawing on Reggio Emilia, we have presented new perspectives and themes, such as pedagogical philosophy, social constructionism and postmodernism, evaluation, management and organization, visions of an encounter, participation and democracy. We have related these themes to concrete examples drawn from the institutions in the core network, including the *atelierista* consultant presenting and discussing work carried out by pedagogues in these institutions. Initially, these lectures were given by the project group. But gradually, pedagogues from the network have become confident enough to present and discuss their own work to their colleagues in the district. Indeed, so self-assured has this group of pedagogues become that in the course of the project they have also been invited to universities and schools of education throughout Sweden to present their documented experiences.

Following Malaguzzi's advice on the importance of involving the whole organization, the project group made other connections with the district, over and above the core network. A coordinating team was established that consisted of the project group, the head of early childhood services and the pedagogical consultant in the district, the manager for the in-service training centre in the district and the head of Åkervägen. Continuous dialogue with the politicians of the district has been established by the project group and the pedagogues in the network, opening up discussion about pedagogical philosophy and practice. We have also started to bring the parents into new forms of participation, in which we seek to challenge common ideas of parents as consumers of services and try to understand what it means to be a participant.

In all these ways, we have created forums or plazas where many debates can take place (Dahlberg and Åsén, 1994: Göthson, 1991), and where the whole district, as well as the project group, can be involved in a process of change and new understanding! In general, the district has welcomed the Project. Beforehand, discussions in the district had been very much about money and budget problems, and many pedagogues felt that they were not listened to and even wanted to leave their jobs. This had created a defensive atmosphere. The project has helped to create a different atmosphere, in which new possibilities can be seen and pursued.

The work has spread beyond Hammarby. During the project, 34 local networks have started throughout Sweden, and one Nordic network has been established. They receive support from the Reggio Emilia Institute, which has close connections to the Stockholm Project. An annual summer symposium is now held, with participants from all over the Nordic countries. There have been other consequences. Some elementary schools have started to take inspiration from the project. A journal, *Modern Childhood*, has been started which disseminates experience from the Project. Several undergraduate and doctorate students have chosen to work in relation to the Project, on subjects such as 'a problematization of the concepts of power, resistance and emancipation in pedagogical documentation work' (Lenz Taguchi, 1998); 'taking a stand towards the modern child and developmental psychology, and formulating an alternative where the child's subjectivity is placed and constructed within a flow of actions and language' (Nordin-Hultman, 1998); and 'loss and meaning in a tradition of representation: difference and ambivalence in the process of knowledge' (Lind, 1998).

A Changing Horizon of Expectations — A New Space, a New Becoming and a New Hope?

Before discussing the work of the project in more detail, it is necessary to consider our general strategy, the project's theory of change, and how we have understood the relationship between the project and Reggio Emilia. How to work in one context with pedagogical ideas from another context, with different conditions, is not self-evident. For reasons already discussed, we have never envisaged a direct translation and application of 'the Reggio approach' into the Swedish context. We have never seen ourselves as engaged in an implementation project; this seems neither desirable nor attainable.

It has always been clear to us that we have to start from where we are in Sweden, from our own traditions and culture. Hence, our understanding of Reggio Emilia — '*our* Reggio Emilia' — is not in any sense a 'true' description of Reggio Emilia, but is rather a construction in which we have built an understanding of their practice in relation to our own Swedish traditions and culture (Dahlberg, 1995). One can say that Reggio has contributed a specific way of thinking, towards which we could relate ourselves with love and/or confrontation: indeed in the Stockholm Project, we have found this statement of Loris Malaguzzi to be very important: 'Pedagogy is not generated by itself, it is only generated if one stands in a loving relationship and/or in confrontation with other expressions of the present.'

In our own work we have used the Reggio Emilia experience as a form of *inspiration*. For us, Reggio Emilia has become, in the words of Melucci, a form of lived utopia,[3] at a time when the welfare state in Sweden has been undergoing great change and questions are being asked about how the rights and position of children can be maintained. We have also used Reggio as a *prism* that, together with postmodern perspectives, has helped us to reflect on and problematize our own tradition and pedagogical practices — and enhancing our ability to reflect and pro-blematize has been a very important part of the project. The idea behind the meta-phor of a prism was that translating a philosophy from one context into another always implies a form of decontexualization and recontextualization of that philo-sophy (Bernstein, 1990; Dahlberg, 1985). A pedagogical philosophy that travels is often seen as something negative, as you can never get the same thing in another context. But like Bauman (1997), we think that one should not regret that there is no possibility to translate something exactly from one context into another. Rather, even if there are many difficulties, we think there are gains to be made if we understand this as a process of co-construction.

When we started this project we were often asked: Why Reggio Emilia? The Swedish early childhood centres are also world famous. Like many others, we originally thought that the Reggio Emilia pedagogy was the same as the Swedish — only they had managed a bit better. Many of the words that we use to describe our pedagogical philosophy in Sweden are similar. As we got to know their work and community, however, we realized that they had transgressed dominant dis-courses, not only in the field of early childhood pedagogy, but also in relation to organization and community!

For us, therefore the Reggio Emilia experience has provided a challenge to the prevalent tradition of early childhood pedagogy, and not only early childhood ped-agogy, but also to pedagogy, education, as a whole. As we have argued throughout the book, early childhood institutions and their pedagogical practices are consti-tuted by dominant discourses in our society and embody thoughts, conceptions and ethics which prevail at a given moment in a given society. Therefore, to change a pedagogical practice, it is necessary to start by problematizing and deconstructing these discourses and to understand and demonstrate how they are related to what is going on in pedagogical practice. Reggio Emilia has helped us to do this and, by so doing, to create a space for the reconstruction of a new vision, offering alternative understandings of the child, the pedagogue and the early childhood institution.

As a first step to understanding these dominant discourses and how the field of early childhood pedagogy in Sweden has been constructed, we focused on the dominant scientific paradigm inherent in social and behavioural science. As researchers, but also as pedagogues, we often get lost in methodological questions, and in doing so lose sight of pedagogy as a cultural and symbolic activity. That pedagogy can be detached from philosophy is due in large measure to the scientific tradition of splitting knowledge from values, a tradition which has been dominant and which has, rather uncritically, been taken as the base for constructing the field of early childhood pedagogy. When Maria Montessori, at the beginning of the century, developed her pedagogical thinking, she paid attention to science but rejected the hopes that were then being raised by the new measurement and technique-oriented research and about their contributions to the training of new teachers. What comes through in her writings is her desire to maintain the value base in pedagogy:

Many have looked upon materialistic and mechanistic science with excessive hopes. It is precisely because of this that we have entered upon a false and narrow way which must be surmounted if we are to revitalize the art of educating future generations . . . I personally believe that we should give more attention to imparting a spirit to teachers than scientific techniques, that is our aim should be towards what is intellectual rather than material. (1967: 4–5)

As a second step we have analysed how the field of early childhood pedagogy and the child has been constructed in Sweden as well as in some other countries. Through this process of deconstruction, we have come to understand how the identities of the child and the pedagogue have been constructed, including some of the constructions discussed in Chapters 3 and 4. We have gone on to analyse how these constructions have become productive in our pedagogical institutions: in our relations to children, to other pedagogues and in the way we have designed the environment, that is, the whole choreographing of the milieu.

This work has illuminated how these dominant discursive regimes and the practices they produce are tied to power. Right from the start, we found it was very difficult to get any tolerance for other ways of thinking about and understanding the field. This we have come to understand in relation to the ideas of Foucault, discussed in Chapter 2. Thus, we are often unaware that we embody a dominant discourse and the constructions it produces (the Idea enthroned as the Truth), or we are unconscious of the power that is connected to action, and that we are, in one way or the other, always participating in acts of power — for example, whether we permit children to have a lot of free, creative play, or permit them to choose by themselves from various Montesorri materials, or if we permit them to work with clay and observe and document their work (Lenz Taguchi, 1996). Categories and concepts function, too, as acts of power in Foucault's perspective. Reggio has helped us to see how we are not only inscribed, both as children and pedagogues, in dominant discourse, but also govern ourselves through these inscriptions.

It is important to emphasize that we are aware that constructions always embody power, and that this is true of the constructions that we have made of the child, and the pedagogical practices that we have produced from these constructions. This is something we never can get around. We cannot pretend to be free of power and to stand outside power relations, we are always within the knowledge/power nexus. Foucault (1970) said 'everything is dangerous', meaning that our constructions are always arbitrary and as such never neutral nor innocent. They always bear social consequences, that is the solutions that we choose have implications not only for the role and position we give the child, but also for how we develop our forms of democracy. In short, processes of construction place a lot of ethical responsibility on all of us.

Many people might consider this talk of power, problematization and (de)construction pessimistic and leading nowhere. However, from our experience in the project, together with the inspiration from Reggio Emilia, we have found them to be quite the opposite, causes for optimism and very productive. It is certainly true that adopting the perspective we have done carries risks and can produce no change at all. But it also bears possibilities and a potential for dynamic change. If we are subject to power, we also have power. If on the one hand conventions and social representations are embodied and always contain power, on the other hand as arbitrary constructions they can always be open for change. This is why it is so important to unmask and trouble the traditions that are embodied in institutions such as schools and early childhood institutions, and by so doing open up for new possibilities and a new space for change and hope. Here concepts and perspectives become tools for constructing alternative understandings and practices.

Through problematizing and deconstructing dominant discourses and constructions we can, as Patti Lather (1991) says, interrupt the values underlying the practices that have been constructed. We can frame the practice in another way, by reinscribing ourselves in another discourse through reconstructing language and practice. In the project, using these methods, we have been able to open up a new space for the reinterpretation and reconstruction not only of the child, now understood as a co-constructor of knowledge and culture, but also of the pedagogue and of the early childhood institution. In that new space, we have also been able to understand the field of early childhood pedagogy from another perspective and to formulate alternative practices, or counter discourses, which could not be articulated in the previous dominant discursive regime. Through an historical understanding and 'situating' of how we have constructed our view of the child and childhood and of knowledge and learning in relation to the process of modernization, we have been able to formulate not only other constructions of the field, of the child and the pedagogue, but also of the role of local authorities, politicians and researchers.

For us, therefore, the central questions in the project have become: How to get another construction of the child, knowledge, learning and the conditions needed for learning? How to reconstruct an early childhood pedagogy which has its starting point in the child's theories, hypotheses, dreams and fantasies and in a view of knowledge and learning as co-construction? How to border cross the project of modernity, holding out the prospect of a continuous and linear progress, certainty and universality, by recognizing uncertainty, diversity, non-linearity, multiple perspectives, temporal and spatial specificities? With inspiration from Reggio Emilia and with the challenges of neopragmatic and postmodern theories we have started to produce provisional answers to these questions, constructing a practice, or daring to play with a practice, which is more varied as well as more self-reflective about itself, its possibilities and its limitations and that does not hide away from uncertainty, multiple perspectives and relationships.

This is demanding work. It questions much of the thinking with which we have constructed the child — and from which we have constructed our ideas of what is of value for pedagogy. We have also needed to create new concepts as the old concepts contain meaning that is related to another construction. Reggio and postmodern thinkers have shown us how we can work with categories and concepts as *provisional* constructs and tools that all the time are open for change.

From the start Reggio helped us to give authority and practical meaning to a construction of the 'rich' child and for that construction to inform the pedagogical work in the early childhood institutions. Our social constructionist perspective implies that child and pedagogue are seen as co-constructors of their own knowledge, their environment and themselves. Learning cannot be seen as an individual cognitive act, something that is taking place in the head of the child, but as a cooperative and communicative act. In this perspective, and in line with the philosophy of Martin Buber (1970), knowledge is not something the individual human has got or owns, but something you find or achieve through placing yourself in relation to the world. The communicative action — the interaction with the You — is therefore a condition of the I, as it is only in relation to a You that the I can be created. Instead of viewing the child's mental structures as an essential part of human nature and permanent, we see the world as mediated through language and our own and others' interpretative work.

By turning towards a social constructionist perspective, we have questioned the essentialist perspective where the child's identity is seen as homogeneous and stable and where children's needs are seen as something inherent — the child as nature. Instead, we have come to see that identity is a construction; it is a discursive practice constructed through language and communication. From a postmodern perspective, the individual does not have privileged access to her or his own identity through introspection: to Alice's question 'Who in the world am I?' (Carroll, 1865, 1973 edition: 24) there is no true answer or true knowledge. Identity is rather a relational and relative concept, and identities are constructed and reconstructed within specific contexts — contexts which are always open for change and where the meaning of what a child is, could be and should be cannot be established once and for all.

We can say that Reggio has helped us to create a crisis in our own thinking, and so helped us to transgress dominant discourses and practices. Through a critical inquiry and through a reflective practice we have been able to understand how our own thinking and practices are inscribed in dominant discourses, which has opened up a new space and helped us to understand that there are other possibilities — alternative discourses or counter-discourses. Working in relation to Reggio has helped us find critical and productive questions: How has the child, knowledge and learning been constructed in the Swedish context? Are there other ways of constructing the child and ourselves as pedagogues which can open up for an emancipatory practice in early childhood institutions? What tools and practices can help this deconstruction and reconstruction of dominant and counter discourses and different pedagogical practices?

Networking

During our work we have realized more and more that networking, combined with pedagogical documentation, have been key tools for opening up a process of analysis and self-reflexion, and hence for change to take place. A networking which opens up for an exchange of experiences and which involves a critical discussion around pedagogical documentation has had a great potential, not only for changing pedagogical practice but also for constructing an ethics of an encounter — a reciprocal relationship which in itself functions both as a means as well as a content and goal.

In our Project we have tried to establish a *co-constructive learning culture* by enhancing self-reflexivity through dialogue, reciprocal relationships among the participants, and pedagogical documentation. It makes possible not only creative meaning making but also the development of friendship, taking responsibility and participation — the most important conditions for democratic relationships. Through co-construction, we open up a new space for ourselves as pedagogues, but also more generally as human beings.

To establish a co-constructive learning culture, characterized by continuous change, we have tried new ways of exchanging experiences, between the pedagogues — but also between the heads of the early childhood institutions and between the managers and politicians of the district's early childhood service. Behind this has been a belief that pedagogical work needs an organization and a pedagogically competent management that is prepared to examine its own work in relation to how it contributes to the support of pedagogical change and to the construction of the child and the pedagogue. To accomplish this management involvement in the Project, we have had regular meetings between the network of the project group and pedagogues and these groups of managers and politicians.

Networking has been central to the Project, becoming for us a way of enacting a more multi-voiced and multi-centred discourse. How have we worked with the network of pedagogues? We began with a two-day session, where we — the pedagogues and the project group — told our stories about our work from an historical perspective. The pedagogues talked about their work over the years and how it had changed, both in terms of practice, but also in relation to theoretical and philosophical ideas and in relation to curriculum and wider changes in society. This was a very important meeting. The pedagogues had never talked before about their work in this way, there was never time or space while at work. Consequently, they felt they had never been seen and listened to.

Given our own tradition in Sweden, and the inspiration of Reggio Emilia, we decided that we should then start with thematic work, documenting what was done in the institutions and bringing the documentation into the network. We wanted to focus on, struggle with and reflect upon everyday pedagogical practice. But after a couple of sessions, we realized that thematic work was too far away from our ideas of change. It easily ran into documenting what we have always done, and not problematizing how we have constructed the learning child and the learning pedagogue. We also realized that documentation in itself was a very difficult tool to use; it needed training and new skills. So we changed tack, and decided that we would work with small-scale situations from the institutions, and observe and document them. We would 'swim in observations'.

This turned out to be very fruitful. With the help of different media and through working with observation and documentation of how children explore and co-construct the world and how their learning processes take place, the pedagogues in the project have begun to critically examine and develop their own pedagogical work. We have used documentation as a tool to understand how the child has been constructed in our early childhood institutions. It has helped us to answer the question: Do we see the child? What do we mean by saying 'to see the child'? This can be seen as a form of deconstructive work in relation to pedagogical practice — what constructions of the child are behind the way we talk about the child and what kind of constructions are behind our way of relating to the child in our practice? How have these constructions shaped how the environment has been ordered? How has the whole pedagogical space been constructed? Are there other constructions to be made? Is this a pedagogical space for the 'rich' child, pedagogue and parent?

What we have found through concentrating our attention on documentation is that we have *not* ended up with our discussion of practice becoming more and more sophisticated, while the pedagogical practice itself remains virtually unchanged. We can easily learn a new language, with new conceptual tools. We can sit in networks and talk, and agree with each other as we always talk in a very abstract way, for example, when we discuss having a 'child-centred' perspective and a pedagogy which takes the 'perspective of the child'. But what does that mean? It is often surface-level talk. New words and concepts do not automatically change practice. A new understanding is not the same as new patterns of action — that is what we earlier have called the difference between the arena of formulation and the arena of realization.

Pedagogical documentation has enabled us to avoid this happening. For if we document our practice and the child's learning we have concrete examples from practice to reflect upon. Pedagogical documentation opens up a possibility for moving back and forth between conceptual tools and practice. As well as deconstruction, documentation has enabled the pedagogues to develop their practice through struggling with a new construction of the child and themselves as pedagogues, and in this way to take more control over their own practice.

When the pedagogues started to listen to the children, and changed their pedagogical relationship, a new construction of the child and the pedagogue appeared. It was a child that, for example, could concentrate on an activity much longer than the pedagogues' earlier constructions had said he or she should be able to, and who was not as egocentric. The children in our project more and more start saying 'look what I can do and know', and the pedagogues are becoming more and more aware of the children's potentialities — what they actually can do and do do rather than what classificatory systems say they should do. The excitement that this has generated among the pedagogues is captured in this comment by one of them: 'I have been working with preschool children for 20 years now and I never thought children know and can do that much. I now have got another child in front of me.'

It is astonishing how changing the construction of the child has contributed to the production of a new practice. Malaguzzi once said about such change: 'in fact this is very simple, but there is someone who has made us think it is so difficult.' Through troubling the dominant discourses and constructions of the child one can open up for 'another child' — a child with lots of capabilities and a child that has got thoughts and theories that are worth listening to both from the perspective of other children but also from the perspective of the adult.

In our project it has become very obvious for us all how the constructions we have made of the child have enormous consequences for how we relate to children pedagogically, how we design and choreograph the milieu as well as how we relate to parents. If we have got a rich child in front of us instead of a problem child this influences everything. It functions as a language that in itself becomes productive. As the pedagogues in Reggio say: 'if we have a rich child in front of us, we also become rich pedagogues and we get rich parents'. We are able to take control over our own learning process and have the right to interpret the world, but also to negotiate interpretations with others.

This work has led to an increasing awareness among the pedagogues of their own potentialities, as well as a new understanding, a new construction of the pedagogue. Giving children the possibility to explore and interpret the surrounding world, and to let children take responsibility for their learning and knowledge construction places a lot of responsibility on the pedagogue. The view of the child as a co-constructor presupposes a view of the pedagogue as a co-constructor of culture and knowledge. This implies both a professional relationship and responsibility, which means being in dialogue and communicative action with children, parents and others, and a reflective and co-constructive relationship with the children and their own work, with the learning process as a starting point. In this process the pedagogue must take a lot of different perspectives, sometimes having to be the director: presenting a problem and initiating project work around a specific theme or introducing new knowledge to enable the project to continue. At other times, the pedagogue is more of an assistant in a process which the children themselves have initiated and directed (Dahlberg and Lenz Taguchi, 1994).

The work of the pedagogue consists largely of being able to listen, seeing and letting oneself be inspired by and learning from what the children say and do. It is important to keep the children's questions, hypotheses, theories — but also their fantasies — alive and to follow and study how they search for answers and make meaning in the world (Lindqvist, 1995; Rodari, 1988). This is part of a wider ethical project of establishing a culture where the children are seen as human beings in their own right, as worth listening to, where we do not impose our own knowledge and categorizations before children have posed their questions and made their own hypotheses.

This does not mean that the pedagogue should not challenge children's curiosity and creativity, their questions, hypotheses and theories. In pedagogical work such as we have developed in the project, the pedagogue becomes very important for bringing in challenges — both in the form of new questions, information and discussions, and in the form of new materials and techniques. The pedagogue must be able to master the difficult art of listening, seeing, hearing, questioning and challenging — and by so doing to enable children to see that there are multiple perspectives, complexities and ambiguities. In this way the pedagogue can enhance children's ability to choose and to construct understanding and meaning, and to see new possibilities in complex situations and to construct knowledge in their own local situation — knowledge being understood not as something you own or as some pre-existing truth to be discovered but as something that is created through being in relation and dialogue with the world. From a pragmatic perspective we should not worry about truth, in the sense of whether or not something is true, but about the choice between different hypotheses. In cultures like ours today that are besotted with the desire for truth, objectivity and certainty (Steier, 1991: 53), we must dare to tolerate the idea of uncertainty, recognizing that life also embodies ambiguities and complexities with which we have to dare to live.

In this view of knowledge and learning the pedagogical process is seen as a communicative context, filled with language and expressions. What the child or the pedagogue are saying must be seen as a complex construction of many negotiations, feelings and memories, which never can be fully reconstructed or reciprocally understood by the other. However, what is said can awaken desires, recognition and curiosity in the other, and for this to happen, the question, 'Have you wondered about something today?', must always be kept alive in the everyday life of the pedagogical practice. Wonder is the primary prerequisite for experience and learning, as many philosophers from Aristotle onwards have recognized. So we must take care of children's wonder about the surrounding world — a world that can be both familiar and strange. In the Project, we often say that children are curious from the start, but can easily lose their curiosity, like they can loose the 'hundred languages' with which they are born. We have to take care of children's curiosity and wonder about human existence and the life that is all around them.

To do this, pedagogues also need to recapture their own wonder, otherwise they will not be able to function as co-constructors together with the children. As adults we need to learn to become curious again. We need to rediscover curiosity and wonder in relation to nature, culture and society, but above all in relation to what children think and do. We need to be full of wonder at what children say and do, and hence curious to continue listening to and hearing what they say and do. As one of the pedagogues in the Project said: 'You have to bow your knees and let yourself wonder over what children can do.' Boredom is the worst enemy of pedagogy. Malaguzzi often referred to Bachelard by saying 'for upbringing to be successful, you need a jester in your pocket', and also quoted Bronfenbrenner, 'for upbringing to be successful, there needs to be at least one crazy uncle around who astonishes' (Dahlberg, 1995: 16).

The work in the early childhood institutions in the network has been carried out in many different ways, due to the different starting points for each institution. Each one has chosen its own journey and developed its own strategy. Each one has discussed where to start. Should we start by changing the milieu, or the pedagogical work with the children? To this question there are no clear answers. Some saw changes in the environment, to make it more like an *atelier*, as the most fruitful way to start and for getting material to discuss within the network, others chose changes in the pedagogical work.

Although there are these differences between the early childhood institutions in the network, some common themes can be discerned. We have laid the base for work that is guided by the pedagogues, and for a pedagogically competent leadership who can open up for change. Through the collaboration within the Project, we have managed to encourage a more reflective and critical attitude towards pedagogical practice. Instead of the common answer when confronted by change 'This is the way we have always done things — why change?', the pedagogues have become open to problematizing their own thinking, to trying out new conceptual tools and changing their pedagogical practice. They have seen that practice can be changed, and realized that they have power over their own practice, that you can think and act by yourself. They have started to confront dominant discourses, and have seen that the child and the pedagogue can be conceptualized and related to in another way.

In this context the importance of *critical dialogue and communication* has become obvious to us. If we want a culture of co-construction and reflection, which always uses the pedagogical work with the children as the starting point, then we have to learn to examine that pedagogical work critically. This proved to be a very demanding part of the project.

To establish a culture of critical dialogue and to enhance self-reflexivity is not easy. In Reggio, they are built into the everyday practice itself, through the process of documentation that every institution undertakes and the stimulation and challenge provided by the *atelieristas* and *pedagogistas*. But it seems as if we, in Sweden, are not used to discussing and critically analysing what we say and do. If we start asking questions about something we as pedagogues have done together with the children, it is very easy for these questions to be taken as some form of criticism of our work or of ourselves as persons, instead of treating them as a way to reconstruct our work. We take these questions personally, as if we have difficulty in distinguishing the person from the issue.

Because we are not used to problematizing, we found in the network that we started talking about a lot of things outside the pedagogical work we were currently undertaking, when what was needed was to focus on and become critical about this work. So, we have struggled with this issue and how to construct and deconstruct meaning and practice. In the project we often return to the comment from Vea Vecchi, the *atelierista* at the Diana early childhood institution in Reggio Emilia, when we asked her how it comes about that they have got such a reflective and exciting atmosphere: *We discuss, and we discuss, and we discuss and we discuss.* We have tried to construct processes of inquiry into the pedagogical practice, requiring a self-reflective attitude from all participants. All this needs time and a lot of work. But despite the hard work, it has also given us a lot of inspiration. It has been a way to take us beyond ourselves, to think the unthinkable and to avoid romanticizing practice.

A key to change has been the idea of *walking on two legs*. Traditions are embodied. One cannot simply throw them all out at once like old baggage. Emphasizing this idea was one way of helping the pedagogues not to despair because change takes such a long time and is such hard work. We talk about how in Reggio they have been working for more than 30 years in the long and continuing struggle to build up their practice. Visiting Reggio can easily give an impression that it is not possible to work like that in our context, we do not have the resources, the support from our management and so on. Yet we can reassure our pedagogues that in Reggio they have the same amount of money as we do. What they have is another perspective, another construction, perhaps also another engagement.

A four-year project is much too short. We have not really managed to change the organization, although we hope that is going on now, and the politicians have become engaged in the pedagogical work. The process of change can easily stop if documentation and self-reflection do not continue. It is easy to start saying now we have found the right way, and to rest on our laurels, when what is needed is continuing co-construction, problematization and documentation. We get so many visitors who want to come, visit the institutions and see what we have done; this shows the great interest in the Project but also leaves too little time to develop the work. The questions for us now are how to ensure that experimental work like this is not petrified? How can the process that has opened up continue?

The Researcher and the Project Leaders as Co-constructors

> The erosion of the legitimation of positivist inquiry has opened up new ways of doing social inquiry . . . Given the postmodern foregrounding of the ways we create our world via language, for perhaps the first time the complex question of political commitment and its relation to scholarly inquiry can be seriously addressed. (Lather, 1991: 14, 172)

During the project work, and in relation to the challenges of postmodern thinking, we have increasingly troubled the concept of empowerment and our perspective of constructing a pedagogy that speaks in the voice of the child. In the project of Enlightenment, the concept of empowerment implied taking control over one's own thinking and acting, but we have also, in earlier chapters, problematized its association with the concepts of reason and the autonomous subject, and its strong relationship to ideas of truth and progress. For us, important questions have been, 'Who is empowering whom?' and 'Who speaks for whom?' (Ellsworth, 1989). Related to this are further questions: How much theory and how many new concepts are needed for change to take place? What role do theoretical perspectives have and what role does the researcher play in a project like this? What is the relationship between researcher and pedagogue? These have not been easy questions for us in the Project, and we think there are no right or wrong answers. They depend to a large extent on goals and visions for our work.

For our work, especially for reflecting on the role of researchers and the researcher–pedagogue relationship, we have drawn much support from postmodern theories, in particular those that relate to what has been described as the crisis of legitimation (see Chapter 2), and problematize the role of the expert as having privileged access to the formulation of problems and meaning. We have paid a lot of attention to, and problematized, the position of science as legitimation of the truth and the concept of the researcher as the expert, the Great Interpreter (Dreyfus and Rabinow, 1980) and the 'master of truth and justice' (Foucault, 1977: 12). We have been influenced by Derrida (1982, quoted in Lather, 1991) when he deconstructs 'enlightenment' as a light-based metaphor or heliocentric view of knowledge which positions the emancipators (e.g. researchers) as 'senders' and the emancipated (e.g. practitioners) as passive 'receivers' of rays.

In the dominant research paradigm that has given this position to science and these roles to researchers, the struggle has been to reach 'the truth' and that which could not be quantified was too difficult to study — although it might be said to be very interesting. This has been a paradigm that has often directed our studies towards methods and their significance and not towards the relevance and meaning of what we study. Scientific research in the early childhood field has to a great extent been characterized by Cartesian dualism, where the object of our studies has been separated from children's and pedagogue's everyday lives in early childhood institutions and schools. Hence, a lot of scientific methods have been produced to study children's lives and development that often put children into very artificial situations or that divide up, fragment and decontextualize the everyday lives of children and pedagogues. Instead of accommodating complexity, these methods give a simplified picture (Dahlberg, 1985). Our argument here is not that methodo-logical discussions are irrelevant, but that they have a tendency to direct and restrict the questions that the researcher poses, to what it is possible to study by means of the prevalent armoury of methods — instead of problematizing and finding new perspectives in relation to the problem itself.

How then can researchers position themselves less as 'masters of truth and justice' and more as creators of a space where those directly involved can act and speak on their own behalf? How can researchers be other than the origin and legitimation of what can be known and done? Who are we to know better than the pedagogues? How can we conduct research about the child and his or her everyday life that recognizes and values complexity and context? Avoiding the researcher as the master voice and researcher-imposed definitions of the Project has not been that simple for us as researchers and scientists, but we have worked hard to do so. As a starting point, as we have already made clear, we have explicitly problematized the role of the researcher in our Project; we have recognized this is a major issue. From there, we have chosen to take the view that researchers, other members of the project group and the pedagogues are co-constructors in the process of change.

Networking, co-construction and documentation, focused on actual pedago-gical work drawn from the everyday lives of the children and pedagogues in their early childhood institutions, have been a form of interactive method which has helped to change the usual relationship between the researcher and the researched, including not situating ourselves, as researchers, at the centre of the Project. These methods can help to break down the sharp distinction between a reflective ped-agogical practice and emancipatory research by producing collaborative work that builds on interpretation and analysis, and neither imposes the researcher's under-standing of reality on to the practitioners, the pedagogues, nor romanticizes ped-agogical practice. We have struggled therefore to work together — researchers and pedagogues — in a process of collaborative co-construction, but at the same time not in a naïve way, remembering that we are never innocent, understanding how politics, knowledge and power are part of an indissoluble relationship so that we can never get away from power.

The relationship between theory, concepts and practice has also been an important issue. To achieve an interactive and reciprocal shaping of theory and practice has been a continuing focus of the Project. While working in the network with the pedagogues, the researchers have all the time had to find a balance between the theoretical perspectives and practice, remembering that the emancipatory objective needs to trouble practice from different perspectives. For us, as researchers, theory has been very important in our praxis-oriented process — but the theoretical concern must not overstep the concerns of practice. It is not enough to get new conceptual tools. They have to be tried out, discussed, negotiated and problematized in practice. A deep theoretical perspective combined with experience from practice opens up beneficial possibilities for dialogue and confrontation.

Some of the questions we have addressed about the relationship between the pedagogues and the researchers are similar to those that have arisen concerning the relationship between the pedagogues and the children. 'Who is the knower-known, who the teacher-taught?' As a project group, we have had a very specific position, being well acquainted with the Reggio Emilia philosophy and practice and, as such, we are frequently asked from all over Sweden to give lectures and to act as advisers. However, we have tried not to see ourselves as representatives of 'the Reggio approach' — not the great interpreters, teachers and knowers whose self-appointed task is to uphold reason and reveal the truth to those unable to see or speak it.

Where the beginning and the end is, there is no answer. We have to try it out! In the network we have tried to go back and forth between theory and practice, very much in line with the view Patti Lather (1991) has taken when she says that such a process raises many questions about vanguard politics and the limits of consciousness-raising. 'The historical role of self-conscious human agency and the efforts of intellectuals to inspire change toward more equitable social arrangements are precisely the aspects of liberatory politics most problematized by postmodernism.'

Some Provisional Understandings

Despite, or perhaps because of, the many challenges and problems we have confronted, we can say that the project has produced some important understandings from the work, about making change in pedagogical practice. Change needs networking combined with documentation and reflection. You need to start with a view, a construction which sees children as rich and competent, and from the work of the children and not the conditions of the pedagogues.

The work needs to be actively driven by the pedagogues, but this commitment needs to be supported. The work of the head of an institution must be centrally concerned with pedagogical practice, and the management of the institutions, in the district, has to be pedagogically competent and willing to analyse, deconstruct and reconstruct — it is not sufficient to confine themselves to administration and super-vision. *Atelieristas* provide invaluable support with knowledge and in producing documentation, and *pedagogistas* are another important source of support: but this tutoring requires a shared view and understanding of the child, knowledge and learning. And while it is always important to reflect on the pedagogical work, it is necessary to be flexible and be prepared to adopt different strategies to find successful ways of doing this.

We are convinced it is necessary to work with institutions which have similar and 'average' conditions, not set up institutions with more resources or other special conditions. Given these conditions, it is important to look at the use of time to ensure work such as documentation gets done. The key to this is to prioritize (for example, we have found that time can be found for staff to work on documentation by not expecting all the pedagogues to be outside with the children or to be eating meals with the children). Given this priority, documentation can both develop inservice training and the formation of public forums for participation, dialogue and confrontation — documentation becomes the focus for both.

Notes

1 Gunilla Dahlberg has been scientific leader for the Stockholm Project, in collaboration with Gunnar Åsén. Anna Barsotti and Harold Göthson, from the Reggio Emilia Institute in Stockholm, have also played leading roles in the development work of the Project. Together with Karin Furnes, who has been an *atelierista* consultant, they have formed the Project team.

2 The Hammarby district is a socially mixed area with a population of around 40,000.

3 Melucci (1989) argues that lived utopias, which he relates to many of today's new social movements, have replaced the old form of grandiose utopia, which are supposed to be realized only in an indefinite future. To live utopias implies a reflexive relationship to the form of organization, in contrast to traditional relationships between ends and means, where the ends justify the means. Melucci says that the forms of action in many of today's social movements express their goals, so that the utopia is embodied in the means, that is how the movement organizes itself and acts for change.

Chapter 7

Pedagogical Documentation:
A Practice for Reflection and Democracy

Pedagogical Documentation as a Practice to Encourage a
Reflective and Democratic Pedagogical Practice

It seems to me that the real political task in a society such as ours is to criticize the workings of institutions which appear to be both neutral and independent; to criticize them in such a manner that the political violence which has always exercised itself obscurely through them will be unmasked so that one can fight them. (Foucault, 1974: 171)

In earlier chapters we have argued for the socially constructed character of knowledge and the situated and embodied nature of the construction of the child, the pedagogue and early childhood pedagogy. This we did by identifying some of the techniques and practices by which we have constructed the child and the pedagogue and the dangers of these actions. From this perspective, it follows that all pedagogical activity can be seen as a social construction by human agents, in which the child, the pedagogue and the whole milieu of the early childhood institution are understood as socially constituted through language. However, this perspective also implies that this activity is open to change; if we choose to construct pedagogical activity in one way, we can also choose to reconstruct it in another.

In this chapter we will further develop this theme of how we can transgress traditions, and constitute an alternative practice within our early childhood institutions. This alternative practice seeks to understand how pedagogues have constructed and represented themselves and the children with whom they work. It offers the possibility to construct new meanings and, by so doing, to transgress boundaries — both in representations and practices. A necessary condition for this practice is forming an active way of opposing and resisting the exercise of the knowledge-power nexus, those regimes of truth which attempt to determine for us what is true or false, right or wrong, what we may or may not think and do.

We have argued earlier that enhancing self-reflexivity has an important part to play in pedagogical practice. By so doing, we can expand our social horizon and construct another relationship to life, work and creativity. How then can we practice a reflective and communicative pedagogy? It presupposes, first and foremost, a reflective practitioner who, together with his or her colleagues, can create a space for a vivid and critical discussion about pedagogical practice and the conditions that it needs. It also requires certain tools. With inspiration from the early childhood institutions in Reggio Emilia in northern Italy, many pedagogues around the world today have begun to use pedagogical documentation as a tool for reflecting on pedagogical practice, and as a means for the construction of an ethical relationship to ourselves, to the Other and the world — what we have termed an ethics of an encounter.

However, the idea and practice of pedagogical documentation has a long history. To take a Swedish example, the idea of documenting practice was an important feature of the pedagogical theory of Elsa Köhler. Like Dewey, Elsa Köhler had a reflective and problematizing approach to pedagogical practice and its related questions. Communication, interaction and observation were at the heart of Köhler's 'activity pedagogy', as well as the idea that the self-reflecting pedagogue should develop an understanding of the constitution of the self. The pedagogue in 'activity pedagogy' was seen as a kind of researcher, and during Köhler's time many pedagogues, because of their involvement in reflection and research, went on to academic studies and writing dissertations (Dahlberg and Lenz Taguchi, 1994; Stafseng, 1994).

This construction of the pedagogue as researcher through reflective practice has also been influential in Reggio Emilia. However, in Reggio they have questioned dominant ideas behind observation and documentation. Instead of seeing observation as being about mapping some universal and objective social reality, they see it as a process of co-construction embedded in concrete and local situations (Kvale, 1992), a shift of concern from

> theories to practices, from theorizing to the provision of practical, instructive accounts . . . The shift from third person observation to second person 'making sense' . . . We become interested in the procedures and devices we use in socially constructing the subject matter . . . We thus move away from the individual, third-person, external, contemplative observer stance, the investigator who collects fragmented data from a position socially 'outside' of the activity observed. (Shotter, 1993: 59, 60)

We have presented pedagogical documentation as a vital tool for the creation of a reflective and democratic pedagogical practice. But pedagogical documentation is important for other reasons. It has a central role in the discourse of meaning making. Rather than rely on some standardized measure of quality, as in the discourse of quality, pedagogical documentation enables us to take responsibility for making our meanings and coming to our own decisions about what is going on.

Pedagogical documentation also contributes to the democratic project of the early childhood institution, which we discussed in Chapter 4, by providing the means for pedagogues and others to engage in dialogue and negotiation about pedagogical work. Through making pedagogical work both visible and a subject for democratic and open debate, pedagogical documentation provides the possibility of early childhood institutions gaining a new legitimacy in society:

> We are convinced that the question of how to restore legitimacy [to early childhood institutions] under existing conditions can only be tackled if the economic aspects are more closely connected with the pedagogical and values-based aspects

of early childhood education. A prerequisite for this is that pedagogical practice and its functions must be made visible outside the world of schools and child care centres and become a part of public discourse . . . As we see it, this requires the participation of a variety of concerned groups and pedagogical practice based on empowerment, participation and reflexive discourse between parents, staff, administrators and politicians. (Dahlberg and Åsén, 1994: 166)

Pedagogical Documentation is not Child Observation

It is important to be clear about what pedagogical documentation is not. It should not be confused with 'child observation'. As we understand it, the purpose of 'child observation' is to assess children's psychological development in relation to already predetermined categories produced from developmental psychology and which define what the normal child should be doing at a particular age. The focus in these observations is not children's learning processes, but more on the idea of classifying and categorizing children in relation to a general schema of developmental levels and stages. Viewed in this way, 'child observations' are a technology of normalization, related to constructions of the child as nature and as reproducer of knowledge. They can also be related to the construction of the early childhood institution as producer of child outcomes, including developmental progress. 'Child observation' therefore is mainly about assessing whether a child is conforming to a set of standards. 'Pedagogical documentation' by contrast is mainly about trying to see and understand what is going on in the pedagogical work and what the child is capable of without any predetermined framework of expectations and norms.

There is another important way in which pedagogical documentation and child observation differ. Adopting a modernist perspective, child observation assumes an objective, external truth that can be recorded and accurately represented. It is located in a traditional objectivist and rationalist view of enquiry and observation, in which the world is understood as an independently existing universe and knowledge is understood as reflecting or corresponding to the world. It takes a view that there are intrinsic, essential qualities within the object of observation, in this case the child, which can be found.

Adopting a postmodern perspective, pedagogical documentation does not claim that what is documented is a direct representation of what children say and do; it is not a true account of what has happened. This challenge to objectivity is, however, not found only within postmodern theories. During the last 30 years, researchers within cybernetic and systems theory are addressing similar issues of knowledge being a social and cultural construction. By exploring the implications of reflexivity and self-reference in social science research these researchers are not only studying circular feedback mechanisms, but also dealing with the process of *observing* as much as with the *observed* (Gergen and Gergen, 1991; Israel, 1992; Steier, 1991; von Foerster, 1991). These researchers, who are said to belong to a second-order cybernetics tradition, lay stress on the responsibility of the observer for her or his observation, descriptions, interpretations and explanations. 'Constructionist inquiry, as human activity, must concern itself with a knowing process as embedded in a reflexive loop that includes the inquirer who is at once an active observer' (Steier, 1991: 163).

Pedagogical documentation is a process of visualization, but what we document does not represent a true reality any more than claims about the social and natural world represent a true reality — it is a social construction, where pedagogues, through what they select as valuable to document are also participative co-constructors. Meaning does not come from seeing or observation alone; 'meaning [is not] lying around in nature waiting to be scooped up by the senses, rather it is constructed. It is produced in acts of interpretation' (Steedman, 1991). When you document you construct a relation between yourself as a pedagogue and the child/ children, whose thinking, saying and acting you document. In this respect the practice of documentation can in no way exist apart from our own involvement in the process. Likewise the staging, that is what we perform of that which we have documented, is also selective, partial and contextual.

What we document represents a choice, a choice among many other choices, a choice in which pedagogues themselves are participating. Likewise, that which we do not choose is also a choice. Carlina Rinaldi, a *pedagogista* from Reggio Emilia, talks about choosing from many possible uncertainties and perspectives, and daring to see ambiguities. The descriptions that we make, and the categories we apply, as well as the understandings that we apply in order to make sense of what is going on, are immersed in tacit conventions, classifications and categories. In short, we co-construct and co-produce the documentation, as active subjects and participators. There is never a single true story.

Consequently, when we document we are co-constructors of children's lives, and we also embody our implied thoughts of what we think are valuable actions in a pedagogical practice. The documentation tells us something about how we have constructed the child, as well as ourselves as pedagogues. Therefore it enables us to see how we ourselves understand and 'read' what is going on in practice; with this as a base, it is easier to see that our own descriptions as pedagogues are constructed descriptions. Hence, they become researchable and open for discussion and change — which means that through documentation we can see how we can relate to the child in another way. From this perspective documentation can be seen as a narrative of self-reflexivity — a self-reflexivity through which self-definition is constructed. The awareness that we are not representing reality, that we make choices in relation to inscribed dominant discourses, makes it easier to critically analyse the constructed character of our documentation and to find methods to counteract and resist the dominant regimes.

We are certainly a long way from the idea of child observation as a true record, an actual representation of the child and his or her development.

What is Pedagogical Documentation?

When we use the term 'pedagogical documentation', we are actually referring to two related subjects: a *process* and an important *content* in that process. 'Pedagogical documentation' as *content* is material which records what the children are saying and doing, the work of the children, and how the pedagogue relates to the children and their work. This material can be produced in many ways and take many forms — for example, hand-written notes of what is said and done, audio recordings and video camera recordings, still photographs, computer graphics, children's work itself including, for example, art done in the *atelier* with the *atelierista*. This material makes the pedagogical work concrete and visible (or audible), and as such it is an important ingredient for the process of pedagogical documentation.

This *process* involves the use of that material as a means to reflect upon the pedagogical work and to do so in a very rigorous, methodical and democratic way. That reflection will be done both by the pedagogue alone and by the pedagogue in relationship with others — other pedagogues, *pedagogistas*, the children themselves, their parents, politicians. In the discussion of the Stockholm Project in the previous chapter, we saw how pedagogical documentation, drawing on small-scale situations from the institutions, became the main work of the network of pedagogues, but that this was not easy — 'it needed training and new skills'. It also presupposes that pedagogues and others can organize their work both to prepare documentation and to make time for these processes of reflection. One conclusion from the Stockholm Project and the work in Reggio Emilia is that this is not just a question of resources, but of prioritizing, making space for pedagogical documentation because it is understood to be of overriding importance.

Pedagogical Documentation as a Learning Process

Before looking in more detail at the theory of pedagogical documentation, we offer an example of pedagogical documentation in practice, based on one piece of work by a pedagogue who was a member of the network in the Stockholm Project. It has not been selected as an illustration of exceptional work or an exceptional pedagogue. It is intended to describe some of the ideas behind the Stockholm Project and the idea behind pedagogical documentation as a learning process, which opens up the possibility of challenging dominant discourses. It is, however, difficult to describe work like this, as it involves so many processes.

The context is that the pedagogues in this early childhood institution, through their participation in the Stockholm Project, are trying to listen to the children's hypotheses and theories, as well as their fantasies. They are also trying to focus, in a more systematic way, on the children's strategies of learning and meaning making, as well as their own way of challenging the children's learning processes. In the case here, Anna, a pedagogue working with an older group of children, starts documenting a project on time, recording what is done and what is said. She takes the documentation home every evening, looks at it and analyses it, reflecting and reinterpreting what is going on, not only amongst the children but also how she has constructed the children and herself as a pedagogue. She can ask questions of the documentation about how the learning child and the learning pedagogue have been constructed in their own practice, how knowledge is constructed and what kind of tools the environment offers for the children's experimenting and symbolizing. What engages these children the most? What kind of theories do these children have? How can I challenge these theories? How is it possible to extend the thematic work over a longer period and deepen the children's learning processes? How should the work continue?

These questions challenge Anna's thinking, and how she plans. If it is used as a tool for reflection, documentation often leads to thematic work taking longer, rather than the pedagogue rushing to the end and jumping into new ideas and content because she has planned in advance what should happen — when in fact the children could continue working far longer on a particular thematic project, deepening their learning processes. This way of working requires a lot of experimenting as well as a lot of interpretive work on the part of the pedagogue, a lot of dialogue with other pedagogues in which multiple perspectives can be introduced, discussed and confronted. In this way, the process can be a way of problematizing one's own understandings and a way of 'working together across differences' (Ellsworth, 1992: 106).

As well as working by herself, Anna takes the documentation back to the children so they can revisit what they did before and find new inspiration and become further engaged in the theme. She puts the documentation up on the wall, and this becomes an important means of engaging parents in the project. Children start coming to the institution with hour glasses and other instruments for telling the time. The children also involve the parents; for example, one day the children ask their parents to run in the corridor and time them. Through the documentation, Anna has also been able to discuss her pedagogical work in the team of pedagogues working at her institution and in the project network and has also shown it to many other pedagogues and to the parents at parents' meetings.

Anna told the network that it was hard to know how she should react to the children's ideas of 'animal time'. It would have been easy to say that animals cannot understand time — but she did not, choosing instead to treat the children's hypothesis in a very serious way. Anna can be said to have worked with a *social constructionist* perspective, rather than a *constructivist* perspective which assumes that the pedagogue has the right and true knowledge, which she should assert before children get the chance to explore their own hypothesis (see Chapter 3 for a fuller discussion of these two perspectives). This is a very difficult task as we are so inscribed in a perspective that assumes the pedagogue already owns the answer and requires her to carefully plan what the children should learn. In this thematic work, Anna has struggled with this, as well as how to find a forum for dialoguing with the other pedagogues at her early childhood institution. (It is also worth noting that during the course of this work the children learned how to tell the time, the sort of 'desirable outcome' that is often sought from early childhood pedagogy — but without the pedagogue needing to do any specific teaching of this competence.)

The project on time started out from a conversation that a group of six 5-year-old children had during their lunch. They had been looking at the clock on the wall and discussing at what time their parents usually picked them up. Anna observed that these children had a real interest in finding out more about the time and the clock. So the next day she took down the clock from the wall and put it on a table in the *atelier* in the institution, in front of the children. She then asked the children 'what is time?' The children answered:

'With the clock you can see what time it is. You need to know the time.'

'There are different types of watches; wrist watches, stop watches, cuckoo clocks that say cuckoo, church clocks that say ding-dong, when the time is 12.'

'The animals get up when we get up — as they do not have their own watches.'

'The watch is at 12 both in the day and in the night and there are only numbers up until 12.'

One child, Johan, also tells the other children a lot of what he knows about the numbers and the hands on the watch, including the hands having different functions. Another child says that now they want to make watches. As they are sitting in the *atelier* they are well aware that they can make different things. Anna has prepared beforehand with round paper plates and she gives them to the children, who start drawing watches with numbers and hands.

Two days later Anna reads back to the children from her documentation of the previous discussion, including the answers that the children had given to her question 'what is time?'. The children start discussing again. During this discussion the children talk a lot about animals and time and Anna asks them how animals can know what time it is. The children answer:

'They get up when they wake up and they cook their breakfast.'

'They wake up when the sun rises and they sleep when the sun goes down.'

'When it is sun here it is dark in Australia. The sun is divided.'

'The sun is the animals' watch.'

Anna continues to follow the children's discussion, documenting all the time what they say. After a while she asks the children if we can measure time by the sun? One child answers, 'No, we can know the time by the watch. Time goes round and round.' Anna then asks, 'Can we measure time at all?', to which Martin replies, 'Yes, when you run — then you can measure time.'

Now the children want to run and measure time so they go into the corridor of the institution. There they decide to have a race. Martin starts counting the seconds while the others run. When it is Johan's turn he uses a watch. He waits until the second hand has reached a marked number, then he counts how long time it takes. The children ask Anna to write down the results. After a while they begin to query why the results were so different when Martin counted. Isak then says that Martin counts very fast and when Johan uses the second hand on the watch it is much slower. They continue to wonder why, but they realize that they cannot solve the problem.

One of the children discovers that the animals also have to have a watch. So he says, 'We have to make a watch for the animals', and they decide that it has to be a round watch with numbers. Björn argues that animals do not have a watch. But Hans insists that they have to make a watch for the animals — so they all do that. They also decide that a lamp could be the sun, but when they direct the lamp on to a paper plate they see nothing and realize that they have to have something to throw a shadow. Then Anna takes out a pen and gives it to them. Johan discovers that by putting the pen on the paper plate they can get a shadow. Johan happily shouts out, 'Oh, it looks like a needle'. But at the same time he says that the animals cannot read numbers.

Isak moves the lamp, and the children realize that the shadow moves. All the children want to try this and they start moving the lamp into different positions to see how the shadow changes.

'We have made a sun watch', says Johan.

'I invented it', says Hans.

But Björn says that the animals do not need a watch as they get up when the sun rises.

Anna could see how interested the children were so she decided that they should continue. Once again she helped them through reading back to them the earlier documentation, to recapitulate what they had done before. They say that they want to make sun watches in another material. Anna gives them clay and tells them not to make the watches too small. The children start, very eagerly, to make round shapes out of the clay. One of the children says that the animals did not need numbers — 'so let's only make dots.' To make needles they used wooden sticks, discovering with the use of a torch that the sticks could serve this function. They start to run and dance around their watches and say that the sun goes up and down. They also observe that the shadow changes when they move the torch and that they can make it longer and shorter and cover several watches.

They make sun watches outside in the garden and they put down a wooden block in the ground to make a sun dial, deciding to continue with that later. Some of the boys also make church clocks with pendulums, starting to explore how the pendulums went back and forth. They say that the whole town could hear the bell when the pendulum went back and forth and they say that people then knew when they had to leave for work or school. Anna asks, 'can we measure time with the pendulum?' She had also brought with her fishing weights and string and the children started to make pendulums out of these materials.

They discover that if they had different lengths of string the pendulum swings differently; when the string is short the pendulum goes faster and when the string is long the pendulum goes slower. They also compare how long a time it takes for different pendulums to stop when they push them. Anna once again asks if they could measure time with the pendulum? 'Yes', one child says, 'like you do when you have an hourglass, like the prisoners in the castle have' (referring to a TV programme that was popular in Sweden just then).

After that the children start to make hour glasses filled with sand, and to compare the hour glasses with the pendulums. They also start to write numbers on the hourglasses, then suddenly go into a role play where they imagine that they are the prisoners in the castle. After this they start to measure everything with the hourglasses. They also make water-filled time glasses, inspired by an example that one of the boys brings from his home.

Anna asks 'does time always exist?' One child replies, 'Birthdays always exist — my mother has to look into her diary to know when I have my birthday and how long is left before the next one.' Another child says that days and hours always exist! 'Can you get the time back?', says the pedagogue. 'No', comes one reply, 'but earlier there were time machines and my mother used to tell how it was in the old times.'

Anna starts talking about the month of September, and then the children start to count the months; they said that it is spring now and that it has been winter. A child says 'Time goes round like the sun. But the same time that comes back is not the same time, because I do not reach five years every time I have my birthday.' 'Winter, spring and autumn, winter, spring and autumn — they go round — that must be human time', observes another child.

Pedagogical Documentation as Challenging the Dominant Discourses

As we discussed earlier, according to Foucauldian thinking we always exercise power over ourselves, which means that we discipline and govern ourselves in our struggles to find knowledge about ourselves and the world. Through documentation we can unmask — identify and visualize — the dominant discourses and regimes which exercise power on and through us, and by which we have constructed the child and ourselves as pedagogues. Pedagogical documentation, therefore, can function as a tool for opening up a critical and reflective practice challenging dominant discourses and constructing *counter-discourses*, through which we can find alternative pedagogies 'which can both be morally and ethically satisfying, but also aesthetically pleasing' (Steedman, 1991: 61). It can be understood as one of the 'technologies of the self', that we discussed in Chapter 2 in relation to 'care of the self', whose use makes it possible to criticize and free ourselves from embodied concepts and produce new concepts; we return to this concept of 'care of the self' later.

Because we discipline ourselves and exercise power over ourselves, we encounter great difficulties in changing our pedagogical practice. As Jennifer Gore notes 'enormous obstacles are faced, and, indeed, created by those who seek (and seek to understand) new pedagogies. Many of these obstacles arise from the fundamental tension in pedagogy itself that requires of those who seek to change it their participation in it' (1993: xi). These obstacles imply that, as a pedagogue, you have to find ways to cross these tensions which result from the fact that the one who is the pedagogue is also the one who is supposed to make the change, i.e. the one who is supposed to reconstruct the pedagogical practice.

Pedagogical documentation can contribute to a deepened self-reflexivity and tell us something about how we have constituted ourselves as pedagogues, as it helps 'telling ourselves a story about ourselves' (Steier, 1991: 3). It can open up a possibility for the pedagogue to see his or her subjectivities and practices as socially constructed, and thus open up an opportunity to break the dominant discourses, as it can broaden our understanding of who we are today and how we have constructed ourselves to be this way, as well as the conditions and dangers of our actions (Gore, 1993). This is a question of taking control over one's own thinking and practice, both as a child and as a pedagogue, in other words being governed less by disciplinary power.

Through documentation we can more easily see, and ask questions about, which image of the child and which discourses we have embodied and produced, and what voice, rights and position the child has got in our early childhood institutions. For example, do we only talk about concepts such as 'child centredness', 'taking responsibility for one's own learning', 'to learn how to learn', 'creativity', 'participation' and a 'reflective practice' — or do they actually permeate the pedagogical practice? Pedagogical documentation enables us to reflect critically on whether these ideas are just at the level of talk or whether they are being put into practice and, if so, in what way are they understood.

The point of departure here is that the greater our awareness of our pedagogical practices, the greater our possibility to change through constructing a new space, where an alternative discourse or counter-discourse can be established producing new practice. It is, above all, a question of getting insight into the possibility of seeing, talking and acting in a different way, and hence cross boundaries, in particular to transgress the grandiose project of modernity and its determination to map all human life in the search for Truth, Beauty and Goodness.

In the process of visualizing and reflecting how we have constructed the child and ourselves lies a critical potential, which in its turn can function as a learning process. This learning process can, at the same time, serve as a starting point for the reconstruction of the pedagogical work. It can operate as a form of in-service training, and as a basis for evaluation along the lines discussed in Chapter 5 in relation to the 'discourse of meaning making'. For pedagogical documentation can provide a critical means for pedagogues, and others, to deepen their understanding of pedagogical work and provide a basis, if required, for making judgments and seeking some degree of agreement on those judgments.

In many ways, using many media, it is possible for the pedagogue to record what the children do and what she as a pedagogue does in relation to the children and their work. Children and pedagogues can, while working, but also afterwards, analyse how the children's learning processes develop. Not only can the pedagogue develop her knowledge and understanding of the children's learning, and how they are producing knowledge, but at the same time, she can deepen her understanding of the consequences of her own actions.

Because documentation can be kept and returned to, and must be seen all the time as a living record of the pedagogical practice, the process of documentation can also function as a way of revisiting and reviewing earlier experiences and events, and by doing so not only create memories, but also new interpretations and reconstructions of what happened in the past. Through this, active pedagogues will be able to build on and utilize well-established experiences and simultaneously take part in constructing new theories concerning children's learning and knowledge construction, with documentation as a base. In other words, the pedagogues can participate in the production of new knowledge. This presupposes, however, that pedagogues engage in continuous self-reflection, something which poses high requirements on their professionalization, but something which also can function as a challenge and inspiration for a deeper engagement.

Visualizing practice requires that the process of documentation becomes an integrated part of the everyday work and not something lying outside. It is work that has to alternate between different focuses: on one's own experiences, on gaining a theoretical understanding of what is going on, and on the philosophical and socio-political values that determine the directions and visions for the pedagogical work. There is a need both for closeness and distance, for continuously working the tensions between high theory and everyday practice (Lather, 1991, cited in Lenz Taguchi, 1997), for a form of spiralling which allows for taking multiple perspectives, for looping between self-reflection and dialogue, for passing between the language of one's professional community (theories and practical wisdom) and one's personal passions, emotions, intuitions and experiences.

Documentation as a learning process, but also as a process of communication, presupposes the creation of a culture of exploration, reflection, dialogue and engagement. A culture where many voices — of children, pedagogues, parents, administrators, politicians and others — participate and can make themselves heard, and through that ensure that a multiplicity of perspectives can be scrutinized and analysed. In this way we can open up a way to make sense of pedagogical work — meaning making as we described it in Chapter 5 — for children, parents and pedagogues.

A hindrance to the development of a reflective pedagogical practice based on multiple perspectives is the very strong influence of what has been called the Jante Law (Boalt-Boethius, 1994). The Jante Law suggests that difference is often handled through finding the lowest common denominator, a response which weakens engagement and militates against other perspectives, other approaches and other voices being examined or given prominence in pedagogical practice. The alternative to the Jante Law, and the reduction of difference that it brings, is to revel in the complexities of multiple realities, multiple understandings and multiple perspectives. Such diversity provides people with alternative perspectives, possibilities to think and act in another way and enlarged possibilities for choice.

The Process of Documentation Can Never Be Neutral

The awareness of the constructed character of documentation also visualizes that the act of documentation never is and never can be an innocent act. Processes of observation and documentation are, as earlier said, never objective and hence not neutral. Or as the bio-physician Heinz von Foerster (cited in Israel, 1992: 19) has expressed it, 'objectivity is a subject's false view that observing can take place without him.' The most important issue here must be that the child and what the child does and says are not objectified and placed within already defined categories, something which has been common within the logocentric and technically rational discourse of modernity. Instead we have to realize and admit that documentation always holds our own subjective feelings, wishes and values. This should not be seen as something negative but rather as something positive (Maturana, 1991), not something to avoid but rather to understand how it enters into processes of documentation.

With documentation as a tool to enable self-reflection we can challenge and offer resistance towards the rational view of observation, as independent of ourselves as observers and of our own processes of construction and implied conventions. However, this presupposes that we, when we document, can live with and accommodate the complexity which always characterizes a pedagogical situation (Dahlberg, 1985). This 'housing' of complexity also presupposes an ability to leave behind a reductionist cause-and-effect relationship between the observer and what is observed and open up instead for understanding the unique, contingent, local and embodied character of our own productions as pedagogues (Ellsworth, 1989).

Starting out from the above perspective, the pedagogue has to regard herself as responsible for the constructions which she makes (von Glasersfeld, 1991). It is a form of reciprocal exchange which can result in many different readings and which presupposes seeing, listening and challenging, as well as having trust in one's own unfinished ideas and thinking. Even if this is a question of daring to open up for uncertainty, ambivalence and multiplicity, it is not a relativistic project, where every construction of reality is seen as good as the other. The housing of complexity rather has to be placed in relation to questions of the relevance of that which is documented, and where the answers are always historically situated in relation to the time we live in and to the direction and vision that we have for our pedagogical work.

Von Glasersfeld proposes that a similar orientation leads to a greater tolerance in social interactions through a realization that neither problems nor solutions are ontological entities, but arise out of particular ways of constructing. Hence, no solution to an experiential problem can be 'right' in an ontological way: 'the world in which the problem arises depends on a way of seeing, a way of experiencing; and where there is one solution there are always others — but this does not entail that one likes them all equally well' (1991: 26).

Pedagogical Documentation as a Dangerous Enterprise

As critical means of resisting the power/knowledge nexus, pedagogical documentation is a dangerous enterprise. As we emphasize time and again, because it is so important, documentation can never be an innocent activity. We do not have any guarantees. We have to see that risks and possibilities are not opposites, but exist at the same time. These processes can never be neutral and innocent — they have always got social and political implications and consequences. They can be dangerous, as Foucault (1970) argued, as they bear political and theoretical significance. Hence the production of knowledge is always related to the production of power.

Documentation is not necessarily radical resistance to the power/knowledge nexus. Whether it becomes so must, from our perspective, be related to whether it realizes its potential for taking in multiple perspectives. If it invites other constructions and perspectives, then documentation has the potential to reveal the embodied character of knowledge construction, and as such functions as an emancipatory practice.

But at the same time there are risks. The classifications and categories that we use also function as tools for inclusion and exclusion — they become productive. We can place children and their doings into categories of normal/non-normal. We can make the Other into the same. The pedagogue, through her influence on the process of the child's identity construction, exercises power and control. So, if we are not alert, documentation may become a practice for exercising, not resisting, control and power. Considering these risks, we always have to pose questions concerning what right we have to interpret and document children's doings and what is ethically legitimate.

An Ethics of an Encounter

Faced by these ethical issues, we seek some answers in the concept of an ethics of an encounter, which we introduced in Chapter 2. It is an ethics, which emanates from respect for each child and recognition of difference and multiplicity, and which struggles to avoid making the Other into the same as oneself. We have to position ourselves 'elsewhere than where the "Other" is the problem for which we are the solution' (Lather, 1991: 138), abjure being the master of truth and justice, the great interpreter.

The art of listening and hearing what the Other is saying, and taking it seriously, is related to an ethics of an encounter. So too is seeing — but what do we mean by seeing? It is all too easy to separate human relationships from their moral significance. As Bauman observes:

> Taking pictures becomes a substitute for seeing. Of course, you have to look in order to direct your lens to the desired object . . . But *looking* is not *seeing*. Seeing is a human function, one of the greatest gifts with which man is endowed; it requires activity, inner openness, interests, patience, concentration. Today *a snapshot* (the aggressive expression is significant) means essentially to transform the act of seeing into an object. (1995: 132–4, original emphasis)

The insight that we enter processes such as pedagogical documentation as participatory subjects, as fellow beings, or in the words of Reeder (1997) as 'the ethical subject of the act', implies a major responsibility. Ethics enters in because we must take responsibility for our acts, including every act of observing, and for our choices. Like Bauman we would argue we are ineluctably moral beings, in that 'we are faced with the challenge of the Other, which is the challenge of responsibility for the Other, a condition of *being-for*' (1995: 1).

In the context of the ethical dimension of documentation, it is also fruitful to go back to Foucault's notion of ethics which he captured in the term 'care of the self' (Foucault, 1986; see also Gore, 1993). By this term, which we introduced in Chapter 2, Foucault does not mean simply being interested in yourself, but whether and how we choose to constitute ourselves — 'the self is not given to us, we have to constitute ourselves as a work of art'. In relation to pedagogical documentation, it is interesting to look more fully into the Greek inspiration that Foucault had for his ideas of 'caring of the self'. The Greco-Roman practice of the self from which Foucault got inspiration is different from a confessional or therapeutic concept; it is also different from what might be called the Californian cult of the self. It is not self-fascination and self-absorption, but self-disentanglement and self-invention, the construction of self rather than self-consciousness. One of the techniques that was used by the Greeks in the constitution of themselves was the *hypomnemata*, notebooks used for constituting a permanent relationship to oneself:

> They do not constitute an 'account of oneself' . . . The point is not to pursue the indescribable, not to reveal the hidden, not to say the non-said, but, on the contrary, to collect the already-said, to reassemble that which one could hear or read, and this to an end which is nothing less than the constitution of oneself . . . Such is the objective of the *hypomnemata*: to make of the recollection of the fragmentary *logos* transmitted by teaching, listening or reading a means to establish as adequate and as perfect a relationship of oneself to oneself as possible. (Foucault, 1986: 365)

Gore, in analysing Foucault's notion of care of the self in relation to teacher education, says that 'exploring the implications and effects of such an approach to journal-keeping vis-à-vis radical pedagogical practice might result in a more thoughtful usage of journals in teacher education . . . What I envision is more an historical tracing of what it means to be a teacher in specific contexts than a personal or biographical account' (1993:151).

Opening Up a Forum

Our social constructionist view of knowledge, making meaning and learning relates to a vision of communicative action and social relations which assumes the Other as equal but not the same and the importance of solidarity between human beings. This in turn assumes a value-based and vivid dialogue and a politics concerning what we want with our early childhood institutions. These institutions must be understood as bearing, but also creating, cultural and symbolic values, as well as being, as we argued in Chapter 4, important institutions in a wider project of democracy. Early childhood pedagogy and early childhood institutions are always related to the philosophical question of what we want for our children here and now and in the future, a question which we have to pose ourselves again and again. The strategies we choose for working with children, our pedagogical practice, tell a lot about our way of conceptualizing children's potentials, position and civic rights in society and hence also how we have constructed our ideas of democracy.

By constructing institutions for children as forums for engagement and dialogue, for an ethics of an encounter, these institutions will get an important role to play in opening up new possibilities, in which a reconstructed welfare state and democracy are based on the visibility and inclusion of children. Viewing institutions for children as forums in civil society and as such providing opportunities for children and adults to come together and engage in discourse — in projects of social, cultural, political and economic significance — gives these institutions a specific meaning: as a *community*, where the life and work of the children can be seen as contributions to that community.

Communication, reflection and action can be seen as a form of cement that connects the pedagogical work, but which can connect the early childhood institution with the surrounding society. The idea of the early childhood institution as a forum, where the child is seen as a citizen and part of a community, presupposes that we formulate and continuously reformulate 'a social contract' between the individual, the public institutions, the state and the market. It requires participatory relationships, so that the early childhood institution becomes a forum in which children, pedagogues, parents, politicians and others are involved. To do this we have to construct forums which embody the ethics of an encounter — an encounter which is characterized by a more tentative and exploratory mode of seeing, listening and challenging.

The role of pedagogical documentation in the construction of such early childhood institutions is critically important. Documentation offers an important starting point for the dialogue, but also for creating trust and legitimacy in relation to the wider community by opening up and making visible the work of these institutions. Thanks to documentation, each child, each pedagogue and each institution can get a public voice and a visible identity. That which is documented can be seen as a narrative of children's, pedagogues' and parents' lives in the early childhood institution, a narrative which can show these institutions' contributions to our society and to the development of our democracy. 'Documentation can offer children and adults alike real moments of democracy. Democracy which has got its origin in the recognition and the visualisation of difference brought about by dialogue. This is a matter of values and ethics' (Rinaldi, 1994).

Chapter 8

Minority Directions in the Majority World: Threats and Possibilities

Introduction

The idea of progress is the major philosophical legacy left by the seventeenth to nineteenth centuries to the contemporary social sciences . . . The core of the concept [is that] with a few temporary deviations, all societies are advancing naturally and consistently 'up', on a route from poverty, barbarism, despotism and ignorance to riches, civilization, democracy, and rationality, the highest expression of which is science . . . The endless and growing diversity of human societies [that Europeans were coming across] had to be made sense of, or at least ordered and categorized, in a way acceptable to its discoverers . . . What produced diversity? The different stages of development of different societies. What was social change? The necessary advance through the different social forms . . . . (Shanin, 1997: 65–6)

The emerging paradigm for human living on and with the Earth brings together decentralization, democracy and diversity. What is local, and what is different, is valued. The trends towards centralization, authoritarianism and homogenization are reversed. Reductionism, linear thinking and standard thinking give way to an inclusive holism, open-systems thinking, and diverse options and actions. (Chambers, 1997: 189)

The preceding chapters have focused primarily on various understandings of young children and early childhood institutions in the Minority World. The influence of that minority is, however, felt around the globe. In particular, we have argued, United States thinking and practice, which is dominated by a particular discipline (developmental psychology) and is located firmly within the project of modernity, is assuming hegemonic proportions on an increasingly global scale, with the increasing likelihood of 'complex globalizations of once localized, western constructions of children' (Stephens, 1995: 8), rationalized through the discipline of developmental psychology which offers a 'Western construction [of childhood] that is now being incorporated, as though it was universal, into aid and development policies' (Burman, 1994: 183). It is ironic that a country that professes grave concerns about the 'toxicity' of its social environments and the well-being of many of its children and families (Garbarino, 1996), as well as about the quality of its early childhood services (Kagan et al., 1996) is looked to as a source of knowledge and guidance about children and services. In such cases, however, hegemonic relationships do not

159

depend on the application of military force or other means of coercion, but rather the influence of economic, cultural and scientific power which combine to produce dominant discourses which dictate that only certain things can be said or thought, as well as matching technologies of normalization — such as measures of quality.

The imperium of the United States is the latest phase of Minority World dominance in relationships with the Majority World, which started several hundred years ago with European expansion and colonialism. This dominance has been sustained by modernist ideas of linear progress and development, certainty and objectivity, universality and totalization, and the reduction of diversity and complexity. Modernity, therefore, has provided a rationale for colonization and hegemony, its structures of knowledge being implicated in forms of oppression (Young, 1990). Modernity has proved equal to this heavy responsibility, being possessed of great self-confidence:

> The positive self-image modern western culture has given to itself, a picture born of the eighteenth century Enlightenment, is of a civilization founded on scientific knowledge of the world and rational knowledge of value, which places the highest premium on individual human life and freedom, and believes that such freedom and rationality will lead to social progress through virtuous, self-controlled work, creating a better material, political and intellectual life for all. (Cahoone, 1996: 12)

Invigorated by such an image, the Minority World has had little compunction in proselytizing such virtues, often with considerable success. The words, thoughts and activities of the colonizers have, in many cases, been absorbed into the lifeways of the colonized, creating a fusion (and in many cases a confusion) of identities. But there has also been a reaction, a growing critique of the project of modernity. Within both the Minority and Majority Worlds the 'positive self-image' noted above is challenged by those who 'see modernity instead as a movement of ethnic and class domination, European imperialism, anthropocentrism, the destruction of nature, the dissolution of community and traditions, the rise of alienation, and the death of individuality in bureaucracy' (Cahoone, 1996: 12).

This reaction is expressed powerfully in the growing problematization and deconstruction of the discourse of 'development' in the Majority World, which began in the 1980s:

> Development fostered a way of conceiving of social life as a technical problem, as a matter of rational decision and management to be entrusted to that group of people — the development professionals — whose specialized knowledge allegedly qualified them for the task. Instead of seeing change as a process rooted in the interpretation of each society's history and cultural tradition . . . these professionals sought to devise mechanisms and procedures to make societies fit a preexisting model that embodied the structures and functions of modernity. Like the sorcerer's apprentices, the development professionals awakened once again the dream of reason that, in their hands, as in earlier instances, produced a troubling reality. (Escobar, 1997: 91)

These development professionals, argues Chambers, reconstruct reality to make it manageable, seeking 'the universal in the diverse, the part in the whole, the simple in the complex, the controllable in the uncontrollable, the measurable in the immeasurable, the abstract in the concrete, the static in the dynamic, permanence in flux' (1997: 55). What we see here, spread out on a much wider canvas, are many of the issues addressed earlier in this book, for example, in relation to the discourse of quality; and just as we suggested that an alternative discourse to quality was possible, so too are 'post-development' writers arguing for alternative discourses and new methods of working and knowing. These discourses and methods attach importance to the local, to complexity, to diversity, to the dynamic and unpredictable, and recognize conditions that are difficult to measure yet demand judgment; the new principles, precepts and practices 'resonate with parallel evolutions in natural sciences, chaos and complexity theory, the social sciences and postmodernism, and business management' (Chambers, 1997: 188).

Just as the concept of *development* in relation to Majority World countries is being questioned for its attempt to prescribe a universal model of progress, so too is the concept of development in relation to children, as has been argued in earlier parts of this book. The tension again is between the concept of development as a universal phenomenon, a predetermined linear sequence that all must follow to achieve full realization, or as a construction specific to and contingent on particular times, places and cultures — between a modernist search for foundations and universals and a postmodern recognition of diversity and contextualization. Issues of universality in child development *and* in global development come together in international activities to promote 'early childhood care and development' (known by the acronym of ECCD). While modernist perspectives, foregrounding the general applicability of 'best practices' largely taken from Minority World experiences and claims to universal knowledge legitimated as the product of scientific enquiry, have dominated much of the discussion, there is a growing swell of support for recognizing and valuing diversity, which might be seen as reflecting a more postmodern perspective.

An example of the ebb and flow of modernist and postmodernist sentiments can be seen in ECCD Seminars held at the UNICEF International Child Development Centre in Florence in 1989 and 1996. In the preface to the 1989 Report on the ECCD Seminar (Landers, 1989), the Director of the Centre employed a decidedly modernist tone:

> Whether early childhood development activities benefit children is no longer a question. The scientific community has held for some time that children whose developmental needs are met do better in life than children who are neglected in this domain. The *developmentally appropriate care* children receive when they are young has a remarkably positive impact. (Himes in Landers 1989: iii, emphasis added)

'Developmentally appropriate' is a term readers may recall from earlier in the book in relation to the policy document *Developmentally Appropriate Practice*

(Bredekamp, 1987), published by the National Association for the Education of Young Children (NAEYC) in the United States. The fact that the terminology of that document, and the thinking that lay behind it, found its way so quickly into this important international forum speaks both to the indirect influence of non-governmental organizations from the United States and the state of international thinking in the early childhood field in the late 1980s.

By the time a follow-up UNICEF seminar was held in 1996, the influence of 'universalist' perspectives was challenged by several of the participants:

> There was considerable critical debate about the cultural and financial preconceptions embedded in many ECCD projects. In particular there was a critique of the view that there was an exportable package of 'scientific' ideas about child development which, with relatively minor adjustments to local conditions, could be used anywhere in the world as a basis for programming and project work. (Penn and Molteno, 1997: 3)

The ranks of those willing to make such a critique of universal approaches to tools, practices and programmes appears to be growing, while at the same time 'best practice' advocates consider ways to advance greater global visibility and influence for their programmes. (For example, NAEYC and Head Start, both United States organizations, have recently considered international 'outreach and training' activities, while the High Scope Foundation, another organization originating in the United States, is well advanced in such work.) As an increasing number of Majority World countries consider the importance of the early years, and its implications for 'labor productivity and national economic prosperity' (A. Choksi, vice-president of the World Bank, preface to Young, 1996), it is important that the voices of those concerned with the limitations of universalism be raised alongside the voices of its proponents.

One of those concerned is Martin Woodhead, an experienced observer of early childhood work in the Minority and Majority Worlds. He has, over the past two decades,

> become increasingly concerned that much of what counts as knowledge and expertise about children is deeply problematic right down to such fundamental ideas as 'early childhood development programme' . . . Those involved in early childhood development must recognize that many of their most cherished beliefs about what is best for children, are cultural constructions. (Woodhead, 1996: 6, 8)

Another critic of universalizing tendencies, writing of her visits to early childhood institutions in South Africa, observes that:

> the written curriculum and pedagogy for the black nurseries were mainly provided by NGOs [non-governmental organizations], almost all of it in English whatever the first language of the recipients. Despite the discrepancies in catchment, funding and organisation of the black and white centres, the curriculum literature and training materials were all derived from western sources, mainly adaptations of

> Montessori and High Scope methods . . . Although materials may be adapted for
> use in educare centres, the western tenets which inform them are generally as-
> sumed to be universal. There is perceived to be little or no ambiguity about what
> constitutes appropriate 'intellectual' or 'social' behaviour. (Penn, 1997a: 107)

Helen Penn expresses concern that, given the significant differences in conceptions
of child rearing between African and Anglo-American cultures, 'the enthusiastic
transmission of "developmentally appropriate practice" and Western models of
nursery education or "educare", far from enhancing competency in young children,
may be damaging to those who use it' (Penn, 1997a: 106–7). Serpell, writing about
East Africa, makes a similar point about 'the potential of carelessly transplanted
forms of day-care for disrupting indigenous cultural values and practices' (1993:
469).

Respected psychologist, Michael Cole, has become similarly concerned that
constructions of child development based in Minority World societies have become
hegemonic throughout the world. In his 1996 publication, *Cultural Psychology: A
Once and Future Discipline*, Cole seeks answers to his overarching question, 'Why
do psychologists find it so difficult to keep culture in mind?' He traces the development of psychology from the 1880s, discerning in its earliest formulation by Wundt
a still-born 'second psychology', the one to which Wundt assigned the task of
understanding how culture enters into psychological processes. Cole's basic thesis
is 'that the scientific issues Wundt identified were not adequately dealt with by
the scientific paradigm that subsequently dominated psychology and the other
behavioural-social sciences' (1996: 7, 8). He argues that 'from at least the seventeenth century on, the dichotomy between historical, universal theories of mind and
historical, locally contingent theories has been bound up with another dichotomy,
the opposition between "natural" and "cultural-historical" sciences' (1996: 19).
Cole paraphrases the contrast made by Berlin (1981) between the assumptions
underlying the natural sciences and cultural-historical approaches noting the former's
belief that: '1) any real question has a single true answer; 2) the method of arriving
at the answers to genuine problems is natural and universally applicable; and 3)
solutions to genuine problems are true universally for all people, at all times in all
places' (p. 20). Mainstream psychology, having chosen to follow the road of the
natural sciences in the decades since its inception, now finds itself estranged from
those for whom behaviour and culture are inseparably intertwined.

Somewhat more cautiously, but still voicing doubts about a universal approach
to children and their development, Save the Children UK (Molteno, 1996) concludes that while some Minority World research on child development may be true
for all children, some of it is bound to be culture- and situation-specific: 'in a world
dominated by global pressures — economic, technological, political — there is a
danger in thinking that one can find universal solutions to social questions' (1996:
4).

Robert Myers, in his influential book *The Twelve who Survive: Strengthening
Programs of Early Childhood Development in the Third World*, undertakes a tentative transition from a primarily universalist, positivist and modernist orientation to

a more indigenous, postpositivist, postmodernist understanding. While his years of experience in the field of international development and early childhood, coupled with his academic training and sensitivity, allow him to appreciate 'both worlds' and the need for bridging frameworks between them, Myers cautions, 'If one had to guess, the guess would be that early childhood programs more often than not are taking their cues from imported models that re-enforce value shifts towards the individualistic, production oriented cultures of the West. Is that where we want to be?' (1992: 29).

Six years later Myer's question remains relevant. At a UNICEF Regional Workshop held in Karachi, Pakistan, in March 1998, and a follow-up meeting at Wye College in Britain in April 1998, the differences between a modernist orientation of 'best practice', non-problematized understandings of 'quality', and the revelatory power of science, seemed at odds with calls at the same meetings for: 'community driven ECCD', respect for 'local diversity', and 'response to the child in context' (UNICEF 1998a,b). These disparate notions ended up as strange bedfellows, uneasily sharing the same sentence: 'Experience indicates that sustainable ECCD programmes begin with what the culture offers; curricula and activities are built on local childrearing attitudes, practices and beliefs, *with what is currently recognized as universal "scientific" messages being added to replace what are deemed as negative practices within the local culture*' (UNICEF, 1998a: 11, emphasis added). But perhaps the bed *is* simply too narrow for two occupants, as the next sentence nudges: 'We need to be cautious about our presumption of what constitutes universal truths, as these "truths" change over time.'

In this context of increasing questioning of universal child and social development being voiced alongside established modernist views on the foundational importance of general laws and principles produced by objective scientific methods, and at a time of wide (even widening) inequalities of power and resources between the Minority and Majority Worlds, the aim of this chapter is to consider to what extent the postmodern perspective we have adopted in this book can contribute to a true dialogue, involving listening and respecting the alterity of the Other, and a retreat of hegemonic tendencies in the field of early childhood. Such discussion is much needed not only between the Minority and Majority Worlds, but also between what some literature refers to as peoples of the Fourth World, that is indigenous populations in Minority-World countries, and the dominant population of these countries. Our argument is not that this book presents an alternative perspective that can or should be universally adopted — many people from the Majority or Fourth Worlds may wish to locate themselves within premodern perspectives or within modernity itself, which continues to exert a powerful influence. Rather, it seems to us that our perspective provides *one* way for enabling early childhood workers from the Minority World to develop dialogic and respectful relationships with their counterparts in the Majority World and among Fourth-World people, a relationship based on recognition of diversity, complexity and contextualization and the ethics of an encounter.

One reason for hoping that a postmodern perspective might contribute to such relationships is the origins of postmodernity in a postwar questioning of Eurocentrism and the part played by Enlightenment thinking in European colonialism. Renewed philosophical interest in the Enlightenment after the Second World War, Foucault (1980b) argued, arose from 'the movement which, at the close of the colonial era, led it to be asked of the West what entitles its culture, its science, its social organization, and finally its rationality itself, to be able to claim universal validity' (54). As a result of this critical re-examination, Eurocentrism was seen to be closely related to Enlightenment thinking and its claims for the universality of its values; postmodernity emerges, in part at least, as a reaction to these claims and their perceived oppressive consequences. Robert Young argues that

> postmodernism can best be defined as European culture's awareness that it is no longer the unquestioned and dominant centre of the world . . . Postmodernism, therefore, becomes a certain self-consciousness about a culture's historical relativity — which begins to explain why, as its critics complain, it also involves the loss of the sense of an absoluteness of any Western account of History . . . Contrary, then, to some of its more overreaching definitions, postmodernism itself could be said to mark not just the cultural effects of a new stage of 'late' capitalism, but the sense of a loss of European history and culture as History and Culture, the loss of their unquestioned place at the centre of the world . . . the loss of Eurocentrism. (1990: 19, 20, 117)

It was this issue — of the relationship between the Enlightenment, its grand projects and universal truth claims on the one hand and the history of European colonialism on the other — that contributed to

> the distrust of totalizing systems of knowledge which depend upon theory and concepts, (which was) so characteristic of Foucault and Lyotard, both of whom have been predominantly concerned with the attempt to isolate and foreground singularity as opposed to universality. This quest for the singular, the contingent event which by definition refuses all conceptualisation, can clearly be related to the project of constructing a form of knowledge that respects the other without absorbing it into the same. (1990: 9–10)

It seems to us that what postmodernity has to offer to relationships between the Minority and Majority Worlds is the infusion, on the Minority World side, of an uncertainty about certainty, a scepticism about claims of universality, and a self-awareness of the relationship between knowledge and power bred of a recognition of the deep complicity in the history of colonialism of Western academic forms of knowledge. If the modernist perspective strives to find universal and objectively 'true' best practices, criteria of quality, developmental norms and methods of measurement, a postmodern perspective embraces the realization that there are many different, inherently subjective and productive understandings of childhood, early childhood institutions, and of 'good' work with children in early childhood institutions — singular and contingent, not universal and decontextual.

The possibility of undertaking cross-national work which adopts this postmodern perspective is well illustrated in the study by Tobin, Wu and Davidson of *Preschool in Three Cultures: Japan, China and the United States.* Their familiarity with the established questions and methods that have guided (and restricted) most Anglo-American early childhood research is evident in their opening statement:

> Our research methods are unlike those used in most comparative research in early child education. We have not tested efficiency of various staffing patterns or ped-agogical approaches. We have not measured the frequency of teacher–student inter-action or computed dollars spent per student . . . or how many minutes a day students spend on reading readiness exercises. Although we touch on all these issues and others in the book, our focus instead has been on eliciting meanings. We have set out not to rate the preschools in the three cultures but to find out what they are meant to do and to be. (1989: 4)

Termed 'multivocal ethnography', their research is far removed from the modernist quest for ultimate 'truth' and the discovery of universals, instead understanding knowledge as constructed through dialogue involving multiple perspectives.

> A telling and retelling of the same event from different perspectives — an ongoing dialogue between insiders and outsiders, between practitioners and researchers, between Americans and Chinese, Americans and Japanese, and Chinese and Japan-ese. In each chapter, the voices, besides our own, are those of Japanese, Chinese and American preschool teachers, administrators, parents, children, and child devel-opment experts. (Tobin et al., 1989: 4)

Our vehicle for exploring the potential of a postmodern perspective for cross-national or cross-cultural work is not a research study, but a Canadian project for training early childhood practitioners, initiated by an Aboriginal (First Nations) Tribal Council and involving work between this group of communities and university faculty and staff from the majority population. Unlike the Stockholm Project, this work was not informed by a prior and deep familiarity with modernist and postmodernist thought and the debate about these two perspectives. But in retro-spect it can be seen to have struggled with issues which have arisen within that debate, being located at least in part within postmodernity and to have problematized certain modernist assumptions. In this respect, the Canadian work may be similar to other projects which, while not seeing themselves theoretically in relation to the modernist/postmodernist debate, in practice challenge dominant assumptions and discourses in the work they undertake. Like the Stockholm Project and the experiences in Reggio Emilia, the Tribal Council work demonstrates the important relationship between postmodernist theory and field-relevant practice.

Many Worlds

In various parts of the world, communities are seeking ways to ensure the survival, or revival, of their cultural beliefs, values and practices, while at the same time in many cases wanting to ensure that their members have access to and competence in the dominant society. In Canada, the more than 600 First Nations, communities of aboriginal peoples colonized by what became a majority non-indigenous society, have experienced generations of cultural suppression taking various forms at various times from genocide to assimilation (Canadian Royal Commission, 1996). Most First Nations' communities in Canada are now actively engaged in reclaiming their culture. Some of those communities are focused primarily on the revival of their traditional culture and do not actively seek contact with non-aboriginal groups. Others, however, wish to prepare their children and young people for growing up in both their own specific culture and community and in the culture and communities of the surrounding society. These communities typically do not seek reproduction of the past, but rather, envision a future that is respectfully informed by a rich past and a multi-faceted present; a new construction with multiple roots and traditions developed through a process over which they have a substantial measure of control through their own agency and actions.

The project described here was initiated in 1988 by the Meadow Lake Tribal Council, which represents First Nations people living in north-central Canada. The Tribal Council sought to prepare their young people, in the words of Louis Opekekew, a tribal elder, 'to walk in both worlds', and sought to do so through establishing a partnership with a university, in the mainstream of the dominant community. The educational approach that emerged through that partnership — termed the Generative Curriculum Model — has now been used with a further six First Nations' organizations which, with the original Meadow Lake group, represent over 25 separate communities. Because each community is itself a complex socio-cultural environment with a unique history and community dynamics, the exact nature and substance of the information that was generated in each partnership could not be identified in advance nor is it the same across all communities. The Generative Curriculum approach embraces diversity and with it a large measure of indeterminacy. Unlike most curricula which are based on a singular construction of pre-established content and outcomes, the Generative Curriculum is a co-construction eliciting the generation of new ideas and possibilities not fully foreseeable in advance.

What follows is the story of an unusual series of partnerships, now extending over almost a decade, but focusing primarily on the very first partnership that was formed and attempting to understand that partnership and the training model that emerged from it through the lens provided in this volume. The story presented is told by one of us, Alan Pence[1], from his own as well as a Minority World perspective. Currently, the First Nations Partnerships Program office, established to support those communities using or wishing to use the Generative Curriculum approach, is engaged in a two-year project to evaluate the Generative Curriculum based largely on the experiences and words of a broad range of communities' members. This project will provide a better understanding of the dynamics of the Generative Curriculum approach across different sites and enable a clearer and more community-to-community response to inquiries from other First Nations. Given the complexity of the Generative Curriculum Model, a roughly chronological approach will be taken in recounting the experiences, with an on-going commentary tying those experiences to the general discourse of this volume.

Meadow Lake and the University: 'What of us is in here?'

In the late 1980s the Meadow Lake Tribal Council of northern Saskatchewan became aware of a Canadian federal government funding initiative that could be used to support a strong interest among its nine communities to provide early childhood institutions, on-reserve, for their community members. At the time, such on-reserve services were virtually non-existent in Saskatchewan, and indeed in most other provinces. Earlier in the 1980s the Tribal Council had determined that the future well-being of their communities rested on the health and well-being of their children, and in 1989 formulated a 'vision statement' that articulated the central role of children and their care:

> The First Nations of the Meadow Lake Tribal Council believe that a child care program developed, administered and operated by their own people is a vital component to their vision of sustainable growth and development. It impacts every sector of their long-term plans as they prepare to enter the twenty-first century. It will be children who inherit the struggle to retain and enhance the people's culture, language and history; who continue the quest for economic progress for a better quality of life; and who move forward with a strengthened resolve to plan their own destiny.

Children and communities are at the heart of this statement. When the Tribal Council began to contact potential educational partners to support their vision of the future by creating courses to train community members to work in their early childhood centres, they found that either the institutions approached did not have an aboriginal Early Childhood Care and Development Programme and were not in a position to develop one, or that if the institution did have a programme, it was preformed and largely immutable. Many of the existing programmes reviewed represented a modification of mainstream programmes with aboriginal 'add-ons' from different tribal groups across the country, making for a pan-aboriginal conglomerate that did not reflect the reality or experience of any one individual group. The implicit question posed to these programmes by the Tribal Council in their search was, 'What of *us* is in these materials?' The answer was 'very little'.

'Very little' is the answer that comes from most curricula, regardless of who asks the question, 'What of us is in here?' The roots of academia are deeply embedded in modernist understandings of knowledge in which the intent is the transmission of ideas and of knowledge *already* established, and the definition of parameters which will guide the creation of 'new knowledge'. Education in the modernist tradition, be it early childhood, primary, secondary or tertiary is funda-mentally *not* about what the learner brings to the enterprise ('What of me is in here?'). That question is irrelevant within the assumptions of modernity, which is based on what learners *lack* rather than what they *bring* to the learning activity. Operating from a position of disregard for either individual or group voices, modernist education is a powerful vehicle for the shaping of uni-vocal rather than multi-vocal understandings of the world. Within such a construction the ways of others cannot be respected, but must be challenged by the one, 'true' way.

Viewed in hindsight, the Tribal Council's implicit question 'What of us is in here?'; the self-evident response of educational institutions, 'not much'; and the resolve of the Tribal Council to continue looking for a suitable partner can be seen as the project's first steps away from a modernist path. Reflecting on that late-1980s event, it is not surprising that these steps were taken by a group with cultural roots very different from those upon which modernity is based. As Cahoone has noted, multiculturalism and postmodernism share 'overlapping tendencies' (1996: 2).

Difference, however, may not be enough. For the power of modernity, and its casting of the world as truth engaged in struggle with not-truth, is such that the argument that its ways are 'best' can, and has, led some in the Majority World to accept the argument and the 'new ways'. For example, a 1985 Thai publication, *Handbook of Asian Child Development and Child Rearing Practices*, notes that:

> Asian parents have a long history of well developed culture behind them. They are mostly agriculturists who are submissive to the earth's physical nature. Thus many of their traditional beliefs and practices prevent them from seeking and using the new scientific knowledge in child rearing.
>
> The Handbook of Child Rearing may require parents to change many of their beliefs, attitudes, values, habits and behaviours. Therefore, many necessary changes will be met with some resistance. For example, giving the child more of the independence the child needs and making less use of power and authority during adolescence will shake the very roots of those Asian families where authoritarian attitudes and practice are emphasized. (Suvannathat et al., 1985, quoted in Woodhead, 1997: 76)

First Nations in Canada have long been the recipients of western 'best practices' and have been shaken to their very roots. Reams of poignant testimony have been collected describing the suffering to parents, to children and to communities of residential schooling, child welfare practices, and other 'helping' services all deemed, at the time, to be in the 'best interests' of the subjected children and families. Born out of this suffering is a distrust of what is deemed 'best' in the eyes of the dominant, western community. What is 'best' has clearly not been good for many First Nations peoples. As the First Nations have begun to exercise greater political control over their futures, they have adopted a path of caution in considering 'best practices' and 'improvements' from the dominant society. While some communities have adopted a path of reformation in the image of the past (not unlike some fundamentalist religious movements), others have embraced the non-determinacy of an emergent path, a path where it is recognized that 'it is children who inherit the struggle . . . to plan *their own* destiny'. How to do so from a position of being informed rather than preformed is one part of that challenge.

The Potential of Not-Knowing

The Tribal Council's search for a partner eventually brought them to the School of Child and Youth Care at the University of Victoria, located on the south-west coast of Canada, far removed from the prairies of the Tribal Council. The School did not have an aboriginal curriculum, and at first it seemed there was no reason to meet with the Council. But the Tribal Council persisted and at the first meeting the depth of the commitment of the Tribal Council's Executive Director to the well-being of the communities' children came through forcefully. So too did his clarity that the Tribal Council was in the 'driver's seat' in this initiative. A university was a desired and necessary passenger, but the steering of the project would be done by the First Nations. The depth of the commitment and the clarity of community responsibility were seen as extremely important and positive elements by the School and a partnership was formed.

Reflecting on this stage of the nascent relationship, what was perhaps most critical was an acceptance of the *powerful potential of not knowing.* In the dualism of modernity, and reflective of its roots in western 'revealed religions', having knowledge is equated with 'good' and not having it or not-knowing as 'bad'. In modernity, and in most Minority World cultures, 'not knowing' is pejoratively equated with 'ignorance' — something to be avoided in oneself and rectified in others. Similarly, 'being' or 'existence' has a presence and utility lacking in 'not being'. Those things that 'exist' become the building blocks of modernity, existence supplants non-existence. Such structures may have physical strength, but they lack light and air. The Taoist concept of 'existence' and 'non-existence' as equally useful, like the window in a wall or the hollow in a cup, is not a familiar part of western thought. Indeed, pre-modernist understandings in some parts of the world can be seen as useful contributors to enhanced understanding of postmodernism, reflecting how, as Hall (1996) suggests, 'pre-modernist may be post-'.

Knowledge is such a 'concrete' building block in Minority-World societies. Knowledge is known to 'exist', and it is valued far more than not-knowing, and while we may have some difficulty pointing out knowledge, or differentiating it from its counterfeit, it is a commodity that is bought, sold and regulated. Institutions are established to 'trade' in knowledge. Freire's analogy (1985) of education to a 'banking system' is apt: there are means by which a deficit in one's account can be infused with the 'appropriate currency', providing 'creditability' and thereby credibility in the socioeconomic system, allowing one's 'fortunes' to rise.

A very different orientation to knowledge, and one that is consistent with postmodernist thought, is that useful knowledge exists only in interaction, or in praxis. Such knowledge is mutable rather than immutable, it takes its form from the environment in which it was created. More like water than block or stone, it is endlessly transforming.

In the particular case of the discussions with the Tribal Council's Executive Director, what appealed was *not* the knowledge of the way forward (for we did not know what this would be), but the *absence* of that knowledge and the opportunity it provided to explore together *a* way forward, to merge the different experiences and different bases of knowledge of our respective communities and see what could be generated out of a new dynamic, a new combination of ideas. Supporting this leap of faith was an understanding that what had been tried before had not worked; the new road was dangerous, but the road more travelled could not take us where we wished to go.

Central to this agreement to proceed into that-which-we-did-not-know was a trust in and resonance with each other. In engaging in *this* process of knowledge creation, an impersonal approach to knowledge transmission, such as often occurs when filling up one mind from another, a banking system of knowledge transfers, will not suffice. The act of co-creation or co-construction requires a level of trust and sharing seldom found and not required in knowledge transfer approaches. By understanding knowledge as a commodity, something that can be bought and traded without engendering personal commitment and sharing, the heart of learning is ignored and with it the affective power within which transformational learning resides. Knowledge accumulation without transformation is a sterile process bereft of progeny. With such wealth one can accumulate, but not create. Such distinctions are critical if we are to move beyond the limited vision of modernity.

With the partnership established and funding secured, the challenge of creating a post-secondary programme for training early childhood workers that was not entrenched on modernist ground was the formidable task at hand. Reviews of existing post-secondary curricula in the human services revealed little that deviated from a preconstructed, knowledge transferral base. Such bases might be critical of other bases, philosophies or theories, but few invited students, and none invited communities, to engage in an *activity of co-construction wherein the outcome was not predetermined.* A number of individuals likened our approach to that of Paulo Freire, and indeed there are similar terms and concepts. However, in reading Freire's *Pedagogy of the Oppressed*, it is clear that his 'critical pedagogy' possesses a specific desired outcome — a revolutionary, emancipatory outcome — but a predetermined outcome or preconstruction nevertheless. The approach sought in the First Nations partnership was one of *indeterminate* co-construction, a cooperative process wherein the result would emerge as part of the process of engagement and would not be predetermined. A distinction between ourselves and Freire was that his 'envisioning' suggests an objective, a product or outcome; whereas our own emphasis on 'emerging' was *process* focused.

The project's openness to 'what will come' has posed a challenge throughout, for example, in employing course developers and instructors. The basis of much Minority World thought and action lies in predictability, in defining pre-established objectives, learning outcomes. It was difficult to find course developers or instructors who were truly understanding or appreciative of the power of indeterminacy. A number of those employed had an outcome in mind, often an outcome that challenged the status quo. In the Generative Model, knowledge and understanding that challenged the status quo was *one* of the possible outcomes. But the outcome might also prove to be consistent with an established conservative order, such as support for the Catholic Church, a long-standing presence in several of the most northern communities.

A Space for Learning

A key characteristic of the curriculum as envisioned by the partnership group was that it must be open to and respectful of information from the Meadow Lake communities, from academia and potentially from other sources as well. The established educational literature and post-secondary practices reviewed had not actively problematized the challenges posed by a respectful coming together of community knowledge and academic knowledge. 'Community' for most educators meant the physical placing of the classroom or the learner in the community — however, the *content* would continue to come *from* academia and from an academic instructor! Such trappings were not sufficient if this approach was to achieve a level of meaning making beyond knowledge imparting. 'Culturally sensitive' was similarly inadequately problematized in most practice, resulting in the academy selecting several readings or inviting in a few 'cultural guests' to augment the core curriculum which remained firmly rooted in dominant academic thought and practice. In both cases, the curriculum and the expected outcomes were predetermined.

For a similar set of reasons (as disconcerting to our more radical critics as the preceding comments may be to the more conservative) the curriculum could not simply be based in or emerge solely from the community either. Rather, this curriculum should be *suspended in the space between* — the void, the space that is *not* filled and is thereby charged with potential. A space where dissimilar ideas might meet, mingle and mutate.

An example of how these various ideas might meet and change over time was provided in the opportunity to visit a practicum site for some of the students in a community-based infant care centre. Initially, only the skin colour of the children and staff would lead one to know that this was not a centre in a white suburb of a major Canadian city. The bright, new cribs with neatly folded blankets, the purchased toys for rolling and pushing, the crawling space with a rail, were all designed to allow exploratory motor behaviour; relatively free movement was possible, even during nap time. Returning some weeks after the Elders had discussed the tradition of the cradle board (a decorated board designed to hold a swaddled infant) and exhibited a number of beautifully crafted and beaded boards with a 'dancing fringe' before the children's eyes, I was surprised to see several beautiful boards lying in the crib, swaddled children sleeping peacefully inside. Upon waking, the child and board were taken out of the crib, the board placed near where the children were crawling and climbing, the board becoming both a functional and symbolic object in the environment that spoke to a vision of 'different traditions'. Over time staff tried out the boards at different times and in different ways, noting not only how each board was different and associated with a particular family, but how each child's relationship to the board was different — some seeming to sleep most comfortably in it, others not. The board was not only a cultural connection between the child and caregiver, but also a connection between parent, caregiver and community. Over time the boards' use and presence varied, continuing indeterminate outcome of a meeting place 'between cultures'.

Looking back over the seven Generative Curriculum projects, the *space between* the many possible worlds of understanding can be seen as the source of energy for much that has transpired. Protecting that space from the belief systems of individuals and groups that fear rather than appreciate the unknown and seek to fill all that is unfilled has been a significant challenge. The power of the space is in its *not* being 'known' or 'owned' by any group or ideology. The space can be used by any, but claimed by none. It is the space where difference is valued, for difference alone is generative, and what is generated can change and transform over time as interaction and dialogue with children, parents, other staff and the broader community bring various thoughts and ideas into the flux of learning.

Starting with Principles

At the outset the Tribal Council/University team could not envision what a generative curriculum would look like. Indeed the term 'generative' would not enter into the discourse for many months. In the initial meetings there was greater clarity regarding what we wished to avoid than what should be embraced. The reality of time pressures, however, meant we must act, for there were only three years to create and deliver a curriculum for a full two-year training course. A decision was made to concentrate initially on identifying a set of general principles that could guide the development process, rather than moving prematurely to create the curriculum itself. A set of six principles were identified, or co-constructed, by the Tribal Council/University partnership team. The principles, in essence navigation points in uncharted waters, included commitments to:

- supporting and re-enforcing community initiative in a community-based setting;
- maintaining bi/multi-cultural respect;
- identifying community and individual strengths as the basis for initiatives;
- ensuring a broad ecological perspective and awareness of the child as part of families and community;
- providing education and career laddering for students such that credit for this course work would be fully applicable to future study and practice;
- creating an awareness that while the immediate focus was on early childhood, this training should provide the basis for broader child, youth, family and community serving training and services.

Some of the principles identified, such as educational laddering, represented structural issues in Canadian post-secondary education that the university partner would need to take the lead in addressing. Most, however, indicated a joint role for both partners.

As the team worked to develop the guiding principles, they were also aware of constraints within which the partnership operated, for example: the need for the programme to be viewed as academically credible and rigorous; the need to meet legislated licensing and accreditation criteria; and at the same time ensuring the appropriateness of the knowledge within a community context. As in the Stockholm Project, we recognized the necessity 'to walk on two legs'. The programme was to be a first in Canada, and whatever was developed would need to be suitable for delivery in other First Nations settings as well. The road ahead was uncertain, but what lay behind had proven inadequate. There was little to lose and much to gain. The partnership emerged from the initial months of planning reinforced in its belief that a cooperative (later understandable as a co-constructionist approach) was not only desirable, but necessary. Having committed ourselves to a position that multiple 'truths' must be respectfully represented in our work, and appreciating that such knowledge is not disembodied but must come through the people who live that truth, the partnership moved beyond commitment to requirement — all paddles must be in and pulling if we were to move. This knowledge that paddling harder on one side would in no way compensate for less paddling on the other provided an internal corrective to asymmetric leadership.

Including Community

Unlike most post-secondary education that requires two main ingredients to commence the activity — students and the post-secondary institution — the approach envisioned with the Generative Curriculum Model required the addition of a third, the students' communities, as an active participant. The inclusion of community added a further unknown to the 'normal' recipe for education.

The decision that, for the vision of the partnership to be realized, the community itself must have a place to speak in the curriculum, became a significant breach in the wall of modernist education that would allow the project to move into relatively unexplored territory. The decision at the time was not seen as radical, but necessary and sensible. No texts or materials existed which could provide information on traditional practices and values within these communities, indeed many of the community members themselves were long estranged from this knowledge. Meadow Lake identified a number of Elders of the communities and some other respected community members as those who could speak to the students about the traditional understandings and ways of the communities.

Initially the words of the Elders were understood as the principal generated component of the Generative Curriculum. Over time our understanding of 'generative' would change and expand forcing a reconceptualization of the initial model used to describe the Generative Curriculum Model. The initial Generative Curriculum Model was a spiral structure (Pence et al., 1993). Each level of the spiral represented a multi-voiced interaction, with the material generated at the previous iteration being incorporated into the successive course offering. This approach to the Generative Curriculum Model proved to be flawed both pragmatically and conceptually.

Pragmatically, because for most of the relatively small First Nations communities that might use the Generative Curriculum Model there would probably be only one cohort of students every five or six years. Annual or successive intakes, it was increasingly clear, were not probable. If there were successive intakes, most likely these students would be drawn from a much broader geographic and cultural area leading to a regional training approach rather than a community-based approach. Such a regional approach, it was feared, would inevitably lead to the same type of pan-aboriginal representations of native beliefs and understandings which had been rejected by the Meadow Lake Council communities in their original search for an educational partner.

Conceptually, the spiral idea reflected a sense of linearity, moving from a less complete to a more complete curriculum over time. Initially, the desire to 'generate' information that had hitherto been largely inaccessible and not recorded for the future use of the communities was a major objective of the project, as was its incorporation into further 'building the curriculum' through successive iterations of courses. However, as the pragmatic problem of successive cohorts became evident, and the probability of the Generative Curriculum's life being that of an itinerant curriculum, the conceptual conflicts became clearer as well. In hindsight the spiral model can be viewed as a hybrid incorporating elements of content *building* sympathetic to modernist notions of knowledge 'refinement', and content *generation* more sympathetic to a postmodern perspective. While the former inextricably moves towards a state of completion, becoming ossified as most curriculum is, the latter has the potential for creating a new and unique generation at each delivery — a 'living curriculum'. In the former model, the term 'generative' had a stronger sense of leading to an *output*, for example, information generated by the community for the use of the community. As the project evolved, however, generative became ever more associated with the *process* of generation, rather than the *products* of generation; this process emphasis continues to the present. At the same time, the model itself shifted from that of a 'spiral staircase', each step building on the one before, to a circular representation (Halldorson and Pence, 1995), with each iteration representing a new and unique coming together of different ideas and interactors. The outcome of such a process can never be known in advance, indeed, the outcome is not singular but multiple — as diverse as the students, instructors and community members who participate. Typically those multiple outcomes are themselves mutable, provisional, transformational, as was the case in the cradle board experience. Not truth, but possibilities emerge from the generative process.

Forums, Plazas, Arenas and Big Houses

The image that began to emerge through the partnership discussion and through daily experiences in the field was that of a 'forum' for learning (or what the Stockholm Project might refer to as 'the arena of realization'). This forum, arena or plaza became increasingly inclusive. By design, Elders had been brought into the class to share their knowledge and wisdom, but increasingly the students wished to play a larger role in shaping the invitations, the questions and thereby the possible dialogues. Students also suggested other community members who they felt could make a useful contribution, and the forum expanded further. The principles of respect and voice identified by the original project team and their lived reality within a caring, supportive and inclusive educational environment, resonate with the discussion in Chapter 6 about the conditions needed for a vivid dialogue and an egalitarian sharing of ideas. Hearing the diverse voices and views — from Elders, texts, community members and instructors — students became more fully aware of their own voices, their own views and how these related to others. Instructors, hearing voices they had not heard before, were similarly challenged and stimulated — all became learners, all became teachers.

All Learners, All Teachers

Skipping ahead many years in this chronology, one of the most powerful experiences in the history of the Generative Curriculum Model was late in 1996 when instructors from four different partnerships (including the original one with Meadow Lake Tribal Council) came together to share, over a two-day period, their stories of the Generative Curriculum experience. A recurring theme was that of transformation, significant personal changes in the instructors' own view of the world and ways of being in it. Participants were moved to laughter and to tears as they reflected on their own journey through a landscape of many voices and different world views. Indeed, this need to share their own story of personal challenge and change has become one of the characteristics the project listens for in introducing new 'instructors' to the programs. Those who are aware of their own learning and transformation are far more likely to be able to support learning and transformation in the 'students'. Those who relate to their own teaching, but not to their own learning, are not suitable for this approach.

At the instructors' gathering, one spoke of how initially the Elders' stories seemed too rambling and off-topic, but then several weeks or even months later, those words would find a place in the course discussion and she or a student would bring them forward, words not bound by time. Another non-aboriginal instructor reflected on her failure to honour Elders in her own family and her resolve to treat her own Elders as respectfully as she would others. A third recounted the relationships she began to observe among Elders, students and other community members outside of class; the forging of relationships surpassed the place and time of the forum. These relationships in turn supported some individuals' involvement in traditional gatherings, such as those within the 'big house', as well as contemporary gatherings around children's birthdays or seeking advice on child and family issues. Reminiscent of Robert Putnam's (1993, 1995) research into the relationship between social and economic well-being, the presence of 'bowling clubs and singing groups' as key indicators of rich 'social capital', the stories of students, instructors and community members interacting in new and meaningful ways provide evidence of the importance of 'meeting places' and the ability of such forums to move out from the setting and condition that created them — be it a post-secondary education forum or an early childhood institution in Reggio or Stockholm — to impact on the lives of individuals and on communities.

Ivory Towers and Fairy Tales

Such a multitude of voices, each speaking their own 'truth' and understanding, is in sharp contrast to 'normal' academia, and its traditional images of ivory towers and fortresses. Such institutions have long posited their role as protectors of unpopular perspectives, but the very walls that have been constructed to protect these views have themselves become prisons, obstacles to hearing, seeing and interacting with others' truths.

This critique of the university as a fortress/prison was not on the minds of the partnership team in the early stages of discussion and formulation. The initial effort was neither deeply philosophical nor critical — it was simply the team's best efforts to follow the lead of the community and the students, within the constraints identified and consistent with the principles employed, while at the same time suspending belief in the importance of colouring inside the lines. In other words this was a pragmatic and heart-felt desire to be true, first and foremost, to the other — the partner.

That commitment to the partner, like so much else in the project, would later be understood to have unlocked a door deserving much deeper investigation and understanding. Different community's and individual's understandings of 'self' and 'other' are central to how children's well-being could be addressed. Seeking to understand the depth and meaning of these differences would become a significant, long-term activity of the project, but the initial motivation was pragmatic — the university did not possess that knowledge, nor was it our place to do so.

The knowledge of the community was held in the community and for that knowledge to come in, the community itself must enter into the place or 'forum' of learning. Taking seriously the question, 'What of us is in here?', it is not possible for one cultural group to render a full and appropriate representation of the values, beliefs and practices of another group. Even if elements of the knowledge may be understood as singular, describable 'artifacts' of a culture, the embedded meaning and the medium of the message (to paraphrase McLuhan) are critical elements of its representation, and they too convey meaning. Even within cultures, different members carry different messages, different knowledge and different forms for conveying that information.

The breaching of the wall that community participation in an educational process represents, provides a broad opportunity for bringing multiple perspectives into the field of early childhood, to create an inclusionary practice in pedagogical work. Through students' exposure to an inclusionary and multi-voiced forum in their training, it is hoped that they will be more sensitive to such an approach in their practice, and there is some evidence to support this hope. Such practice would not rely on 'one best way' and the authority of the early childhood worker, but would seek instead to bring multiple perspectives — of children, parents and others in the community — to the task of understanding or making meaning of pedagogical work with young children and engaging in on-going dialogue about what we want for our children. This potential influence of the Generative Curriculum on practice will be discussed further later in the chapter. I will return now to some additional descriptions of the Generative Curriculum Model as it evolved within the Meadow Lake project.

Learning Evolving

These further extensions of the Generative Curriculum Model were not fully understood in these formative stages of the work. The major effort in the early work was to follow and to support the community's lead; to respect not only what we, the academy, would bring, but what the community must provide as well. To this end, the instructors who the community had searched for and had employed (in consultation with the university) reported back to the development team (based at the university but including a key community leader) on all facets of the curriculum delivery including student activity, Elder presentations and other community involvement. This information was critical in the shaping of an approach to curriculum that was specifically inclusive and multi-vocal in nature.

Initially, and perhaps ironically, the course materials that began to be produced were quite heavily scripted. Student learning and teacher delivery packages typically numbered 100 to 150 pages per course in each community. Each course included 13 weeks of 3 hours a week instruction plus homework and outside class projects. In this respect the courses could be seen as consistent with modernist education packages such as those found in many print-based, distance education courses. The reason for this heavy scripting related primarily to the different approach taken by the Generative Curriculum Model in terms of what students and community brought to the learning. Scripts and suggestions regarding how one might elicit, support and extend community-based information contributed significantly to the size of the course materials. Not insignificantly, the bulk of the materials contributed to their credibility; in a society like Canada where numbers matter, the thick text mattered to those who count pages. However, the Generative Curriculum materials deviated from 'normal' practice to a significant degree in the nature of the assignments and in the augmentation of instructor and text information with Elder, student and community information. This approach to an 'opening up' of curriculum came to be described later as an 'open-architecture' approach to curriculum design (Pence, 1999).

In the original partnership, one afternoon was set aside each week for the Elders to speak. Initially the topics had been suggested by the course writers, complementing the course materials for that week. For example, an Elder midwife would speak on her understandings, experiences and knowledge during the week the course addressed peri-natal care. But over time, the students themselves identified the topics they wished to hear addressed. Often the Elders spoke in Cree or

Dene, the mother tongue that many students did not fully understand. The talks were translated and written down by one of the instructors or a community member. After the programme had been running for about a year, many of the Elders consented to having the sessions discretely video-taped with the tapes becoming the start of a Tribal Council archive on the 'Words of the Elders'. The presentations were also transcribed into a Tribal Council publication, materials *generated* through the Generative Curriculum process (Greenwood et al., 1994).

Consistent with the principles developed by the partnership team, whenever possible the words of the community serve as the starting point for other parts of the discussion, which include those that follow from Minority World texts and instructors whose degrees are generally based on largely modernist perspectives. It is the intent of the programme to provide an orientation for the instructors to the Generative Curriculum approach before they commence their activities. This second part of the process is the representation of the 'other' world of the dominant culture. In that world the theories, interventions and understandings typically conveyed in an academic course are introduced — not as 'truth' or 'best' practice, but as one way, one practice, ideas to be shared, respected and considered along with other respected ideas and ways of understanding already introduced. Often there is a convergence or a complementarity across information sources, but sometimes not. The effort is to appreciate the context from which different information emerges as well as the context of the communities and individuals. Final agreement or a group consensus is not the intention — dialogue, personal awareness and reflection are. It is the *process*, the recursive consideration of these different views, the seeking out of what Freire would call 'new knowledge', that represents the heart of the Generative Curriculum Model. Freire's formulation of the 'circle of knowledge' is complementary to our own: 'The circle of knowledge has but two moments . . . the moment of the cognition of existing, already produced, knowledge, and the moment of our production of new knowledge . . . both are moments of the same circle' (1997: 192).

Elders' Words

Initially, the Generative Curriculum Model saw the Elders' presentations as a balancing of traditional community knowledge with academic, text-based knowledge, providing that knowledge in ways that would be more contextually appropriate through the community-base rather than a distant academic base. But this approach to knowledge and the conveying of knowledge exemplified in many Elders' stories also links with postmodernist discourses on language. Philosopher David Hall (1996) comments on postmodernist language:

> If we are to have a language that evokes difference, however, we must find a new sort of metaphor. In place of metaphors which extend the literal sense of a term, we shall have to employ 'allusive metaphors'. Allusive metaphors are distinct from the expressive variety since they are not tied to a literal or objective signification.

They are free-floating hints and suggestions. They *allude*; they do not *express*. (p. 705)

Students and instructors often commented on the Elders' use of stories to teach, stories that might seem to have little relationship to the immediate topic at hand, but which at some later point would ring powerfully. Consistent with Hall's analysis of premodernist thought in China and postmodernist critiques of language, it would appear that Elders' stories resonate with the Taoist idea 'that the thing that can be named, is not the thing'.

The Generative Curriculum approach, in line with a postmodernist perspective, sees the knowledge of the dominant group as a particular construction based on certain assumptions and experiences. From the perspective of the Tribal Council this construction and these assumptions are valuable as they inform and shape patterns of behaviour and understanding in the dominant Minority World. But also valuable are the assumptions, behaviours and understandings that inform their own communities, which are also not static but evolving. An image that one Elder used to describe the Generative Curriculum Model was that of a feather — there are two sides to a feather, and both are needed to fly.

Flight is an apt analogy for the Partnership Projects. Many First Nations communities believe they have lost the ability to soar above their troubles, to hope and to dream. The suicide rate among First Nations young people is three to four times that among the rest of Canadian society. In one western province First Nations people accounted for less than 10 per cent of the population but over two-thirds of the children in care. On some reserves a significant percentage of children born suffer from Fetal Alcohol Effects or Fetal Alcohol Syndrome (Assembly of First Nations, 1989; Canadian Royal Commission, 1996). The social science literature on First Nations in Canada is a litany of woe, some of the most disturbing and depressing literature in existence. When First Nations communities look at why it is so hard to fly above the pain and sorrow, some Elders see feathers that have been damaged on their traditional side, sheared of their strength and beauty.

It is clear to many First Nations that if they are to fly again, this damage must be repaired and that only those programmes and approaches that nourish that which has been damaged will provide them with the necessary strength to go on, to try to rise above. Yet despite, at some level, an awareness among the social science and education communities of the Minority World that great damage has been done, that something fundamental has been broken and must be repaired, the reaction to presentations on the Generative Curriculum partnership approach invariably produces alarm within a substantial part of the academic community attending. The basis of the alarm is that First Nations communities do not know how to heal themselves; implicit in this position is that they, the professionals and experts, do. One can only sit in stunned disbelief that intelligent and well-intentioned individuals can truly believe that they know more about what a community needs than the community itself. Such is the power of modernist belief that it can erase the evidence of history, the generations of well-meaningness that have reduced a population to death and despair, and still sincerely believe that *this* time it will be different, *this* time they will be proved right, *this* time it will work.

Evaluation as Practical Wisdom

As the project entered its third and final year and students neared completion of the two-year academic programme, the Meadow Lake Tribal Council was obliged by the funding body (the federal government) to formally evaluate the program, to determine if the partnership and Generative Curriculum approach had worked and had met its 'objectives'. These objectives were a required part of the original application and focused to a large extent on concrete things that could be counted (e.g. students registered, services established, and so on). The Tribal Council employed a respected Elder to do an evaluation, an individual who was not from the Meadow Lake area but who knew the communities well. In her evaluation she highlighted the importance of 'unanticipated outcomes':

> Some of the greatest benefits of the MLTC Indian Child Care Program are those that were not included in the list of eight basic objectives . . . these spinoffs have had a significant impact on the lifestyle and community spirits.
> The involvement of the Elders in the Indian Child Care Program and subsequently into all community events and undertakings has led to a revitalization of cultural pride and traditional value systems. These individuals are those that hold the fabric of community life together. They have increased the awareness of the need to work together, to have self respect and respect for others, that unless there is a healthy community environment there cannot be healthy community members, and that traditional values and ceremonies have a rightful place in the modern world. (Jette, 1993: 58, 59)

The Elder evaluator not only discussed the intended and unintended outcomes of the project, but provided eloquent testimony to the limitations of established ways of knowing and measuring:

> [The unanticipated outcomes] cannot be measured in dollars and cents but are perhaps more important to the people of First Nations than achievement in the more measurable and tangible areas. To visit the Meadow Lake Tribal Council district and to feel the new vitality and resurgence of cultural pride and self respect is to know that this program has been successful. (1993: 60)

The Elder evaluator's words, as the Generative Curriculum project itself, is not framed in postmodernist vocabulary, but a critique of modernity is there nevertheless. Embodying Schwandt's (1996a) concern that 'many social scientists believe that method offers a kind of clarity on the path to truth that philosophy does not' (p. 60), she consistently steps outside the narrow pathway of pre-established objectives and outcomes. She looks for and listens to voices that fall outside the power structure and the normal participants; she is not led by a predetermined understanding of 'best practices'; and she is sensitive to diversity and difference. She and the project itself were led by a pragmatic desire, or what Schwandt refers to as 'practical wisdom', to be 'true to the thing itself', not some external or *a priori* representation of what should be. Neither she, nor the project, knew what 'the thing itself' would be, but they trusted that it would emerge from openness and honest engagement. The starting point for the project was 'not knowing' and excitement to enter that place. She resonated with that beginning, quietly addressed the objectives that the funder identified, and then began her search for making meaning of this work through listening to the voices of the community, not knowing what she would find.

She and the project itself were led by such pragmatic impulses, and those impulses are not modernist in nature. They are not fully rational, they are not fixed, they do not await discovery like some monoliths on an ancient shore. Rather, they emerge in the doing, they are part of a praxis in the moment, yet their mark may remain while they themselves have gone, like tide lines on a beach. Her effort was to identify their mark, to see where they had passed, and to comment on it. In this effort she is more postmodernist than modernist, yet she would probably identify her process as coming from an 'old' place, not a 'new' place. In the same way that Hall suggests that Chinese premodernist thought has similarities to postmodernist thought, the Elder evaluator seems to be tapping into an older discourse which resonates with a postmodern perspective.

Elements of modernist and postmodernist thought have been with us a very long time. They wear various guises at various times, but the essential drama is the very human one of knowing and not knowing, certainty and uncertainty. Some Hebraic traditions, for example Judaism, Christianity and Islam, cast these forces as an oppositional dualism. Other traditions, such as Taoism, perceive in them a necessary complementarity and synergy of the whole. By extending this volume's discussion beyond the Minority World into the Majority World we open a door, which allows us to encounter ways of understanding and socio-philosophical dynamics, which can contribute to and extend postmodernist thought.

The case of the Generative Curriculum, with its bringing together of the two different worlds of western academia and tribal communities, is one illustration of efforts to step outside a modernist approach — albeit this is more apparent in retrospect, than at the time. In doing so, plausible alternatives to normal, modernist ways of proceeding have been encountered, many of which build on each other, stimulating additional changes and new directions as the approach evolves. These alternative approaches have also revealed glimpses of an alternative world view that are profoundly non-modernist, based not on postmodernist construction, but ancient premodernist understandings some of which resonate with postmodernist orientations. Further exploration of such pre-, post- and other- convergences is beyond the scope of this volume, which will now briefly consider further extensions of the Generative Curriculum approach beyond post-secondary training, linking those extensions with other recent writings in the Majority World development literature.

Ripples and Further Extensions

The Elder evaluator focused much of her commentary on the broader community impact of the Generative Curriculum Model. One of the community members interviewed likened it to 'a ripple effect, impacting on all other programmes . . . in the district'. In retrospect, those ripples' movements were made possible by the project's efforts to meaningfully *bring in* the community — to engage community members in a forum of idea sharing, or practical discourse, involving the future of their communities and children's key role in that future: 'It will be the children who inherit the struggle' (Meadow Lake Tribal Council, 1989). Through the Elder evaluator's focus on the unintended outcomes, and finding there the most significant influences of the programme, the university partnership team began to shift their understanding of the Generative Curriculum Model from that of a tertiary education project, to a community development project that employed tertiary education as a tool. Unexpected or unspecified outcomes have since become a major area of interest for the team, and those dynamics are currently being investigated in a major evaluation project.

The evaluation focuses on hearing from the community itself what participation in the project has meant. Not only participating students, instructors and Elders are interviewed as part of the process, but also family members, tribal administrators, service providers and other community members. The effort is to hear not only what various community members have to say, but also to have them hear from each other and to promote broader and potentially on-going dialogues regarding the well-being of children and families within and among communities. The image of ripples generating out from initial points of contact, and then working to understand the interaction of diverse ripples with each other over time is part of the intent of the evaluation. Some describe such work as *ecological* in nature, the communities often use the word *holistic*. In either case the intent is far removed from a modernist process of evaluating predefined outcomes, based on predetermined points of interest, utilizing preselected tools.

Worlds Beyond

The approach taken in the Generative Curriculum Model breaks with traditional modernist assumptions regarding the role and practices of post-secondary education. By valuing more highly being true to the spirit of the partnership and the desires of the community to reclaim, reconstruct and co-construct, the approach violates assumptions that reach back over the centuries to doctrines of revealed truth — a bedrock of modernity and a source of its enduring strength. As long as truth is conceived in this way, as singular and revealed rather than multiple and constructed, there is little room in it for accommodation to the beliefs and values of others. Focusing on the necessity to challenge and confront established assumptions in a forum that depends on community involvement and dialogue, the Generative

Curriculum Model provides elements of a postmodern model of education that imbues learners with a respect for 'many truths', many bedrocks of understanding.

Starting with the *training* of early childhood workers, rather than with pedagogical work with young children, the project highlights the many entry points that can be used to advance alternative discourses. Utilizing a *process-driven*, rather than a 'product-driven', approach to education, the Generative Curriculum approach models and supports the skills and processes required for effective, community-supportive and community-involving practices. Such community-involving skills are largely absent from mainstream, modernist, human services in education, reinforcing an implicit philosophy of 'doing to' rather than 'doing with'. Utilizing a modernist frame of reference and orientation to practice, the calls for community that dominate services to children and families in North America find a limited capacity for response from those who have been taught that the answers lie without, not within, the specific community.

Cross-national and cross-cultural early childhood relationships and work, such as the Meadow Lake Project, can draw inspiration and in turn inspire those seeking new approaches and methods for development work in the Majority World. Although Chambers focuses on rural development, the challenges and changes he identifies fit well the challenge for early childhood workers in the Majority World and beyond.

> The practices are personal and professional, requiring changes which are radical but surprisingly practicable: to question our values; to be self-critically aware; to see simple as often optimal; to help people do their own analyses . . . to test and use participatory approaches, methods and procedures; to encourage decentralization and diversity; to put people before things. (1994: ix)

Chambers' critique and recommendations, like the Generative Curriculum Model, do not originate from a postmodernist perspective, but both seek to move from a place that can be clearly understood as a modernist orientation to one that is not. Reminiscent of Tribal Administrator Vern Bachiu's comments (1993), 'what we are trying to do is turn the world upside down', for Chambers the way forward represents a 'turning upside down' of 'normal practice' and moving to a respectful inclusion of the relevant community. An approach advocated by Chambers in the early 1990s is Participatory Rural Appraisal (PRA).

> PRA is a growing family of approaches and methods to enable people to share, enhance and analyse their knowledge of life and conditions, and to plan, act, monitor and evaluate. Its extensive and growing menu of methods includes visuals such as mapping and diagramming. (Chambers, 1997: 102)

> With PRA it is less outsiders, and more local people themselves, who map, model, diagram, score, observe, interview, analyse and plan. Experiences with PRA in South Asia, East and West Africa and elsewhere, have shown that local people are better at these activities . . . we have witnessed a discovery of capabilities which earlier were little expressed and little expected by outsider professionals. (Chambers, 1994: 97)

Chambers' recognition of indigenous strengths and abilities is similar to Malaguzzi's description of children born with 100 languages and losing 99. It is not the children or the local population who are dramatically limited, but rather the professionals and experts whose ability to listen, to see, and to create is blocked by what they 'know'. Neither Malaguzzi nor Chambers would say that there is no role for professionals to play, whether in early childhood pedagogy or rural development. But what that role is must be examined closely and deeply, it must be problematized and open to reinterpretation, to voices too seldom heard, and to insights that are paradigmatically different from what has come before. The inclusion of those most affected will bring the power of pragmatic, thoughtful action into the discussion and give 'legs' to the abstract, connecting it to practical decisions 'on the ground'. Or as Patti Lather (1991) says, such inclusion allows for 'working the tensions between high theory and everyday practice'.

Participatory Rural Appraisal has been complemented by Participatory Learning and Action, and the creation of *PLA Notes* in 1988, a clearinghouse for a growing number of approaches committed to the 'common theme . . . of the full *participation* of people in the processes of *learning* about their needs and opportunities, and in the *action* required to address them' (PLA notes, 1996: cover page). The February 1996 edition was a special issue on 'Children's Participation'. With the emergence of that literature from the Majority World, describing children and communities as powerful, knowledgeable and capable, we find much in common with the perspectives adopted by Loris Malaguzzi in Reggio Emilia and in the Stockholm and Meadow Lake Projects. In all of these cases we can begin to see the potential for a productive relationship between postmodernist theory and practice — whether in rural development, pedagogical work or training early childhood workers, we can see a world of possibilities, a world filled with potential.

Such potential flows from diversity and complexity, the celebration of multiplicity and uncertainty, not from attempts to standardize, normalize and simplify. This diversity and complexity will flow not only from the individual voices of diverse peoples, but from the 'little narratives' of local knowledge that Lyotard (1984) proposes to replace the 'meta-narrative' of modernity. The dream of universality can also be understood as the nightmare of uniformity and the vulnerability of similarity. It is diversity, not similarity, that is the fount of creativity. To diminish diversity is to diminish possibility. But possibility also requires the coming together of diversity, the exchange of ideas and insights, forums of interaction and dialogue. They suggest the potential of the local, of the forum in civil society, where knowledge and understanding can be produced in fresh, creative and useful ways. Through refocusing our attention from the dream of universality, to the potential of diversity, doors to the future will open that are as yet unimagined.

We started the book with what we called the dominant language of early childhood, a language with its own particular vocabulary and that produces a particular type of conversation and question. The rest of the book has been about the possibilities for talking about early childhood differently, using a different language, having different conversations, asking other questions. We have talked about the rich child, the co-constructing child, the child as citizen; about the early childhood institution as a forum in civil society, with possibilities for many and varied projects, a place for children and childhood; about meaning making and pedagogical documentation and generative curricula; about power and freedom; about dialogue, confrontation and reflection; about plurality, singularity, uncertainty and contingency; about the ethics of an encounter and relating to the Other. Through this different language, and the postmodern perspectives we have used, we have found new ways of understanding, new opportunities for practice, new spaces where new issues can be explored — so that when we look now at early childhood it is as if we know 'the place for the first time'.

Clearly, we are exhilarated by the possibilities offered by working with postmodern perspectives. But some may not be so sure. Instead of new possibilities, they may see chaos and risk. In some respects they are right, for as Foucault noted 'everything is dangerous' because nothing is neutral, power is everywhere and uncertainty is our only certainty.

Modernity has comforted those who fear an unpredictable and complex world, allayed their concerns with images of knowability, predictability and order. But like Shakespeare's *Tempest*, 'the baseless fabric of this vision shall dissolve . . . we are such stuff as dreams are made on'. Indeed, the dream is already over. The dream to create foundations that could support the weight of universal truths and certainties — in understanding children's development, in knowing the ingredients of quality care, in evaluating environments, in predicting child outcomes and more — never was more than a dream. A dream born out of the promise of modernity.

For some the awakening is a nightmare, but it need not be so. Modernity was never risk free; quite the opposite. Postmodernity is not, can never be, a panacea; but neither is it unproductive. There are theories that can lead us in fruitful directions. There are now sufficient examples that indicate the opportunities that exist from working with different understandings of ourselves and the world. There is evidence that great potentials lie untapped, not from more of the same but from some of the other. The risk we face is not in exploring the unknown, but in retreating to the comfort of the 'known'.

Note

1   Alan Pence is coordinator of the First Nations Partnership Programs, which has involved partnerships with seven geographically and culturally diverse tribal organizations, starting with the Meadow Lake Tribal Council in 1988. The team at the University of Victoria working in this field has varied in size and membership over the 10-year period, but Lynette Halldorson and Jessica Ball have been key contributors.

References

ADORNO, T. and HORKHEIMER, M. (1944, 1997 English edn.) *Dialectic of Enlightenment*, London: Verso.

ANDERSSON, A.E. and SYLWANS, P. (1997) *Framtidens arbete och liv (Work and Life of the Future)*, Stockholm: Natur och Kultur.

APPLE, M. (1991) Series Editor's Introduction to LATHER, P.: *Getting Smart: Feminist Research and Pedagogy with/in the Postmodern*, London: Routledge.

ASPLUND, J. (1983) *Tid, rum och kollektiv (Time, Space and Collective)*, Stockholm: Liber.

ASSEMBLY of FIRST NATIONS (1989) *Report on the National Inquiry Into First Nations Child Care*, Ottawa: A.F.N.

BACHIU, V. (1993) in *Children Are Our Future, Informational booklet for First Nations Partnerships Program*, Victoria, B.C.: University of Victoria.

BALAGUER, I., MESTRES, J. and PENN, H. (1992) *Quality in Services for Young Children*, Brussels: European Commission Equal Opportunities Unit.

BANK, J. (1992) *The Essence of Total Quality Management*, London: Prentice Hall.

BATESON, G. (1988) *Ande och natur: En nödvändig enhet*, Stockholm: Symposium.

BARSOTTI, A. (1986) *Hoppet över muren (The Jump over the Wall)*, Stockholm: Mariedamfilm och HB Barsotti.

BARSOTTI, A. (1997) *D- som i Robin Hoods pilbåge*, Stockholm: HLS Förlag.

BARSOTTI, C. (1981) *Ett barn har hundra språk men herövas nittionio (A Child has got a Hundred Languages but Ninety-Nine are Lost)*, Stockholm: UR och Mariedamfilm AB.

BARSOTTI, C. (1986) *Staden och regnet (The Town and the Rain)*, Stockholm: Mariedamfilm och HB Barsotti.

BARSOTTI, C. (1994) *Mannen från Reggio Emilia (The Man from Reggio Emilia)*, Stockholm: Mandragola Film AB.

BAUMAN, Z. (1991) *Modernity and Ambivalence*, Cambridge: Polity Press.

BAUMAN, Z. (1993) *Postmodern Ethics*, Oxford: Blackwell.

BAUMAN, Z. (1995) *Life in Fragments*, Oxford: Blackwell.

BAUMAN, Z. (1997) *Postmodernity and its Discontents*, Cambridge: Polity Press.

BECK, U. (English edn. 1992) *Risk Society: Towards a New Modernity*, London: Sage.

BEDEIAN, A. (1993) *Management (Third Edn.)*, Fort Worth TX: Dryden Press.

BELL, D. (1987) 'The world and the United States in 2013', *Daedalus*, **116**, pp. 1–31.

BENHABIB, S. (1990) 'Communication ethics and current controversies in practical philosophy', in BENHABIB, S. and DALLMAYER, F. (eds) *The Communicative Ethics Controversy*, Cambridge, MA: MIT Press.

BENHANBIB, S. (1992) *Situating the Self*, Cambridge: Polity Press.

BERLIN, I. (1981) *Against the Current: Essays in the History of Ideas*, Oxford: Oxford University Press.

BERGER, P. and LUCKMAN, T. (1966) *The Social Construction of Reality*, New York: Doubleday.

BERNSTEIN, B. (1990) *The Structuring of Pedagogic Discourse, Volume IV*, London: Routledge.

BOALT-BOETHIUS, S. (1984) *Arbetslag på daghem (Teams in Day Care Centres)*, Stockholm: Institute of Psychology, University of Stockholm.

BOWLBY, J. (1969) *Attachment and Loss. Volume 1: Attachment*, London: Hogarth Press.

BREDEKAMP, S. (ed.) (1987) *Developmentally Appropriate Practice in Early Childhood Programs Serving Children Through Birth to 8 Years*, Washington, DC: NAEYC.

BREDEKAMP, S. and COPPLE, C. (eds) (1997) *Developmentally Appropriate Practice in Early Childhood Programs (Revised Edn.)*, Washington, DC: NAEYC.

BRONFENBRENNER, U., KESSEL, F., KESSEN, W. and WHITE, S. (1986) 'Towards a critical social history of developmental psychology', *American Psychologist*, **41(11)**, pp. 1218–30.

BROPHY, J. and STATHAM, J. (1994) 'Measure for measure: Values, quality and evaluation', in MOSS, P. and PENCE, A. (eds) *Valuing Quality in Early Childhood Services*, London: Paul Chapman Publishing, New York: Teachers College Press.

BUBER, M. (1970) *I and Thou*, New York: Scribners.

BUSH, J. and PHILLIPS, D. (1996) 'International approaches to defining quality', in KAGAN, S. and COHEN, N. (eds) *Reinventing Early Care and Education: A Vision for a Quality System*, San Francisco: Jossey-Bass.

BURMAN, E. (1994) *Deconstructing Developmental Psychology*, London: Routledge.

BUTLER, J. (1993) *Bodies that Matter: On the Discourse limits of 'Sex'*, New York: Routledge.

CAHOONE, L. (1996) *From Modernism to Postmodernism: An Anthology*, Cambridge, MA: Blackwell.

CALLEWÆRT, S. and KALLÓS, D. (1976) 'Den rosa vågen i svensk pedagogik (The Rose Wave in Swedish Pedagogy)', *Forskning om utbildning*, **1**.

CANADIAN ROYAL COMMISSION ON ABORIGINAL ISSUES (1996) *Report on the Royal Commission on Aboriginal Peoples*, Ottawa: Government of Canada.

CARLEHEDEN, M. (1996) *Det andra moderna: Om Jurgen habermas och den samhällsteoretiska diskursen om det moderna* (Second Modernity: Jurgen Habermas and the Social Theoretical Discourse of Modernity), Göteborg: Bokförlaget daidalos AB.

CARROLL, L. (1865, 1961 edn) *Alice's Adventures in Wonderland*, London: The Folio Society.

CARROLL, L. (1893, 1973 edn) *Sylvio and Bruno Concluded*, in *Lewis Carroll, the Complete Works*, London: The Nonesuch Press.

CHAMBERS, R. (1994) *Challenging the Professions*, London: Intermediate Technology Publications.

CHAMBERS, R. (1997) *Whose Reality Counts?* London: Intermediate Technology Publications.

CHERRYHOLMES, C.H. (1988) *Power and Criticism: Post-structural Investigations in Education*, New York: Teachers College Press.

CHERRYHOLMES, C.H. (1994) 'Dialogue, pragmatism, poststructuralism and socially useful theorizing', *Curriculum Inquiry*, **24(2)**, pp. 194–213.

CLARKE, A. (1995) 'Paradigms and methods: Quantity and quality in evaluative research', paper given at the UK Evaluation Society National Conference, London, September.

COCHRAN, M. (ed.) (1993) *International Handbook of Child Care Policies and Programs*, Westport, CT: Greenwood Press.

COCKS, J. (1989) *The Oppositional Imagination: Feminism, Critique and Political Theory*, New York: Routledge.

COHEN, J. and ARATO, A. (1992) *Civil Society and Political Theory*, Cambridge, MA: The MIT Press.

COLE, M. (1996) *Cultural Psychology: A Once and Future Discipline*, Cambridge, MA: The Belknap Press of Harvard University Press.

DAHLBERG, G. (1985) *Context and the Child's Orientation to Meaning: A Study of the Child's Way of Organizing the Surrounding World in Relation to Public Institutionalized Socialization*, Stockholm: Almqvist and Wiksell.

DAHLBERG, G. (1992) 'The parent-child relationship and socialization in the context of modern childhood: The case of Sweden', in ROOPNARINE, J.L. and CARTER, D.B. (eds) *Parent-Child Relations in Diverse Cultural Settings*, Norwood, NJ: Ablex.

DAHLBERG, G. (1995) 'Everything is a beginning and everything is dangerous: Some reflections on the Reggio Emilia experience', paper given at an international seminar *Nostalgio del Futuro* in honour of Loris Malaguzzi, Milan, October.

DAHLBERG, G. (1997) 'Images of the Child, Knowledge and Learning', lecture given at a Summer Institute of the School of Child and Youth Care, University of Victoria, BC, July.

DAHLBERG, G. (1998) 'From the "Home of the People" — *Folkhemmet* — to the Enterprise: Reflections on the constitution and reconstitution of the field of early childhood pedagogy in Sweden', in POPKEWITZ, T. (ed.) *Educational Knowledge: Changing Relationships between the State, Civil Society and the Educational Community*.

DAHLBERG, G. and ÅSÉN, G. (1994) 'Evaluation and regulation: A question of empowerment', in Moss, P. and PENCE, A. (eds) *Valuing Quality in Early*

Childhood Services, London: Paul Chapman Publishing, New York: Teachers College Press.

DAHLBERG, G. and LENZ TAGUCHI, H. (1994) *Förskola och skola — om två skilda traditioner och om visionen om en mötesplats (Preschool and school — two different traditions and a vision of an encounter)*, Stockholm: HLS Förlag.

DAHLBERG, G., LUNDGREN, U.P. and ÅSÉN, G. (1991) 'Att utvärdera barnomsorg (To evaluate early childhood education and care)', Stockholm, HLS Förlag.

DALAIS, C., LANDERS, C. and FUERTES, P. (1996) *Early Childhood Development Revisited. Report of a follow-up to the 1989 Innocenti Global Seminar*, Florence: UNICEF Innocenti Centre.

DENCIK, L. (1989) 'Growing up in the postmodern age: on the child's situation in the modern family and the position of the family in the modern welfare state', *Acta Sociologica*, **32**, pp. 155–80.

DENCIK, L. (1997) 'Modernization — a challenge to early childhood education', keynote lecture given at the 7th European Conference on the Quality of Early Childhood Education, Munich, September.

DEPARTMENT FOR EDUCATION AND EMPLOYMENT (England) (1997) *Excellence in Schools* (Cmnd.3681), London: Department for Education and Employment.

DEVEN, F., INGLIS, S., MOSS, P. and PETRIE, P. (1998) *State of the Art Review on Reconciliation of Work and Family Responsibilities and Quality in Care Services (DfEE Research Report No.57)*, London: Department for Education and Employment.

DICKSON, T. (1995) 'Quality and beyond: an Overview', in CRAINER, S. (ed.) *The FT Handbook of Management*, London: FT Pitman Publishing.

DOCKER, J. (1994) *Postmodernism and Popular Culture: A Cultural History*, Cambridge: Cambridge University Press.

DREYFUS, H. and RABINOW, P. (1980) *Michel Foucault: Beyond Structuralism and Hermeneutics*, Chicago, IL: University of Chicago Press.

EDWARDS, C., GANDINI, L. and FORMAN, G. (eds) (1993) *The Hundred Languages of Children*, Norwood, NJ: Ablex.

ELDER, G., MODELL, J and PARKE, R. (eds) (1993) *Children in Time and Place*, Cambridge: Cambridge University Press.

ELLSWORTH, E. (1989) 'Why doesn't this feel empowering? Working through the repressive myths of critical pedagogy', *Harvard Educational Review*, **59(3)**, pp. 297–324.

ESCOBAR, A. (1997) *Encountering Development: The Making and Unmaking of the Third World*, Princeton, NJ: Princeton University Press.

VON EULER, G. (1975) 'Om observationer (On observations)', in SOU: 1975 *Utbildning i samspel (Education for Relationships)*, Stockholm: Allmänna Förlaget.

EUROPEAN COMMISSION CHILDCARE NETWORK (1996a) *A Review of Services for Young Children in the European Union 1990–1995*, Brussels: European Commission Equal Opportunities Unit.

EUROPEAN COMMISSION CHILDCARE NETWORK (1996b) *Quality Targets in Services for Young Children*, Brussels: European Commission Equal Opportunities Unit.

EVANS, J. (1994) 'Quality in ECCD: Everyone's concern', *Coordinators' Note-book*, **15**, pp. 1–32.

EVERS, A. (1997) 'Quality development — part of a changing culture of care', in EVERS, A., HAVERINEN, R., LEICHSENRING, K. and WISOW, G. (eds) *Developing Quality in Personal Social Services: Concepts, Cases and Comments*, Aldershot: Ashgate.

FARQUHAR, S. (1993) 'Breaking new ground in the study of quality', paper given at the NZARE Conference, Hamilton.

FISHMAN, D. (1995) 'Postmodernism comes to program evaluation II: A review of Denzin and Lincoln's *Handbook of Qualitative Research. Evaluation and Programme Planning*', **18(3)**, pp. 301–10.

FLAX, J. (1990) *Thinking Fragments: Psychoanalysis, Feminism and Postmodernism in the Contemporary West*, Berkeley and Los Angeles: University of California Press.

VON FOERSTER, H. (1991) 'Through the eyes of the other', in STEIER, F. (ed.) *Research and Reflexivity*, London: Sage.

FOUCAULT, M. (1965 English edn.) *Madness and Civilisation: A History of Insanity in the Age of Reason*, New York: Pantheon.

FOUCAULT, M. (1970 English edn.) *The Order of Things: An Archaeology of the Human Sciences*, New York: Random House.

FOUCAULT, M. (1972 English edn.) *The Birth of the Clinic: An Archaeology of Medical Perceptions*, New York: Vintage.

FOUCAULT, M. (1974) 'Human nature: Justice versus power', in ELDERS, F. (ed.) *Reflexive Water: The Basic Concerns of Mankind*, London: Souvenir Press.

FOUCAULT, M. (1977 English edn.) *Discipline and Punish: The Birth of the Prison*, Harmondsworth: Penguin.

FOUCAULT, M. (1980a) *Power/Knowledge: Selected Interviews and Other Writings, 1972–1977* (GORDON, C. ed.), London: Harvester Wheatsheaf.

FOUCAULT, M. (1980b) 'Georges Canguilhem: Philosopher of Error', *Ideology and Consciousness*, **7**, pp. 53–4.

FOUCAULT, M. (1980c) 'The Subject and power', an afterword in DREYFUS, H. and RABINOW, P. *Michel Foucault: Beyond Structuralism and Hermeneutics*, Chicago, IL: University of Chicago Press.

FOUCAULT, M. (1986 English edn.) *The Care of the Self*, New York: Pantheon.

FOUCAULT, M. (1988) *Politics, Philosophy, Culture: Interviews and Other Writings, 1977–1984* (L. Kritzman ed.), New York: Routledge.

FOUCAULT, M. (1990) 'Qu'est-ce que la critique?' *Bulletin de la Société Française de Philosophie*, **84**, pp. 35–63.

FREIRE, P. (1985 English edn.) *Pedagogy of the Oppressed*, Harmondsworth: Penguin.

FREIRE, P. (1996 English edn.) *Letters to Christina: Reflections on my Life and Work*, London: Routledge.

FREIRE, P. (1997 English edn.) *Pedagogy of Hope*, New York: The Continuum Publishing Co.

FROMM, E. (1942) *The Fear of Freedom*, London: Routledge and Kegan Paul.

GARBARINO, J. (1996*) Raising Children in a Socially Toxic Environment*, San Francisco: Jossey-Bass.

GASTER, L. (1991) 'Quality and decentralisation — are they connected?' *Policy and Politics*, **19(4)**, pp. 257–67.

GELLNER, E. (1992) *Postmodernism, Reason and Religion*, London: Routledge.

GERGEN, K. (1992) 'Towards a postmodern psychology', in KVALE, S. (ed.) *Psychology and Postmodernism*, London: Sage.

GERGEN, K. and GERGEN, M. (1991) 'Toward reflexive methodologies', in STEIER, F. (ed.) *Research and Reflexivity*, London: Sage.

GESELL, A. and ILG, F. (1946) *The Child from Five to Ten*, New York: Harper and Row.

GIDDENS, A. (1990) *The Consequences of Modernity*, Cambridge: Polity Press.

GIDDENS, A. (1991) *Modernity and Self-Identity*, Cambridge: Polity Press.

GINSBURG, C. (1989) *Ledtrådar, Essäer om Konst, förbjuden kunskap och dold historia* (*Threads, Essays on Art, Forbidden Knowledge and Hidden History*), Stockholm: Häften för Kritiska studier.

GIROUX, H. (1989) *Schooling for Democracy: Critical Pedagogy in the Modern Age.* London: Routledge.

VON GLASERSFELD, E. (1991) 'Knowing without metaphysics; aspects of the radical constructivist position', in STEIER, F. (ed.) *Research and Reflexivity*, London: Sage.

GORE, J. (1993) *The Struggle for Pedagogics: Critical and Feminist Discourses as Regimes of Truth*, New York: Routledge.

GÖTHSON, H. (1991) *Från gamla svar till nya frågor (From Old Answers to New Questions)*, Stockholm: Socialstyrelsen.

GREENWOOD, M., OPIKOKEW, L., OPEKOKEW, M.R. and McINTYRE, M.R. (1994) *The Elders Speak: Of the Past, Of Children and Families*, Meadow Lake Tribal Council.

HABERMAS, J. (1983) 'Modernity: an incomplete project', in FOSTER, H. (ed.) *The Anti-aesthetic; Essays on Postmodern Culture*, Port Townsend: Washington.

HALL, D. (1996) 'Modern China and the postmodern West', in CAHOONE, L. (ed.) *From Modernism to Postmodernism*, Cambridge, MA: Blackwells.

HALL, S. and JACQUES, M. (eds) (1989) *New Times: The Changing Face of Politics in the 1990s*, London: Lawrence and Wishart.

HALLDORSON, L. and PENCE, A. (1995) *Program Guidebook to the Generative Curriculum*, Victoria, BC: University of Victoria.

HAMBLETON, R. and HOGGART, P. (1990) *Beyond Excellence: Quality of Local Government in the 1990s (Working Paper 85)*, Bristol: School for Advanced Urban Studies.

HARMS, T. and CLIFFORD, R. (1980) *Early Childhood Environment Rating Scale*, New York: Teachers College Press.

HARVEY, D. (1989) *The Condition of Postmodernity*, Oxford: Blackwell.

HATCH, J.A. (1995) 'Studying childhood as a cultural invention: A rationale and framework', in J.A. HATCH (ed.) *Qualitiative Research in Early Childhood Settings*, Westport, CT: Praeger.

HAUG, P. (1992) *Educational Reform by Experiment: The Norwegian Experimental Educational Program for 6 Year Olds (1986–1990) and the Subsequent Reform*, Stockholm: HLS Förlag.

HEDENQVIST, J.-A. (1987) *Språklig interaktion i förskolan (Interaction in the Preschool)*, Stockholm: Lärarhögskolan i Stockholm.

HENRIQUES, J., HOLLOWAY, W., URWIN, C., VENN, C. and WALKERDINE, V. (1984) *Changing the Subject: Psychology, Social Regulation and Subjectivity*, London: Methuen.

HULTQVIST, K. (1990) *Förskolebarnet: En konstruktion för gemenskapen och den individuella frigörelsen (The Swedish Pre-school Child: a Construction for the Spirit of Community and Individual Freedom)*, Stockholm: Symposion.

HULTQVIST, K. (1995) 'En nutidshistoria om barns välfärd i Sverige. Från Fröbel till dagens centraliseringsprojekt', in DAHLGREN, L. and HULTQVIST, K. (eds) *Seendet och seendets villkor. En bok om barns och ungas välfärd*, Stockholm: HLS Förlag.

HUTTON, W. (1995) *The State We Are In*, London: Jonathan Cape.

ISRAEL, J. (1992) *Martin Buber: Dialogfilosof och sionist (Martin Buber: Dialogoe Philosopher and Zionist)*, Stockholm: Natur och Kultur.

JENKS, C. (1982) *The Sociology Of Childhood — Essential Readings*, London: Batsford Academic.

JENSEN, C. (1994) 'Fragments for a discussion about quality', in MOSS, P. and PENCE, A. (eds) *Valuing Quality in Early Childhood Services*, London: Paul Chapman Publishing, New York: Teachers College Press.

JENSEN, J. (1996) *Men as Workers in Childcare Services*, Brussels: European Commission Equal Opportunities Unit.

JETTE, D.I. (1993) 'Meadow Lake Tribal Council Indian Child Care Program Evaluation', unpublished report to the Meadow Lake Tribal Council.

JOWELL, R., CURTICE, J., PARK, A., BROOK, L. and AHRENDT, D. (eds) (1995) *British Social Attitudes Survey: the 12th Report*, Aldershot: Dartmouth.

KAGAN, S., COHEN, N. and NEUMAN, M. (1996) 'Introduction: The changing context of American early care and education', in KAGAN, S. and COHEN, N. (eds) *Reinventing Early Care and Education: A Vision for a Quality System*, San Francisco: Jossey-Bass.

KARLSSON, O. (1995) Att utvärdera mot vad? Om kriterie problemet vid intressentutvärdering (To evaluate against what? On the criteria problem in stakeholder evaluations), Stockholm: HLS Förlag.

KATZ, L. (1993) 'What can we learn from Reggio-Emilia?', in EDWARDS, C., GANDINI, L. and FORMAN, G. (eds) *The Hundred Languages of Children*, Norwood, NJ: Ablex.

KEMP, P. (1992) *Emmanual Levinas: En introduktion (Emmanuel Levinas: An Introduction)*, Göteborg: Daidolos.

KESSEN, W. (1979) 'The American child and other cultural inventions', *American Psychologist*, **24**, pp. 815–20.

KESSEN, W. (1983) 'The child and other cultural inventions', in KESSEL, F. and SIEGEL, A. (eds) *The Child and other Cultural Inventions: Houston Symposium 4*, New York: Praeger.

KESSLER, S.A. and SWADENER, B. (eds) (1992) *Reconceptualising the Early Childhood Curriculum: Beginning the Dialogue*, New York: Teachers College Press.

KUMAR, K. (1995) *From Post-Industrial to Postmodern Society: New Theories of the Contemporary World*, Oxford: Blackwell.

KVALE, S. (ed.) (1992) *Psychology and Postmodernism*, London: Sage.

LAMB, M., STERNBERG, K., HWANG, C.-P. and BROBERG, A. (eds) (1992) *Child Care in Context*, Hillsdale, NJ: Lawrence Erlbaum Associates.

LANDERS, C. (1989) *Early Child Development Summary Report*, New York: UNICEF.

LARNER, M. and PHILLIPS, S. (1994) 'Defining and valuing quality as a parent', in MOSS, P. and PENCE, A. (eds) *Valuing Quality in Early Childhood Service*, London: Paul Chapman Publishing, New York: Teachers College Press.

LATHER, P. (1991) *Getting Smart: Feminist Research and Pedagogy with/in the Postmodern*, London: Routledge.

LATHER, P. (1992) 'Postmodernity and the human sciences', in KVALE, S. (ed.) *Psychology and Postmodernism*, London: Sage.

LAURIDSEN, S. (1995) 'Training of child care and social care workers in Denmark', paper given at a conference in Madrid, November.

LENZ TAGUCHI, H. (1997) *Varför pedagogisk dokumentation? (Why Pedagogical Documentation?)*, Stockholm: HLS Förlag.

LENZ TAGUCHI, H. (1998) 'A problematisation of "Power", "Resistance" and "Emancipation" in pedagogical documentation work', paper given at a research symposium on Theoretical Spaces, at Stockholm Institute of Education, November.

LIEDMAN, S.-E. (1997) *I skuggan av framtiden (In the shadow of the future)*, Stockholm: Bonnier Alba.

LIND, U. (1998) 'Loss and meaning in a tradition of representation: On the construction of difference and ambivalence in the process of knowledge', paper given at a research symposium on Theoretical Spaces, at Stockholm Institute of Education, November.

LINDENSJÖ, B. and LUNDGREN, U.P. (1986) Politisk styrning och utbildningsreformer (Political governing and educational reforms), Stockholm: Liber.

LINDQVIST, G. (1995) *Från fakta till fantasi (From Fact to Fantasy)*, Lund: Studentlitteratur.

LUBECK, S. (1996) 'Deconstructing "child development knowledge" and "teacher preparation"', *Early Childhood Research Quarterly*, **11**, pp. 147–67.

LUNDGREN, U.P. (1990) 'Educational policy making decentralisation and evaluation', in GRANHEIM, M., KOGAN, M. and LUNDGREN, U.P. (eds) *Evaluation as Policymaking: Introducing Evaluation into a National Decentralised System*, London: Jessica Kingsley.

LYOTARD, J.-F. (1984) *The Postmodern Condition: A Report on Knowledge*, Minneapolis, MN: University of Minneapolis Press.

MALAGUZZI, L. (1993a) 'For an education based on relationships', *Young Children*, **11/93**, pp. 9–13.

MALAGUZZI, L. (1993b) 'History, ideas and basic philosophy', in EDWARDS, C., GANDINI, L. and FORMAN, G. (eds) *The Hundred Languages of Children*, Norwood, NJ: Ablex.

MALPAS, N. and LAMBERT, P.-Y. (1993) The Europeans and the family; Results of an opinion survey (Eurobarometer 39), Brussels: European Commission.

MÄNTYSAARI, M. (1997) 'Quality management in Finland — problems and possibilities', in EVERS, A., HAVERINEN, R., LEICHSENRING, K. and WISOW, G. (eds) *Developing Quality in Personal Social Services: Concepts, Cases and Comments*, Aldershot: Ashgate.

MARQUAND, D. (1998) 'May's magic still lingers as Blair faces hard choices', *The Guardian*, 2 May.

MATURANA, H. (1991) 'Science and daily life: the ontology of scientific explanations', in STEIER, F. (ed.) *Research and Reflexivity*, London: Sage.

MAYALL, B. (1996) *Children, Health and the Social Order*, Buckingham: Open University Press.

McGURK, H., CAPLAN, M., HENNESSY, E. and MOSS, P. (1993) 'Controversy, theory and social context in contemporary day care research', *Journal of Child Psychology and Psychiatry*, **34**, pp. 3–23.

MEADOW LAKE TRIBAL COUNCIL (1989) 'Vision Statement, MLTC Program Report', unpublished report.

MELUCCI, A. (1989) *Nomads of the Present: Social Movements and Individual Needs in Contemporary Society*, Philadelphia, PA: Temple University Press.

MILLER, P. and ROSE, N. (1993) 'Governing economic life', in GANE, M. and JOHNSTON, T. (eds) *Foucault's New Domains*, London: Routledge.

MOLTENO, M. (1966) *Starting Young: Principles and Practice in Early Childhood Development*, London: Save the Children UK.

MONTESSORI, M. (1967) *The Discovery of the Child*, New York: Ballantine Books.

MOONEY, A. and MUNTON, A. (1997) *Research and Policy in Early Childhood Services: Time for a New Agenda*, London: Institute of Education, University of London.

MORSS, J. (1996) *Growing Critical*, London: Routledge.

MOSS, P. and PENCE, A. (eds) (1994) *Valuing Quality in Early Childhood Services*, London: Paul Chapman.

MOSS, P. and PENN, H. (1996) *Transforming Nursery Education*, London: Paul Chapman.

MOUFFE, C. (1996a) *Deconstruction and Pragmatism*, London: Routledge.

MOUFFE, C. (1996b) 'Democracy, power and difference', in BENHABIB, S. (ed.) *Democracy and Difference: Contesting the Boundaries of the Political*, Princeton, NJ: Princeton University Press.

MUNTON, A., MOONEY, A. and ROWLAND, L. (1995) 'Deconstructing quality: A conceptual framework for the new paradigm in day care provision for the under eights', *Early Child Development and Care*, **114**, pp. 11–23.

MYERS, R. (1992) *The Twelve Who Survive: Strengthening Programmes of Early Childhood Development in the Third World*, London: Routledge.

NEW, R. (1993) 'Cultural variations in developmentally appropriate practice', in EDWARDS, C., GANDINI, L. and FORMAN, G. (eds) *The Hundred Languages of Children*, Norwood, NJ: Ablex.

NORDIN-HULTMAN, E. (1998) 'To confront the concept of identity within developmental psychology, and to explore an alternative where subjectivity is placed and constructed within situations, in a flow of actions and language', paper given at a research symposium on Theoretical Spaces, at Stockholm Institute of Education, November.

PASCAL, C., BERTRAM, A. and RAMSDEN, F. (1994) *The Effective Early Learning Research Project: the Quality, Evaluation and Development Process*, Worcester: Worcester College of Higher Education.

PENCE, A. (1989) 'In the shadow of mother-care: Contexts for an understanding of child day care in Canada', *Canadian Psychology*, **30(2)**, pp. 140–7.

PENCE, A. (1992) 'Quality care: thoughts on R/rulers', paper given at a workshop on Defining and Assessing Quality, Seville, September.

PENCE, A. (1999) '"It takes a village . . .". and new roads to get there', in KEATING, D. and C. HERTZMAN (eds) *Developmental Health as the Wealth of Nations*, New York: Guilford.

PENCE, A., KUEHNE, V., GREENWOOD, M. and OPEKOKEW, M.R. (1993) 'Generative curriculum: A model of university and first nations cooperative. Post-Secondary Education', *International Journal of Educational Development*, **13(4)**, pp. 339–49.

PENCE, A. and MOSS, P. (1994) 'Towards an inclusionary approach in defining quality', in MOSS, P. and PENCE, A. (eds) *Valuing Quality in Early Childhood Services*, London: Paul Chapman Publishing, New York: Teachers College Press.

PENN, H. (1997a) 'Inclusivity and diversity in early childhood services in South Africa', *International Journal of Inclusive Education*, **1(1)**, pp. 101–14.

PENN, H. (1997b) *Comparing Nurseries*, London: Paul Chapman.

PENN, H. and MOLTENO, M. (1997) 'Sustainability in early childhood development projects', unpublished paper for UNICEF.

PHILLIPS, D. (1996) 'Reframing the quality issue', in KAGAN, S. and COHEN, N. (eds) *Reinventing Early Care and Education: A Vision for a Quality System*, San Francisco: Jossey-Bass.

PHOENIX, A. and OWEN, C. (1996) 'From miscegenation to hybridity: Mixed relationships and mixed-parentage in profile', in BERNSTEIN, B. and BRANNEN, J. (eds) *Children Research and Policy*, London: Taylor and Francis.

PLA NOTES (1996) 'Special issue on children's participation', Number 25, February, International Institute for Environment and Development.

POLLITT, C. (1988) 'Bringing consumers into performance measurement: Concepts, consequences and constraints', *Policy and Politics*, **16(2)**, pp. 77–87.

POLLITT, C. (1997) 'Business and professional approaches to quality improvement', in EVERS, A., HAVERINEN, R. LEICHSENRING, K. and WISOW, G. (eds)

Developing Quality in Personal Social Services: Concepts, Cases and Comments, Aldershot: Ashgate.

POPKEWITZ, T. (1990) 'Some problems and problematics in the production of evaluation', in GRANHEIM, M., KOGAN, M. and LUNDGREN, U.P. (eds) *Evaluation as Policymaking: Introducing Evaluation into a National Decentralised System*, London: Jessica Kingsley.

POPKEWITZ, T. (ed.) (1993) *Changing Patterns of Power: Social Regulation and Teacher Education Reform*, Albany, NY: State University of New York Press.

POPKEWITZ, T. (1994) Systems of Ideas in Historical Spaces: Vygotsky, Educational Constructivism and Changing Problems in the Regulation of the 'Self', manuscript, University of Wisconsin.

POPKEWITZ, T. (1997) 'A changing terrain of knowledge and power in educational research: A social epistemology', in POPKEWITZ, T. (ed.) *Critical Theory and Educational Discourse*, Johannesburg, SA: Heinemann.

POPKEWITZ, T. (1998a) *Struggling for the Soul: The Politics of Schooling and the Construction of the Teacher*, New York: Teachers' College Press.

POPKEWITZ, T. (1998b) 'The culture of redemption and the administration of freedom in educational research', *The Review of Educational Research*, Spring issue, pp. 1–35.

POPKEWITZ, T. and BRENNAN, M. (1998) 'Restructuring of social and political theory in education: Foucault and a social epistemology of school practices', in POPKEWITIZ, T. and BRENNAN, M. (eds) *Foucault's Challenge: Discourse, Knowledge and Power in Education*, New York: Teachers College Press.

PORTER, T. (1995) *Trust in Numbers*, Princeton, NJ: Princeton University Press.

PRIESTLEY, M. (1995) 'Dropping "E's": the missing link in quality assurance for disabled people', *Critical Social Policy*, **44/45**, pp. 7–21.

PROUT, A. and JAMES, A. (1990) 'A new paradigm for the sociology of childhood?', in JAMES, A. and PROUT, A. (eds) *Constructing and Deconstructing Childhood: Contemporary Issues in the Sociological Study of Childhood*, Brighton: Falmer Press.

PUTNAM, R. (1993) *Making Democracy Work: Civic Traditions in Modern Italy*, Princeton, NJ: Princeton University Press.

PUTNAM, R. (1995) 'Bowling alone; America's declining social capital', *Journal of Democracy*, **6**, pp. 65–78.

QVORTRUP, J., BARDY, J., SGRITTA, G. and WINTERSBERGER, H. (eds) (1994) *Childhood Matters: Social Theory, Practice and Politics*, Aldershot: Avebury.

RABINOW, P. (ed.) (1984) *The Foucault Reader*, New York: Pantheon.

RANSOM, J. (1997) *Foucault's Discipline*, Durham, NC: Duke University Press.

READINGS, B. (1996) *The University in the Ruins*, Cambridge, MA: Harvard University Press.

REEDER, J. (1997) 'Tolkandets gränser (The boundaries of interpretation)', paper given at the Research Conference, Reggio Emilia, June.

RICHARDSON, V. (ed.) (1997) *Constructivist Teacher Education*, London: Falmer Press.

RINALDI, C. (1993) 'The emergent curriculum and social constructivism', in EDWARDS, C., GANDINI, L. and FORMAN, G. (eds) *The Hundred Languages of Children*, Norwood, NJ: Ablex.

RINALDI, C. (1994) 'Observation and documentation', paper given at the *Research Conference*, Reggio Emilia, June 1995.

RODARI, G. (1988) *Fantasins grammatik (The Grammar of Fantasy)*, Göteborg: Korpen.

ROGOFF, B. and CHAVAJAY, P. (1995) 'What's become of research on the cultural basis of cognitive development?', *American Psychologist*, **50(10)**, pp. 859–77.

RORTY, R. (1980) *Philosophy and the Mirror of Nature*, Oxford: Blackwell.

RORTY, R. (1982) *Consequences of Pragmatism*, Brighton: The Harvester Press.

RORTY, R. (1989) *Contingency, Irony and Solidarity*, Cambridge: Cambridge University Press.

RUBENSTEIN REICH, L. (1993) *Samling i förskolan*, Lund: Almqvist and Wiksell.

SAID, E. (1993) *Culture and Imperialism*, London: Chatto and Windus.

SCARR, S. (1998) 'American child care today', *American Psychologist*, **53(2)**, pp. 95–108.

SCHWANDT, T. (1996a) 'Farewell to criteriology', *Qualitative Inquiry*, **2(1)**, pp. 58–72.

SCHWANDT, T. (1996b) 'The landscape of values in evaluation: Chartered terrain and unexplored territory', paper given at the Annual Meeting of the American Evaluation Association, Atlanta, GA, November.

SCHWEINHART, L., BARNES, H. and WEIKART, D. (1993) *Significant Benefits: The High/Scope Perry Preschool Study Through Age 27*, Ypsilanti, MI: The High/Scope Press.

SCHYL-BJURMAN, G. and STRÖMBERG-LIND, K. (1977) *Dialogpedagogik (Dialogue Pedagogy)*, Köpenhamn: Fremad.

SELANDER, S. (1984) *Textum institutionis: Den pedagogiska väven (The Pedagogical Web)*, Stockholm: Gleerup.

SERPELL, R. (1993) *The Significance of Schooling: Life Journeys in an African Society*, Cambridge: Cambridge University Press.

SHADISH, W. (1995) 'Philosophy of science and the quantitative-qualitative debates: thirteen common errors', *Evaluation and Programme Planning*, **18(1)**, pp. 63–75.

SHANIN, T. (1997) 'The idea of progress', in RAHMENA, M. and BAWTREE, V. (eds) *The Post-development Reader*, London: Zed Books.

SHOTTER, J. (1992) ' "Getting in touch": The meta-methodology of a postmodern science of mental Life', in KVALE, S. (ed.) *Psychology and Postmodernism*, London: Sage.

SINGER, E. (1993) 'Shared care for children', *Theory and Psychology*, **3(4)**, pp. 429–49.

SORLIN, S. (1996) *Universiteten som drivkrafter: Globalisering, kunskapspolitik och den nya intellektuella geografin (The Universities as forces: Globalisation, Politics of Knowledge and the New Intellectual Geography)*, Stockholm: SNS Förlag.

SOU (1972) *Förskolan del 1 och 2 (The Preschool, Volumes 1 and 2)*, Stockholm: Allmänna Förlaget.

SOU (1975) Utbilding i samspel (Education for relationships), Stockholm: Allmänna Förlaget.

SPANOS, W. (1987) *Repetitions: The Postmodern Occasion in Literature and Culture*, Baton Rouge, LA: Louisiana State University Press.

STAFSENG, O. (1994) *Den historiske konstrucktion av moderne ungdom (The Historical Construction of the Modern Youngster)*, Oslo: Cappelen Akademisk Förlag.

STEDMAN, P.H. (1991) 'On the relations between seeing, interpreting and knowing', in STEIER, F. (ed.) *Research and Reflexivity*, London: Sage.

STEIER, F. (ed.) (1991) *Research and Reflexivity*, London: Sage.

STEPHENS, S. (ed.) (1995) *Children and the Politics of Culture*, Princeton, NJ: Princeton University Press.

SUVANNATHAT, C., BHANTHUMNAVIN, D., BHUAPIROM, L. and KEATS, D.M. (eds) (1985) *Handbook of Asian Child Development and Child Rearing Practices*, Bangkok: Srinakharinwirot University, Behavioural Science Research Institute.

TOBIN, J. (1995) 'Post-structural research in early childhood education', in HATCH, J.A. (ed.) *Qualitiative Research in Early Childhood Settings*, Westport, CT: Praeger.

TOBIN, J. (1997) 'The missing discourse of pleasure and desire', in TOBIN, J. (ed.) *Making a Place for Pleasure in Early Childhood Education*, New Haven, CT: Yale University Press.

TOBIN, J., WU, D. and DAVIDSON, D. (1989) *Preschool in Three Cultures: Japan, China and the United States*, New Haven, CT: Yale University Press.

TOULMIN, S. (1990) *Cosmopolis: the Hidden Agenda of Modernity*, Chicago, IL: University of Chicago Press.

UNICEF (1998a) 'UNICEF regional workshop on early childhood care and development (ECCD)', unpublished report from a workshop held in Karachi, Pakistan, March.

UNICEF (1998b) 'UNICEF Futures Group: early childhood care and development', unpublished report from a meeting held in Wye College, Britain, April.

VADEBONCOEUR, J. (1997) 'Child development and the purpose of education', in RICHARDSON, V. (ed.) *Constructivist Teacher Education*, London: Falmer Press.

WALKERDINE, V. (1984) 'Developmental psychology and the child-centred pedagogy: The insertion of Piaget into early education', in HENRIQUES, J., HOLLOWAY, W., URWIN, C., VENN, C. and WALKERDINE, V. *Changing the Subject: Psychology, Social Regulation and Subjectivity*, London: Methuen.

WALLIN, K. (1996) *Reggio Emilia och de hundra språken (Reggio Emilia and the Hundred Languages)*, Lund: Liber.

WALLIN, K., MAECHEL, I. and BARSOTTI, A. (1981) *Ett barn har hundra språk. Om skapande pedagogik på kommunala daghemmen I Reggio Emilia, Italien (A Child has got a Hundred Languages: on Creative Pedagogy in the Scuola Comunale, Reggio Emilia, Italy)*, Stockholm: Utbildningsradion.

WALZER, M. (1992) 'The Civil Society argument', in MOUFFE, C. (ed.) *Dimensions of Radical Democracy: Pluralism, Citizenship, Community*, London: Verso.

WEILER, H. (1990) 'Decentralisation in educational governance: An exercise in contradiction', in GRANHEIM, M., KOGAN, M. and LUNDGREN, U.P. (eds) *Evaluation as Policymaking: Introducing Evaluation into a National Decentralised System*, London: Jessica Kingsley.

WEISNER, T.S. and GALLIMORE, R. (1977) 'My brother's keeper: Child and sibling caretakers', *Current Anthropology*, **18(2)**, pp. 169–180.

WILLIAMS, P. (1994) *Making Sense of Quality: A Review of Approaches to Quality in Early Childhood Services*, London: National Children's Bureau.

WOODHEAD, M. (1996) *In Search of the Rainbow: Pathways to Quality in Large Scale Programmes for Young Disadvantaged Children*, The Hague: Bernard van Leer Foundation.

WOODHEAD, M. (1997) 'Psychology and the cultural construction of children's needs', in JAMES, A. and PROUT, A. (eds) *Constructing and Deconstructing the Child: Contemporary Issues in the Sociological Study of Childhood*, London: Falmer Press.

WOODILL, G., BERNHARD, J.K. and PROCHNER, L. (eds) (1992) *International Handbook of Early Childhood Education*, New York: Garland.

YOUNG, M.E. (1996) *Early Child Development: Investing in the Future*, Washington DC: The World Bank.

YOUNG, R. (1990) *White Mythologies: Writing History and the West*, London: Routledge.

ZIEHE, T. (1989) *Kulturanalyser: ungdom, utbildning, modernitet (Cultural Analysis: Youngsters, Education and Modernity)*, Stockholm: Norstedts Förlag.

ZUCKERMAN, M. (1993) 'History and developmental psychology, a dangerous liaison: A historian's perspective', in ELDER, G., MODELL, J. and PARKE, R. (eds) *Children in Time and Place*, Cambridge: Cambridge University Press.

Index